IRAQ:
THE SEARCH FOR NATIONAL IDENTITY

IRAQ

THE SEARCH FOR NATIONAL IDENTITY

Liora Lukitz

FRANK CASS
LONDON

First published in 1995 in Great Britain by
FRANK CASS & CO. LTD.
Newbury House, 900 Eastern Avenue, London, IG2 7HH

and in the United States of America by
FRANK CASS
c/o ISBS, 5804 N.E. Hassalo Street, Portland, Oregon 97213-3644

Copyright © 1995 Liora Lukitz

British Library Cataloguing in Publication Data

Lukitz, Liora
   Iraq: Search for National Identity
   I. Title
   956.704

      ISBN 0-7146-4550-8 (cloth)
      ISBN 0-7146-4128-6 (paper)

Library of Congress Cataloging in Publication Data

Lukitz, Liora,
   Iraq : the search for national identity / Liora Lukitz
      p.   cm.
   Includes bibliographical references and index.
   ISBN 0-7146-4550-8 (cloth) : ISBN 0-7146-4128-6 (paper)
   1. Nationalism—Iraq.   2. Iraq—Politics and government.
   I. Title.
   DS79.L85   1995
   320.5′4′09567—dc20   94-31533
                                    CIP

Typeset by Regent Typesetting, London
Printed in Great Britain by
Bookcraft (Bath) Ltd, Midsomer Norton, Avon

To the memory of my father,
Moshé Lokiec,
whose own life was
a cycle in history

Nationalism is chameleon-like. It takes its colour from its context.

Anthony D. Smith,
National Identity

Contents

Abbreviations

AOC	–	Air Officer Commanding
AHQ	–	Air Headquarters of the RAF units in Iraq
AIR	–	Air Ministry Files
CIC	–	Commander-in-Chief
CO	–	Colonial Office Files
FO	–	Foreign Office Files
LP&S	–	India Office Letters, Political and Secret
SSO	–	Special Service Office
RAF	–	Royal Air Force
RIAF	–	Royal Iraqi Air Force
890 goo	–	US National Archives Files

Preface

The 1991–92 events in the Gulf focused the world's attention on Iraq, raising many questions about the attitudes of the country's leadership in particular and the dynamics of Iraqi politics in general.

The debate that followed the post-war events in the northern and southern provinces centred on the question whether the rebellion of the Kurds and the Shi'is was just a reaction to the policies of Iraq's current regime or a variant of structural problems preventing the integration of Iraq's population.

The very framing of the problems as structural provoked a reaction from those who believed in a steady and progressive integration of all sectors in Iraq's population in spite of the constant upheavals characterizing its political life since its inception as a modern state in the early 1920s. To them the presentation of the problems as structural indicated an inclination to reify them and to prevent their solution. Any emphasis on the roots of the problems was seen as anti-progressive and hence inconsistent with the general idea of nation-building pervading the current historiography on Iraq.

Although I was aware of these problems when I started this research as a PhD student, I could not have imagined years ago that the story of Iraq's formation – as viewed by the population of the provinces – would arouse so much interest and bring about so many emotion-laden reactions.

The sensitivity surrounding the near-dismemberment of Iraq in the aftermath of the war was so profound that a book focusing on the population of the provinces was seen not just as an attempt to shed light on some obscure aspects of a well-known story but as a political statement. An account of the divisions in Iraq's population was seen as reflecting a personal position, and not as echoing historical evidence and realities on the ground. I hope that at this juncture emotions have already calmed down a little, making the presentation of the different aspects of the problem possible.

Some of the questions that arose at the time of my first encounter with the subject acquired years later a controversial political connotation focused on the reasons behind Iraq's fragility and on their possible dating back to mandatorial times. Was the preservation of Iraq's territorial continuity just an outcome of Britain's interest in the area? Did territorial continuity imply the cultural integration of Iraq's population? How was Baghdad's writ extended to the provinces? What was Britain's role in promoting Sunni hegemony over the country? How did it contribute to the delineation of a still amorphous Iraqi identity?

All these questions pointed to divisiveness, reflecting at the time more a guess than a certitude. Before attempting to deal with them, I should like to point out that divisiveness represented, during the period studied, one side of the coin. My choice to focus on it stemmed from the need to counterbalance the priority given to cohesiveness in modern Iraq's historiography. I should also like to note that by pointing to divisiveness I am not necessarily hinting at its perpetuation. Ethnic loyalties, class interests, communal identities are solidarities or links that interact in theory as well as in practice. The attempt to highlight one of them at any given period in time does not mean totally overriding the others. Overlapping identities and shifting loyalties coexist, pointing to the fact that in history 'human groups change ... sometimes quite radically in their own estimation'.[1]

Change, however, does not occur overnight, and the lingering effect of old loyalties is sometimes felt well after the emergence of newer ones. Loyalties are part of the mass of feelings, beliefs and motivations that – like the submerged base of an iceberg – determine the direction and movement of a human group. In Iraq's case, politics are even more difficult to explain, given the existence of various masses sometimes moving in opposite directions or clashing altogether. Thus the apparently inexplicable moves of the Sunnis, Shi'is and Kurds are in fact conditioned by a submerged mass of memories, loyalties and designs that are not always perceived by others.

To measure the width of the iceberg's base, one has to plunge beneath the surface, to plunge into history. Such a fascinating adventure cannot be accomplished without the help of others. I am very grateful to all those who helped me accomplish it. First and foremost, I should like to acknowledge the late Professor Elie Kedourie's sharp insights given years ago. These proved so valuable that they continued to guide me during the long process of turning an apparently outdated PhD dissertation into a most timely book. Professor Kedourie's passing away left his former students with a sense of great loss and at the same time of responsibility towards historical evidence and its not always convenient implications.

I am also grateful to Professor Roy Mottahedeh, who spared no effort to help me feel at home at the Center for Middle Eastern Studies at Harvard University. His seminal work *Loyalty and Leadership in an Early Islamic Society* (Princeton, 1980) was a great source of inspiration, pointing to the intrinsic and not always discerned ties and connections that keep members of a society together.

I should also like to thank Dr Suzan Gibson Miller, the Center's assistant director, for her friendship and special assistance during the last stages of my writing. Barbara Henson and Helen Ives were wonderful with their advice and support in all technical matters. Lynne Gay, Dalia Geffen and Haya Naor edited this manuscript at different stages without sparing time or effort. Following the advice of the late Professor Kedourie regarding transliteration from Arabic to English, I have disregarded diacritical marks (except for the hamza and ain), and have retained the names in common usage when referring to well-known people and places. I am also grateful to Helga Lokiec for her help with translations from German sources. My recognition goes to all of them as well as my apologies for the remaining errors, for which I alone am responsible. The Truman Institute at the Hebrew University in Jerusalem awarded me a grant that permitted the final polishing of the manuscript, for which I am grateful.

Above all, I should like to thank my immediate family: my brother, Franklin, who understood; my mother, Esther, who believed; and my two sons, Irad and Yanai, who grew up so wisely and handsomely in the process.

Introduction

This book is an analysis of political dynamics in Iraq from its inception as a separate political entity in 1921 until 1958, when the old system was overthrown and new revolutionary forces came to power. The idea for the book arose from a need to understand better some of the events in the history of Iraq that look like recidivistic problems when viewed from an historical perspective. This book is therefore a search in Iraq's past in order to understand its present better. This search was undertaken by using two parallel methods, namely, reassessing previous approaches to Iraq as a society and correcting some of the historical misconceptions that had led to many errors in the present. With these two methods in mind, I tried to offer a different image of Iraq, one in which its complex web of social, ethnic and religious connections can be seen more clearly.

In almost all studies on Iraq published in the last two decades, connections and divisions were the main topic. However, the real nature of these divisions, as well as their political expression, was in most cases misinterpreted. The divisiveness of Iraq's population was evaluated in terms of greater or lesser national integration and/or social cohesion, without offering precise answers as to how divisiveness, national integration and social cohesion should be measured in each particular case. Iraq and the dynamics of its politics remain a riddle, mostly because these divisions were explained not only in terms of ethnic, sectarian, religious and linguistic categories, but also in terms of economic interests and class affiliations.

Even when these explanations proved insufficient, no re-evaluation was made, and 'integration' and 'cohesion' were seen as the natural outcomes of a continuous process towards the crystallization of a national identity that supposedly reflected the designs of all the factions in Iraq's population. An increasing allegiance to the state and its institutions seemed to be the inevitable result of a process in which primordial loyalties, to the village, town and a religious or ethnic group, would gradually be replaced by loyalty to the state and the nation.[1]

The establishment of strong, centralist regimes and the dissemination of a radical ideology helped to suggest that the state-formation process in Iraq was advanced enough to neutralize the re-emergence of separatist tendencies. Such impressions were strengthened by the current assumptions that modernization could not help but lead to the formation of a nation in which all the sectors of the population would express themselves politically.

Before proceeding any further, it may be useful to define some of the concepts that pervade the text of this book. Among these, the concepts of state, nation and national identity should be considered.

I have chosen Anthony D. Smith's definitions as working formulas. He defines *state* as the assemblage of public institutions exercising a monopoly of coercion and extraction in a given territory.[2] *State-formation* is the process in which these institutions (legislature, executive, judiciary and armed forces) are formed. It also implies an organized effort towards internal cohesion. The concept *nation* refers to a definite social space within which its members live and work. The concept of nation implies historical and territorial continuities that locate the nation's population in time and space.[3] At the same time, the concept of nation implies integration and encapsulates the idea of a common destiny.[4] *Nationalism* is the doctrine that makes the nation the object of every political endeavour[5] and it is a political reaction to an external presence, whereas *national identity* refers to the collective self-image of the members of a national unit and to their distinctive cultural system, shared by the majority of the population.

To clarify these concepts further, it may be worth noting that states are not nations, that nationalism is a doctrine (or a movement) and that the term national identity implies the legitimation of social order and common solidarities.

It is perhaps also important to note – again for the sake of clarity – that the newly formed states created after the First World War (including Iraq) are, up to now, considered states in formation, in which all the different communities forming their heterogeneous populations rally around the idea of *nation*, as it is defined and diffused by a *nationalistic* doctrine. The doctrine then is supposed to function like a glue, assembling all the groups (ethnic/linguistic/religious) together and persuading their members to take part in the process of building a state and creating a new, more appealing system of values which, while drawing from the traditional cultural values, adapts them to the requirements of modernity. The general impression is that nationalism is a historical necessity and is recognized as such by a population willing to collaborate in the endeavour of building a state. Once the state is built or established, the task of creating (or 'inventing') a nation is more easily accomplished. The sense of historical continuity is instilled through education, and a common culture is propagated by the diffusion of a common language. The economic, cultural and political integration of the population lays the grounds for a common national identity.

This sequence of developments corresponds, however, more to theory than to reality. The complex nature of human configurations and the difficulty of finding common denominators cast many shadows on the various stages of the process.

In the case of Iraq, many variants co-exist, making the categorization of human groups more difficult and the analysis of their participation in the process even more complex. To these difficulties, one must add the natural fluidity of identities (ethnic/communal and others) and each group's particular vision of the national process and their part in it.

It is also important to note again that national integration is not an irreversible process and that group identities are not unidimensional. If we refocus our attention on Iraq and the various groups comprising its population, we see how difficult it is to define the elements categorizing each group and, consequently, to foresee the political behaviour of its members. If we take the Iraqi Shi'is as an example, we see how complex a task it is to measure the intermittent effects of ethnicity and religious affiliation on their political behaviour. As an instance one can refer to the alignment of the Shi'is with the Iraqi government during the Iran–Iraq war (1980–88). Their position was explained at the time in terms of the precedence of loyalty to the state over loyalty to religion. That was particularly important at a time when the attraction of Shi'i Islam was at its zenith.[6] This loyalty to the state was seen as the result of the Shi'is' gradual integration into Iraq's political system and cultural life.

The Shi'is' position reinforced the opinion that the Sunni–Shi'i conflict was, and still is, political in its essence. Stemming originally from a political controversy over the right method for choosing the successor to the Prophet, the Sunni–Shi'i conflict was, also in the context of modern Iraq, reduced to a contention over 'fruits of office' and deprived of its historical and religious dimensions. The religious factor was undermined and subordinated to the ethnic one. Emphasis was put on the fact that Iraq's Sunnis and Shi'is are Arabs, speak the same language and take pride in Arab history and culture.

3

This explanation, although correct, especially for the urbanized and secularly educated sectors of Iraq's Shi'i population today, fails to explain why the Shi'i community as a whole is not yet totally integrated in all echelons of Iraqi society. It also fails to explain why the Shi'is, although subscribing to the idea of an Iraqi state, do not fully identify with the version of Iraqi identity propagated by official circles. The proof of this are the constant upheavals whose eruptions express the tension and conflict which continue to exist today.

Without dwelling, at this point of the debate, on all the causes for tension, I should like to refer to the cultural dimension of Islam – or, in this case, Islams – as a basic component of identities.

The influence of the idea of Islam as an ingredient in the formation of local cultural identities is immense, and at this point it is worth introducing the idea of culture in its anthropological dimension.

As explained by Clifford Geertz in *The Interpretation of Cultures* (1973 and 1993), culture is the webs of significance established by men which forge their collective behaviour. In Geertz's quotation from Claude Kluckhohn's *Mirror for Man*, culture is a total way of life of a group and its way of thinking, feeling and behaving.[7] In other words, culture is a system whose core symbols are the basis upon which a whole social structure is erected.[8] If we define culture as a complex of symbols recommending a style of life, of rituals and beliefs, one can more easily understand the immense power of Islam (or of religion in general) in the forging of a group's identity. This was particularly true at a period in time – such as the one studied here – when groups were mainly defined according to their members' religious affiliation.

This was a period when the lingering effects of the millet system still determined allegiances, loyalties, identities. The passage from the Ottoman era to modern statehood was in the making, while contradictory influences, values and interests clashed continuously.

This was a passage to a new era in which religion was no longer accepted as the main element forging a group's identity. Attention was turned to other factors acting in the process, and their growing or declining influence which varied according to the challenges put forth by changing circumstances.

Another, totally different example of the way in which ethnic, cultural and religious factors interacted (and still do) in the shaping of the relationships between two distinct groups is the conflict between Kurds and Arabs. There is no disagreement regarding the classification of Kurds and Arabs as ethnically and linguistically distinct. The question as to whether the Iraqi Kurds subscribe to the idea of an Iraqi national identity which is Arab in essence remains, however, a source of contention. Some scholars base their argument on the fact that the 1970 agreement establishing the principle of administrative autonomy in the Kurdish areas paved the way for the Kurds' acceptance of the Iraqi identity.

Without entering, at this point, into a larger debate over the question of administrative autonomy for the Kurdish areas, I should like to point out that – when seen in the context of the long-lasting conflict between the Kurds and the Iraqi government – the 1970 agreement (which is viewed by some as the ultimate proof of the Kurds' acceptance of an Iraqi identity) appears more as a political arrangement, pragmatic in essence. It was instrumental for the preservation of the Kurds' cultural characteristics on the one hand and for avoiding their total separation from Iraq on the other.

The same rationale is used in analysing the identification of Iraq's other communities with the model of nation propagated by the Sunnis from the earliest stages of Iraq's formation. The current view is that Iraq's Christians, Turkmen, Yazidis and other indigenous groups have gradually adopted and consequently contributed to the crystallization of an Iraqi identity.

The integration of the different Christian communities in Iraq's society is usually brought up as an example of successful nation-building and is mainly attributed to the ethnic factor in their identity and to the deep roots these communities have in the ancestral territory. The rationale is that the members of the different Christian minorities are Arabs, indigenous and, as such, totally identified with the state in its modern version and with the nation in a historical context. An exception is made in the case of the Assyrians, a Christian minority originally from eastern Turkey, whose painful settlement in Iraq cannot be accounted for as an example of voluntary participation in the nation-building process.

The current view is that in modern Iraq religious affiliation is a secondary and not a primary type of loyalty. Drawing from the principles of modern citizenship, many believe that loyalty goes first and foremost to the state and cannot be shared on an almost equal level of intensity with loyalties to the community. That is to say that there is no place in a modern state for group definitions along communal or religious lines. All this holds true when the point of departure is a steady and voluntary participation of all these elements in the state-building process and when the lingering effects of old loyalties do not interfere in the course of events. However, constant 'bumps in the road' remind us that the way to statehood is not as smooth as the one described above.

Various attempts were made to explain the nature of the obstacles standing in Iraq's way to a fully crystallized common identity. Michael C. Hudson, in *Arab Politics: The Search for Legitimacy*, maintains that the instability of a political system is generally the result of too little support given to the country's ruler by the population. This support can come about when the 'new scale of beliefs' implemented by the state brings a shift of allegiance 'from building blocks of primary legitimacy (kinship and religion) to more complex ones such as nationalism and modernity'.[9] The legitimacy of the government of the day, and, by implication, of the state, is thereafter guaranteed and the stability of the whole political system assured. Accordingly, the blend of ingredients, such as literacy, urbanization and education, in the 'social mobilization package' should lead, at the end of the day, to the identification of all sectors in the population with the state and its institutions.

However, the increasing instability of Iraqi politics led to a search for different explanations. Hanna Batatu, in *The Old Social Classes and the Revolutionary Movements of Iraq*,[10] provided a contrasting definition of the nature of divisions and associations in Iraqi society. In his book, division lines were traced horizontally, with social position and economic interests as the main determinants in political dynamics. Vertical categories of ethnic and religious affiliation were subordinated to the horizontal, class-structured ones. These vertical lines were supposed to fade as society evolved. The application of this model to a Middle Eastern society was important, as it tried to offer a closer description of how politics were determined from below, by the population and not just by the rulers and policy-makers.

Although Batatu recognized that all classes in monarchic Iraq 'remained purely economic in character without [carrying] a political aspect',[11] he reconsidered this statement further on by referring to the 'unconscious effects' of class affiliation on the political awareness of its members. The difficulty of measuring the intensity of these unconscious effects, however, led Batatu to conclude that political positions were determined by factors other than economic ones. That is because classes were no more than 'parallel structures within the recognized religious communities'.[12] Subtle as the argument was, it could not establish the reasons that induced different sectors of the population to opt for determined political stands at determined political junctures. The overlapping of hierarchies of wealth and ethnic affiliation suggests that the vertical ethnic/religious divisions are more resilient than the horizontal socio-economic ones.

Such an interplay of vertical and horizontal cleavages led to the next step in the discussion, namely, the fundamental changes brought about by the 1958 revolution which supposedly led to the rotation of the axis from a vertical to a horizontal position. The assumption was that in the post-1958 era most of the problems would disappear and no questions would arise regarding the endemic character of some of the problems registered during the monarchy.

Partial answers to these questions were found in séveral studies appearing during the late 1980s that explained the re-emergence of tension between the different communities by focusing on 'ethnic politics'.[13] Ethnicity was then rediscovered and used as a key to decode political behaviour. It challenged previous assumptions that modernization of the political system led inevitably to integration and democracy. This key was used to explain the lack of a uniform national identity and to specify the origins of distinct versions of collective identity.

Thus the ethnic approach replaced class-oriented analyses in the reformulation of the rules of Iraq's political game. Its main flaw, however, lay in the looseness of its terminology. By leaving the definition of ethnic characteristics somewhat vague, the ethnic approach blurred the distinctions between the characteristics that mattered politically and those that did not. By the same token, the impossibility of offering clear-cut divisions made this approach inappropriate when it came to defining cross-cutting categories, such as Shi'i Arabs and Sunni Kurds, and to evaluating each group's position in a political system ruled by Sunni and Arab cultural values.

Moreover, the ethnic approach, while defining some of the constitutive elements of the 'ethnic identity' (common myths, memoirs, symbols and values)[14] wrapped in the 'cultural package', proved insufficient when it came to evaluating its political implications in the specific Iraqi context. This evaluation was sometimes effectuated by inserting the whole package into a 'perennialist' perspective, one that focused on the nation's historic continuity.[15] However, the *de facto* autonomy of the Kurds and the Shi'is in Ottoman times made it difficult to present them as part of a perennial Iraqi nation. By the same token, the 'ethnic key' by itself could not indicate why, in Iraq's case, traditional structures could not subsist within contemporary models of social and political organization or explain why nationalism, the 'culture of the elites', did not seem to reach the country's 'peasantry'.[16]

The difficulty of finding answers to many of the above questions by using the ethnic key brought about the rediscovery of another one: Islam. The advent of the Islamic Revolution in Iran refocused attention on religion and on its role as the main catalyst in the reversal of political systems in the Middle East. It was then assumed that the Iraqi Shi'is would be attracted to the Iranian model.[17] Some comparative studies tried to find common characteristics between the Shi'i radical movement in Iraq and its Sunni equivalents in Syria and Egypt.[18] Although interesting parallels were traced, a more careful examination of the cases in question revealed basic differences. This was because these comparisons failed to highlight the basic differences between these movements when interacting with different social and political environments. In other words, these comparisons underrated the fundamental differences between a Shi'i movement in conflict with a political system embedded in Sunni values, and a Sunni radical movement performing within a system ruled by Sunni traditions and culture.[19]

The Islamic key in itself failed therefore to offer a complete explanation of the reasons why the Shi'i radical movement rejected nationalism in its secular as well as its ethnic dimension, whereas the Syrian Sunni radical movement accepted Pan-Arabism, dismissing only its secular characteristics. The Islamic key in itself did not offer a more viable explanation of the Shi'is' 'traditional activism' or 'traditional quietism'[20] when no further indication was offered regarding the historical context in which these contradictory attitudes manifested themselves.

Hence, each key in itself could not offer satisfactory answers to the questions that continued to arise. A more accurate and complete approach was needed, one that could apply each of these methods and combine their findings. This is not an easy task. A *partial* solution can be found by recourse to history. By trying to discover how these 'keys' interacted in the past, we could perhaps trace some analogies as to their interactions in the present.

History, or its imprint on collective memories, offers a more complete approach to an understanding of the attitudes of the three main contestants in the Iraqi arena – the Sunnis, the Shi'is and the Kurds – and helps explain why a different perception of the past brings a different perception of the present and, implicitly, of the future. By delving into the past, we rediscover three 'self-absorbed and feebly interconnected societies',[21] each with different collective memories and different notions of identity. These were communal identities shaped by factors internal to each community, further reinforced by opposition to the other communities and then to the state. This was so because the state represented not only a monopoly of power in the hands of the Sunnis but also a political expression of Sunni cultural values.

8

This book is not yet an attempt to find the 'key' to decipher all the riddles in Iraq's politics. This book purports to tell a story, the story of Iraq's inception as a state as viewed by the inhabitants of the provinces. In this story, ethnicity, Islam and state-building intertwine and react to each other, providing some indication as to their weight in past times.

The first chapter focuses on the way in which Iraq was 'invented' and on the treaties and agreement formalizing its creation. Chapters 2 and 3 focus on the reaction of the main ethnic/religious groups to the state, its institutions and the hegemony of culture implied in state-building. These chapters also point out Baghdad's difficulties in extending its writ throught the rest of the country.

Chapter 4 centres on the crystallization of three different models of Iraqi nationalism: one that grows in opposition to Britain – the matrix upon which the Iraqi state and institutions were modelled; a second that grows through resentment towards Britain and is inspired by the German model of nation and nationalism; and a third, ephemeral but yet very present, a current that adopted the motto 'Iraq first' and purported to emulate the Turkish model.

Part II opens with a description of Iraq's educational system and its role in forging an Iraqi national identity. Chapters 6 and 7 deal with the reactions in the provinces to education, nationalism and the idea of state developed after the first two decades of 'nation-building' through state education and administrative centralism. Chapter 8 reassesses the effects of the process at midway and the alternatives – ideological and others – adopted by inhabitants in the provinces.

Without dwelling extensively on theory, the stories told refer to some of the main theoretical points raised in this introduction. Even though a focus on the different communities may seem at first glance to be a use of the 'ethnic key', a more careful reading will indicate that the 'key' actually used was that of history, or the historical context in which ethnic, religious and social explanations intertwined and found expression. This revision of the current, Baghdad-centred version of Iraq's formation could only be based on documents describing the situation and the atmosphere in the Iraqi provinces at the time. British and, in a lesser measure, American files containing reports, pamphlets, journals, newspapers and petitions collected in the provinces were therefore used as main sources for this study.

Few Arab primary sources could be used for this purpose, whereas the secondary ones (mainly the memoirs of Sunni politicians fully engaged in the process of state-making) could hardly portray the feelings, hopes and disillusions of the inhabitants of the provinces during the period under revision.

Refraining from adopting a deterministic position while writing history, I shall abstain from referring to the events and developments described in the following pages as the roots for Iraq's constant tendency to divisiveness. My purpose is to tell a story and let readers, draw their own conclusions.

Part I

1

Formal Independence and Informal Implications: Treaties, Agreements and State-formation

At the end of the First World War the British found themselves in possession of three former Ottoman vilayets – Baghdad, Basra and Mosul – without having a defined policy for their future.

Britain's interests in the area went back to the eighteenth century, centring on trade from India to the Gulf and vice versa. After the First World War the need to guarantee a continued British presence in the Gulf area became imperative for two reasons: to safeguard the air route connecting the various parts of the British Empire and to retain control of the Persian oil fields and the Mosul vilayet. In both cases, strategic and economic interests were intertwined, as Mosul's oil, although commercially unexplored, already weighed as a factor in British political considerations.

The question of how to safeguard military achievements and control the new territory (with frontiers extending 1,600 miles and a population of more than three million) remained unanswered, given Britain's economic problems caused by heavy wartime expenses.

The decision to replace the British mandate (prescribed by the League of Nations at the San Remo Conference in 1920) with a less expensive formula that would legalize the British military presence and preserve British political and economic interests in the area was an outcome of the above impasse. This chapter describes the steps leading to a series of treaties and agreements between Britain and the new rulers of Iraq – the Emir Feisal of the Hijaz and his entourage of Sherifian officers, whose most important figures were Nuri al Sa'id and Ja'far al 'Askari.

The relevance of these treaties and agreements transcends the realm of politics, as they eventually brought changes in all spheres of life. They introduced new political and administrative measures that would eventually lead to a new system of allegiances and loyalties. The institutionalization of Sunni dominance over the various ethnic, sectarian and linguistic groups populating the three geographically distinct areas artificially united after the war was meant to create a united and homogeneous society.

However, the difficulty of imposing such radical changes on a heterogeneous population was clear.[1] The vilayets had developed a system of direct communication with Istanbul. By the same token the Ottoman Empire's traditional policy of non-intervention in day-to-day life helped preserve local customs and practices as well as the social position and authority of the local leadership. The government's intervention was sporadic at best while tribal sheikhs and Kurdish aghas remained traditional opponents to a central government that would undermine their own authority. Even the Tanzimat reforms, implemented throughout the empire during the second half of the nineteenth century, did not change this state of affairs.

Such a population, so bound by tradition, could hardly accept the imposition of a Western-style political system or the idea of a constitutional monarchy headed by a foreign king, who hailed from the Hijaz via Syria and enjoyed little support inside the country. The British attempt to impose both could not but stir discontent at all levels of society.

Emir Feisal's arrival in 1921 turned the history of modern Iraq in a totally different direction, suiting mainly the personal perceptions of the British officials involved in the process. During the 1920s these officials – led by Percy Cox, Gertrude Bell, A. T. Wilson, Henry Dobbs and Ken Cornwallis among others – carried out Britain's official policy on the spot, leaving their personal imprint on the country's formative years.

The treaties engineered by these officials sought to legitimize British presence in the area and at the same time served as a means to define the country over which the new rulers would rule. In parallel with the establishment of norms between Britain and Iraq's new rulers, there were protests from Baghdad's more radical nationalist circles and from inhabitants of the provinces, mainly the Kurds and the Shi'is.

The first treaty that bestowed legitimacy upon Britain's presence in Iraq was signed in October 1922. With its ratifying protocol of June 1924, the treaty provided an option for Britain to exchange its mandatory rule – established in 1920 at the San Remo Conference –

14

for a friendship treaty preserving nearly all the mandatory privileges, under a different cover. The duration of the treaty was 20 years, with revisions to be made every four years. The treaty was ratified by a constituent assembly elected through indirect elections after the establishment of a constitution under the Organic Law of 1924.

The British sought control on two levels: the military and the administrative. Militarily, Britain's forces enjoyed maximum freedom of manoeuvre and facilities such as fuel storage and the use of roads, railways, waterways and ports. The 1922 treaty also permitted British control over the nascent Iraqi army by a network of British officers, supervised by a British inspector general.[2]

On the administrative level, a network of advisers controlled ministries and key institutions, such as the departments of irrigation and public works, land registry, police and others.

The 1922 treaty had two annexes. The first, a judicial agreement drawn up under Article 9, safeguarded the interests of foreigners, retaining in some ways the immunities and privileges they enjoyed under the Ottoman system of capitulations. To this end, British judges were invested with effective powers making it possible for foreigners to be tried by a court including at least one British judge.[3]

The second annex to the 1922 treaty was a financial agreement providing for the transfer to Iraq's government of all public works built by the British, including roads, bridges and irrigation canals. The railway system and the port of Basra, considered as strategic assets, remained under British control. A joint British–Iraqi directorate was in charge of the administration of the railway and the port's trust.[4]

A military agreement, also signed in 1924, forwarded responsibility for internal order and external defence to the Iraqi government in four years' time.[5] There was, however, a hidden catch in the military agreement. The need to secure the free movement of British troops and to maintain the network of communications made Britain as interested in the country's stability as the Iraqi authorities themselves. The question of Iraq's security was complex, as it encompassed external threats to its newly established borders (threats emanating mainly from the tribes of Nejd and from Kemalist Turkey) and internal threats (coming from the ethnic and religious groups forming the population in the provinces). The danger of dismemberment from within was far greater than any danger from outside the borders.

The Sunni government's proposal to create an army by conscription – as a tool for defence and national sovereignty on the one hand and as a means to consolidate its own position on the other – provoked a reaction from the British, who preferred a small professional and mobile army.[6] Such a reaction was caused by the certitude that conscription would lead to the mobilization of poorly trained troops,[7] and also by the apprehension that Iraq could not cope with an increased military budget.[8] The British wanted the funds to go to the construction of roads and railways,[9] essential for the country's development and indispensable for the mobility of their own troops in Iraq. The Sunni authorities, for their part, believed that the British position stemmed from the desire to retain control over the country and the Iraqi army, and from a basic disbelief in the government's capacity to control the provinces.[10] Such a lack of confidence in the Iraqi army was at the basis of the air force officers' pressure to remain in Iraq for the years to come, in spite of the cost of maintaining Royal Air Force units and conciliary forces in Iraq's territory.[11]

The debate over conscription aroused waves of antagonism all over the country. The Shi'i leaders saw conscription as a threat to their position and an instrument for perpetuating Sunni domination for decades to come. This position stemmed from the belief that the illiterate Shi'i tribesmen would remain the army's rank and file, whereas the officer class would be drawn from the Sunnis.

The Kurds and Yazidis also opposed conscription, and for much the same reasons, whereas the Jews and the Christians considered emigration as a means to escape the draft. A good illustration of the impasse thus created is a letter written in October 1927 by E. L. Ellington, from Air Headquarters in Baghdad, to Sir Henry Dobbs, the High Commissioner: 'In fact, the only ones who profess to be in favour of it [conscription] are those who will not be conscripted.'[12]

Ellington echoed here, as in other documents, the opinion of his colleagues at the Air Ministry, namely, that the country's security should be based first and foremost on an air scheme. The air officers' lack of confidence in Iraq's army and its new rulers reinforced the tendency prevalent in Britain's official circles to turn the RAF into the backbone of the country's security system.[13] This option, however, had far-reaching consequences. An air defence scheme implied secure bases, guarded by troops other than those that could be drawn from the newly formed Iraqi armed forces.

Moreover, this reliance on the air scheme undermined the necessity to conscript a large local army and implied a *de facto* abrogation of the controversial points in the military agreement. In effect, the air scheme, if correctly implemented, would reduce Iraq's *de jure* and *de facto* responsibility for internal security and allow funds to be transferred to the development of the communication network so looked for by the air authorities.

16

As the years passed, the debate around the scheme expanded, becoming one of the main points of discussion among the air authorities, the Colonial Office, the Treasury and local nationalist circles.[14] The tension thus created induced the British to divert attention to other points under discussion, among them the question of the Mosul vilayet.

THE MOSUL QUESTION

The composition of Mosul's population (Kurds and Turkmen, mostly Sunnis) was already an important factor in former plans to annexe the former vilayet of Mosul to Iraq. This annexation would prevent the Shi'is from constituting a majority and endangering the Sunnis' hegemony over the country. Annexation, however, was not a simple matter. The Kurds, the main group in the area, were unwilling to be ruled by the Arabs and asked for the promises of autonomy made by Britain during and after the First World War to be honoured.

The Kurds' second choice was to become part of Turkey. This option was supported by the Turks' claim to Mosul on the basis of its occupation by Britain in the last days of the war, when the armistice had already taken effect. The Turks also dwelt on the legitimacy of their presence when confronted with the difficulty of the new Iraqi authorities in retaining control over Mosul without the active help of the RAF.[15] In other words, the Mosul vilayet could be attached to Iraq only if a British presence was legally maintained. However, legality could be drawn only from a mandate accorded to Britain by the local population. To this end, a commission appointed by the League of Nations was sent to Mosul. Its formal mission was to inquire into the population's wishes. Although aware of the impossibility of learning the population's real desires, the commission's members decided to attach Mosul to Iraq on the condition that Britain remain the country's mandatory power for another 25 years (beginning in December 1925). However, this condition was circumvented by a later proviso stipulating that the nomination of Iraq to the League of Nations would put an end to the mandate and abrogate the treaty. This proviso implied the extension of Baghdad's writ to Mosul in spite of the resistance of the local population. How Baghdad's control over the provinces would come into effect, and whether Iraq was prepared for independence, remained open questions.[16]

Article 5 of a new treaty, signed in January 1926, granted the British sites for new air bases near Basra and west of the Euphrates and permitted them to remain in Hinaidi and Mosul for another five years.[17] The terms of this article provided the answers for the above questions, without, however, referring to the controversy over the government's ability to maintain order in the provinces. It was therefore clear that the RAF would assume a *de facto* responsibility for the extension of Baghdad's authority to the provinces.

Once the maintenance of order was guaranteed and the authority of the government and the reputation of its armed forces ensured, renewed pressures were exerted on the King by the nationalist forces. The nationalists wanted the abrogation of the 1926 treaty and based their claim on the British undertaking to revise the terms of the treaty after four years. The revision of the treaty was obtained during Feisal's visit to Europe, as a result of his refusal to return to Iraq without a trophy to ease the pressure from Baghdad's nationalists. The British promise to support Iraq's candidacy to the League of Nations in 1932 was thus obtained.[18]

The prospect of premature independence met the opposition of the Air Ministry, which wanted to retain the air bases on Iraq's soil and have the Assyrian Levies as the guards of those bases.[19] The reason for the appointment of Levies – troops recruited during the war from among the Assyrians – as guards for the British air bases was twofold: their maintenance as special troops would, on the one hand, help avoid a reliance on the Iraqi army for the defence of the bases and, on the other hand, prevent the Levies' conscription in the Iraqi army. Even more indicative of the Air Ministry's lack of confidence in the Iraqi army was the requirement that the Air Officer Commanding be recognized as the officer supervising any joint military ground–air action of Iraqi and British forces. These measures were intended to retain some control over the army and control of the government's moves in the provinces.[20]

These conditions aroused protests in Baghdad and led to calls for the abrogation of the 1926 treaty and a return to the old treaty of 1922.[21] One possible compromise – an informal extension of the status quo – met the Air Ministry's opposition. This was because the possibility of leaving the air forces unsecured by a treaty[22] was less palatable to the air authorities than to the Colonial Office.

The air authorities reiterated the importance of the RAF in face of the inability of the nascent Iraqi army to cope with insurrection. In effect the scarcity of British ground troops (two armoured sections in Baghdad, three in Basra and one in Mosul)[23] induced even the Iraqi authorities to recognize the necessity of keeping the RAF as a means to preserve the government's authority in the provinces.[24]

The government's dependence on the RAF did not, however,

prevent the nationalists from pressing further for the attainment of total independence.[25] The complex situation thus created led to a deadlock that lasted until September 1929, when the advent of a Labour government in England brought the suspension of the 1926 treaty. This did not, however, change the situation radically, as the main problems remained unsolved. The most important one was the continuing quarrel over the nature of relations between the RAF and the Iraqi army after independence.

This impasse was finally solved by Nuri al Sa'id's secret proposition to Henry Dobbs, the British High Commissioner, on 27 October 1928, under which the retention of the air bases by Britain was assured,[26] as was freedom of movement and action for British air forces in Iraqi territory. Accordingly the RAF would enjoy 'all the privileges as if it were in Britain or in India'[27] and be completely free of any possible intervention on the part of the Iraqi government.

In return, Britain would accept the idea of a conscripted army. These secret agreements paved the way for Iraq's independence, letting Britain interfere in Iraq's internal affairs. The parameters of British–Iraqi relations after independence were thus established, as were relations between Baghdad and the provinces in the following years.

THE ADVISERS' ISSUE

The main obstacle was thus removed, leaving only one troublesome question still to be solved: the presence of British advisers. Iraqi rulers and officials resented the advisers' presence and their intervention in state affairs. The British, however, wished to retain this valuable source of information and influence, before and after independence.

The antagonism this issue engendered was aggravated by a secret programme initiated in September 1929 by 'Abd al Muhsin Sa'dun's fourth cabinet. Although its contents were never released, the programme apparently stipulated a reduction in the number and authority of British officials employed in governmental departments. The sensibility around the issue continued, however, to fuel tension, and the pressure exerted by both sides on 'Abd al Muhsin led the Prime Minister to commit suicide.

Despite the antagonism and bitterness created by the advisership issue,[28] the British still hoped that the Iraqi rulers would recognize their inability to run affairs of state.

There will be a complete cessation of payment of revenues and tribal areas taxes in the Euphrates and Kurdish area [as well as an] increase of brigandage and rise of tribes. When the tribes rise and revenue has failed the Iraqis will demand the help of the RAF. We must refrain until they admit formally that they must collaborate with us and then we will step into the arena again with increased reputation.[29]

In fact the government's dependence on British advisers was disputable. However, even recognizing that 'either the Chamber must stop [the advisers] from going on leave or it must change the time of the annual opening of Parliament',[30] the Iraqi authorities disputed the quantity of advice to be accepted from Britain, as the proposed reduction in the number of advisers from 150 to 18 did not seem to appease the nationalist circles.

A secret accord between Feisal and the British then brought the impasse to an end, as the King promised that current information on issues of strategic importance to Britain, such as the oil fields, the railways and the port of Basra, would continue to flow to the British after independence. The last obstacle to the signing of the 1930 treaty was thus removed.[31]

THE 1930 TREATY

The new treaty was signed on 30 June 1930. Nuri al Sa'id was then Prime Minister and Minister of Foreign Affairs, and Ja'far al 'Askari was Minister of Defence. This convenient composition of government, led by two ex-Sherifian officers known as pro-British, coupled with the temporary paralysis of the anti-British opposition because of personal rivalry between Yasin al Hashimi and Rashid 'Ali al Gailani, led to the signing of the 1930 treaty. Iraq's independence, achieved despite the government's difficulties on the administrative level and on internal security issues, resulted in a *de facto* interdependence between Iraq's political leadership and Britain.[32] This interdependence blurred the vision of both sides in relation to some basic definitions. Among those, the term 'civilian population' was redefined by the British in order to suit their policy and interests.[33] 'Civilian population' was seen by the British as having a different meaning in Iraq from the one it had in other parts of the world, as it referred mainly to armed tribesmen, Shi'i and Kurds. As a result, aerial bombardment of the civilian population was accepted by both sides as a norm, especially when it served to safeguard British interests.[34]

These definitions and patterns of action became thereafter a permanent part of Iraq's political reality.

The British were not totally unaware of the possible implications of this line of policy on the country's future. Henry Dobbs, the former High Commissioner, when reassessing the 1930 treaty and its contradictions, seemed especially concerned about the Iraqi government's inability to fulfil the functions bestowed upon it by the old military agreement, particularly in the maintenances of order in the provinces. At the same time he was worried about the growing involvement of British forces in support of the government's policies in the provinces. 'The British forces would be used', stated Dobbs, against those subjects 'deprived of the natural remedy against tyranny – the hope of a successful insurrection.'[35] Later events added weight to his predictions.

This short account of the developments that launched the state-making process and gave official recognition to Sunni hegemony over the country contradicts the current thesis which maintains that a colonial power is always interested in keeping ethnic consciousness alive as a means of perpetuating its mandate over the country. In Iraq's case, the evidence contradicts the assumption that the principle of divide and rule prevailed in all types of colonial policy. What we see is that Britain – in its eagerness to get rid of a direct responsibility for, and the costs of, Iraq's internal affairs – opted for an arrangement which secured order by the use of the RAF. The subordination of the provinces to Baghdad was therefore artificially maintained.

On the administrative level Britain sought indirect control of Iraq's affairs – and ultimately achieved it – through the advisership system. The perpetuation of this anomalous situation was possible only through Britain's tacit alliance with the ruling minority at the expense of the country's majority. This is not, therefore, a case of divide and rule just for the sake of colonial interests but rather a case of state-building and compulsory integration for the very same purposes.

2

The Northern Provinces in the 1920s and 1930s

THE ASSYRIAN AND OTHER CHRISTIAN COMMUNITIES: STATE-FORMATION, TRIAL AND ERROR

The first test for independent Iraq was the Assyrian affair. It was cited as an example of the government's first breach of promises made to the League of Nations preserving the rights of the minorities after independence.

The fact that the text of the 1930 treaty made no mention of Iraq's minorities proved – among other things – the determination of the Sunni leadership to construct an Iraqi identity that would draw mainly upon the Sunni Arab cultural reservoir. It also suggested that the politically dominant group was entitled to shape the country's cultural values and political life.

For nationalist circles, independence meant national assertiveness and the possibility to shape the state's institutions and cultural life according to the values of a renascent Arab nation.

From the British side, the omission of any reference to the minorities meant Britain's definite decision to subordinate her former pledges to the various communities for the sake of safeguarding British economic and strategic interests in Iraq. However, the text of the treaty could not reflect the anxiety of an inexperienced leadership concerned about the difficulties of establishing state authority over groups accustomed to self-government.

The first to suffer from this complex situation were the Assyrians. Their case was even more problematic, given the fact that their position as a *de jure* minority was controversial at best. Their arrival in Iraq after the war (in late 1918) and their status as refugees backed by the British contributed to growing opposition among the nationalist circles to Britain's protégés. The mosaic-like population in the area and the rising nationalist feelings among the Arab Sunni population in the town of Mosul made integration of the Assyrian refugees in Iraq even more difficult. The roots of the Assyrian problem can be found in the web of complexities that preceded the outbreak of the First World War, complexities resulting from British attempts to seek out allies among the local population to help them drive a wedge into Ottoman defences. The promises made to these allies before and during the war became problematic because they clashed with the new realities in its aftermath.

The Assyrian question began in 1915 with their expulsion by the Turks from their homeland in the Hakkari Mountains. This was the result of escalating tension between them – as a Christian belligerent minority – and a nascent, assertive Turkish nationalism. The rise of the Young Turks and the advent of the idea of a Turkish modern nation implied the redefinition by the former 'millets' members of their relations with the Turkish state. This revision was not easy, as it implied relinquishing privileges preserved during centuries of Ottoman rule for not yet clearly grasped benefits. This was a revision that the Assyrians were not so eager to undertake.

Believing themselves to be the descendants of the ancient Assyrian empire, this Christian minority had managed to maintain cultural and administrative autonomy over the centuries. They were governed by tribal councils headed by maliks (tribal leaders), while a supreme religious authority, the Mar Sham'un, acted as a link between the community and the Ottoman government when the need arose. This state of affairs was disturbed in 1908 by the implementation of a centralist policy by the Young Turks. Relations between the Assyrians and the Turkish authorities worsened with the outbreak of war, when the massacres of the Armenians fuelled fears of a jihad against all the Christians of the Ottoman Empire. Heeding British promises, the Assyrians rose against the Ottomans in May 1915. Their villages were burned by Turkish troops, and the Assyrians fled to Urmiya, a district already under Russian control. The collapse of the Russian front after the Bolshevik Revolution and the assassination of the Mar Sham'un by Agha Simko, chief of the Shikak Kurds, weakened the Assyrians politically and socially.

The opening in 1917 of a new offensive against the Allies under the command of a Turkish general, 'Ali Muhsin Beg, induced the British to use the Assyrians as a spearhead in their attempt to drive the Turks back to Rowanduz. Britain's failure to back the Assyrians during this operation caused the latter to withdraw in panic. The gathering of 90,000 Assyrians, in the summer of 1918, in the Ba'quba camp north of Baghdad[1] and the poor conditions in the camp demoralized the refugees, who were already suffering from the break-up of a traditionally supportive social system. The enlistment of men, in most cases heads of families, in the Levies further aggravated the refugees' feelings of being uprooted.

It is important to recall that the Levies, formed at the Cairo Conference in 1921, were at the time essentially Assyrian troops[2] modelled on the Indian army. The financial reasons that led to their creation proved unprofitable, and they became another example of financial considerations leading to big political mistakes. The rationale behind their creation was that native troops would be cheaper to maintain than British forces abroad. This view, even if economically valid, proved to be politically wrong. The employment of these Christian troops as a *de facto* British force contributed to the disavowal of the Assyrian community as a whole by the Muslim population.

The first incident between the two parties occurred in Kirkuk in 1923 when an attack on the refugees triggered the Levies' reaction.[3] This fuelled the feelings of mistrust between the two communities, further reducing the likelihood of the Assyrians' integration into Iraq.

In fact, their settlement in the Mosul vilayet was not a simple question. On the other hand, the Assyrians' desire to return to the Hakkari Mountains, which had remained part of the Turkish territory, could not easily be met. British efforts to include the district in Iraq's territory failed, and the Brussels Line established as the northern frontier of the vilayet by the League Commission of 1925[4] remained the official boundary. The delicate position of the Assyrians contributed to the League's decision to grant the vilayet to Iraq, but Mosul's annexation was made conditional on a continuous British presence in the area for 25 years.[5] The commission's decision was interpreted by the Assyrians as an informal promise that encompassed, among other things, the preservation of their rights as a millet. This assumption was based mainly on the special relations that had developed between them and the British during the war and by their privileged status as a Christian minority protected by the Archbishop of Canterbury. The League's recommendation regarding the collective settlement of the Assyrians in northern Iraq was viewed by the Iraqi government as impracticable. The government's position was due not only to its interest in dismembering a resentful community but also to the fact that no available land could be found in the northern districts to permit a collective settlement. According to government sources, this could be achieved only by the confiscation of

Kurdish lands or the settlement of the Assyrians as tenants of Kurdish aghas.[6]

The Assyrians' refusal to submit socially and economically to the Kurds (by preferring short-term leases rather than long-term ones)[7] helped to perpetuate their precarious condition. Their refusal also reinforced the government's argument that the Assyrians were unwilling to commit themselves to norms of conduct appropriate to modern states[8] and continuing to behave according to the rules of tribal societies.

This was partly true, but there were other aspects to be considered. First of all, the Assyrians were unwilling to relinquish their status as dhimmis – Christians protected by force of Islamic law, with well-defined rights which had been preserved for generations by the Ottomans. No amorphous notion of citizenship could replace the privileges of their former status, mainly because it would also imply the loss of their even higher status as Christians, which during the war had been placed on an almost equal footing with the British. Added to all that was the traditional animosity between the Assyrians and the Kurds, fuelled by memories of feuds and clashes that had occurred during and after the First World War.

In fact the animosity between the two communities had been artificially exacerbated, as some of the feuds had been instigated first by the Turks and then by the British. The following quotation from a telegram sent in October 1920 by the political officer at 'Aqra to Agha Petros, the military chief of the Assyrians, confirms this supposition: 'I am glad to hear of your successes on the Zab and hope you will be able to catch the Zibari and Barzani sheikhs and aghawat soon. I am sure the British government will be very grateful to you if you do so.'[9]

At the time, Agha Petros played the game of the British, further complicating the relations between the two communities. The expectation that such an intricate web of relations would radically change when modern norms of conduct were introduced was a naive one. What in fact happened was an increase in resentment and antagonism, leading to redefinition of each community as a 'nation' *per se.*

The confusion surrounding the term 'nation' and its obvious misapplication in this case should be attributed to the misunderstanding of the principle of self-determination as it developed after the First World War. The idea launched by US President Woodrow Wilson, that any self-differentiating people had the right to political autonomy, led to great confusion among the communities and to an increase of intercommunal tension. The confusion was further compounded by the intermingling of the concepts 'nation' and 'state'. The peoples in the area could hardly internalize the fact that the term 'state' implied loyalty to and identification with an effective government and its institutions, whereas the term 'nation', encompassing a sense of cultural distinctiveness, did not necessarily imply any political substantiation.

The Assyrians' self-definition as a 'nation' grew in opposition to the development of the concept of an Iraqi state. It also drew on the idea of culturally homogeneous nations propagated by Ataturk. An example of the above was the drawing up of the Assyrian National Pact in 1932, mirroring the Turkish National Pact signed years earlier. This document, following the dispersion of the Levies, was presented as a protest against Britain's 'failure to ensure the Assyrians' future as a nation',[10] or, in a more practical sense, to guarantee their incorporation into Iraq as a homogeneous collective:[11]

> We have now come to the real understanding that all the services done by our nation during the war and those of the Levies after the war have been obliterated ... for the reason that Iraq is getting its independence.[12]

In this document, the Levies expressed their commitment to the community, agreeing to meet the High Commissioner only after obtaining the Mar Sham'un's approval. This move was meant to emphasize their submission to the community's traditional leadership by defying the authority of their immediate superiors – the British officers. Their move was also intended to defy the Iraqi government's authority. The Levies insisted on the recognition of the Assyrians as a millet, implying the preservation of their political and cultural autonomy even in the framework of a modern Iraqi state. This authority was embodied in the preservation of Mar Sham'un's temporal and spiritual authority. In other words, the Levies required the different heirs of the empire – the states created after the First World War, and Iraq in particular – to recognize the community's rights along the same lines as in Ottoman times.[13]

On the other hand, the manifesto amounted to a retreat from a previously irrevocable position, namely the return to the Hakkari Mountains. However, the Iraqi authorities could not consider it as a compromise. They viewed the relinquishing of the Assyrians' claim to the Hakkari Mountains mainly as a slackening of Assyrian pressure on the British and a way out of a deadlock created by Britain's unfruitful attempts to annexe the area to Iraqi territory. The Iraqi authorities were less concerned about the Turks' refusal to give in to British territorial claims than about the fact that the Assyrians might jeopardize the extension of Baghdad's authority to the northern provinces.

Moreover, the Iraqi government considered the Assyrians as a burden inherited from the Ottomans and the British. In their view, Iraq, a sovereign state, was not obliged to pay for its predecessors' mistakes. The Iraqi government agreed to preserve the administrative advantages accorded to the Assyrians, in the late 1920s, namely exemption from taxes, provision of special funds for schools and hospitals and the use of church endowments for the promotion of the community's interests.[14] However, and this was a point of principle, the state-building process launched after independence implied the integration of the Assyrians as individuals not as a collective. This was the rationale behind the promotion of the Baradost project in Arbil liwa' in the early 1930s.[15] However, this settlement plan was considered by the Assyrians as another attempt to dismember their community, since only a small number of the refugees could be transferred to Baradost.[16] The project was subsequently abandoned and the Assyrian problem remained unsolved.

A second point of discord was due to the Assyrians' unwillingness to relinquish their cultural patrimony. The Assyrians strove for the implementation of a special curriculum in their primary schools whereby Syriac would be preserved as the official language and the fundamentals of their religion would be considered as cultural and national determinants. These claims were a reaction to Article 28 of the 1930 Public Education Law which imposed a curriculum in which Arabic, Iraqi history and geography were predominant.[17]

These measures affected not only the Assyrians, whose status in Iraq was problematic, but also the schools of the native Christian communities in the Mosul area, the Chaldeans, Syrians and Jacobites. This was the first attempt to impose a uniform cultural programme whose final goal was to create a culturally homogeneous population that would – with time – subscribe to a common national-cultural identity. This goal, however, was difficult to reach. Culture and religion were so interwined that a modern national scheme of education could not easily replace them.

The problem was even more complex as each Christian community was an entity *per se*, making it impossible to refer to a single Christian community. Although some confusion still exists over the ramifications, it is important to note that in Ottoman times Christian communities were often referred to as *Masihiun* in a more collective sense. During the period studied, the fact that the three main communities – the Chaldeans, the Catholic branch of the Nestorians (60,000); the Assyrians (40,000); and the Syrian Catholics, Jacobites and Armenians (10,000) – did not stem from a single cultural source or adhere to the same churches was even more conspicuous. The Chaldeans' traditional connections with the Vatican, the Roman Catholics' links with France and the Assyrians' links with Britain accorded each of these communities a distinct set of references.[18] The Assyrians, as we have seen, found themselves in a much more precarious situation than the native Christian communities. The Assyrians were still trying to achieve the position and circumstances that the other Christian communities were struggling to maintain. The common denominator in this complex equation was the efforts made by the different communities to preserve their own characteristics in face of the attempts to institutionalize uniformity.

The institution of national schools and the replacement of priests by Muslim teachers trained in Baghdad's normal school were seen by all the Christians as an attempt to uproot their traditional sets of beliefs and references. Their claim was that in many cases the government's policy contributed to widening the gap between the communities instead of bridging it. A memorandum sent to the League of Nations in September 1930 by a Chaldean priest[19] points to the growing gap between the communities, a result of the spreading of the national education scheme in the Mosul area. Contacts between children of different communities lessened when Muslim children who had previously attended Christian schools run by Dominican priests began attending the schools set up by the state. A new education law establishing a network of schools to replace local schools (which previously belonged to the dominant community in a village) deprived 125,000 Christian children (Syrian and Chaldean) of their communal schools.

The government's policy 'reinforced, rather than weakened communal feelings', claimed the writer of the memorandum to the League of Nations, and the attempts to strip the communal leaders (in this case, priests and patriarchs) of their social role as mediators between Christian peasants or Chaldean craftsmen and the Iraqi authorities only tightened the links between community members and the clergy.[20] In fact, the government's policy of speeding up integration through national education and a more centralized administration had an immediate opposite effect. The government also rejected all claims for members of the communities to be appointed as administrative officials, as the measure was considered an affront to the state's sovereignty.

On this point, the Iraqi government was adamant, especially in relation to the Assyrians.[21] Since they were not even a native minority, the Assyrians were viewed as less entitled than the other Christian

minorities to enjoy any kind of administrative privileges. The Assyrians, accustomed to settling their problems through the mediation
of the High Commissioner, saw in this new dependence on Arab
officials a loss of status.[22] Their demand that the League's representative should act as intermediary was, however, considered by the Iraqi
government as an external interference not to be tolerated by an
independent state.[23]

The Assyrians sent endless petitions to the League of Nations,
claiming the loss of political, educational and administrative rights.[24]
The petitioners accused the Iraqi government of preventing the
development of a network of communications with the Medi-
terranean coast, namely Lebanon and Syria, isolating Mosul from its
natural markets, increasing its dependence on Baghdad and aggravat-
ing the hardship of the inhabitants.[25]

Although generally considered as foreigners, the Assyrians had the
support of Chaldeans, Jacobites, Protestants, Syrian Catholics, Armenians and even Yazidis and Jews in their claims.[26] Even if these
groups had not eventually backed the Assyrians' cause, their support
was a protest against the administrative and economic measures
implemented by the authorities.

Renewed claims by the Assyrians refocused the discussion on the
Mar Sham'un's status after independence.[27] The claims were based on
the government's undertaking to preserve the rights of Ottoman
subjects residing in Iraq before 1924,[28] a category into which the
Assyrians fell after Mosul's annexation in 1926. This point acquired
renewed significance after 1930, because granting the Mar Sham'un
the status of a political leader set precedents for other communities
and religious groups.[29] For their part, the Assyrians emphasized the
fact that the 1923 negotiations between the government and the
Levies had *de facto* confirmed the Mar Sham'un's special political
position.

The government of 1932, headed by Rashid 'Ali al Gailani, one of
the most ardent nationalists, responded to the Assyrians not only in
terms of practical policy, that is, the need to reduce the sheikhs' and
aghas' authority, but also in conceptual terms, namely the need to
consolidate the state and its authority.[30] The state was to become the
primordial focus of allegiance and the recipient of all loyalties. The
preservation of parallel and even competing focuses of allegiance
could endanger the state-building process and should be viewed as a
luxury that could not be afforded while the state's foundations were
still so shaky.

The tension that followed was aggravated by the crossing into Syria of a group of Assyrians led by Yaco, son of one of the most powerful maliks. This was an attempt to obtain help from the French or, alternatively, to investigate the possibilities of a settlement in Syria. The Iraqi authorities, however, saw it as an illegal movement of armed men, and their return to Iraq was made conditional on the surrender of their personal weapons.[31] The Assyrians were not willing to accept this condition, as it meant relinquishing all former signs of status and virility, even implying physical extinction. This was especially true in an environment where all other tribesmen carried arms. Clashes between the Assyrians and the Iraqi army led to the looting of Assyrian villages by Arabs and Kurds and the massacre by Iraqi soldiers of Assyrian villagers in Simmel.[32] Rather than establishing new standards of political behaviour, this incident epitomized the complexity of a situation in which state-making implies 'nation-destroying'. On a more factual level, this incident confirmed Britain's subordination of the Assyrians and other communities or 'nations' to the Arab Sunni government for the sake of building a modern state.[33] In a minute written in August 1932, J. E. W. Flood from the Colonial Office clearly expressed current opinion in British circles:

> The Assyrians are really seeking what is impossible [to achieve] on general grounds. Their demand is to live in Iraq without taking their place as Iraqi citizens. This is not possible. The aim of His Majesty's Government is to create an Iraqi state and nation.[34]

This was also the opinion at the Foreign Office. George Rendel, head of the Eastern Department, wrote on 1 February 1932:

> If the separate character of the minorities were to be emphasised, and they were to come to be regarded as the standing excuse for European intervention – no legal safeguards, however elaborate, would really be of much value.[35]

By 'European intervention' Rendel meant the League of Nations, as the British were also opposed to letting a special League commission monitor the conditions of the minorities after independence.[36]

It is important to note once more that distinct standards characterized the government's policies towards the Assyrians (as a non-local and belligerent minority) and the native Christian minorities. The differences between both groups, which emerge clearly with the perspective of time, remain blurred in the documents of these years. There are various reasons for this, the main one stemming from different notions of borders, particularly those separating one

Ottoman vilayet from another. The distinction between modern Turkey and modern Iraq was not then as deeply rooted in the consciousness of the inhabitants of the area as it is now. In other words, the 'Iraqi' identity of the local Christian minorities, so evident to some observers today, was less well-defined during the first years of independence. By the same token, the collective identity of the Christian minorities was determined by religion and by the administrative implications of their former status as a millet. This is the reason why, in the documents of the time, the different Christian groups were qualified as 'Christians' in a more collective sense of the term. This is also the reason why the Simmel incident evoked great concern among other Christian groups in the Mosul area.

Other reasons contributed to the lumping together of these different Christian communities. Among them was the growing pauperization afflicting the Christians more than others. The hardships that spread throughout the area were caused by a slump in grain prices and other economic difficulties related to the crisis on the international market. However, coupled with the general economic depression, there were local causes stemming from government policies. Among these was the government's decision to draw tax revenues from the provinces and to invest the monies in the Baghdad area.[37] The changes introduced in the system of taxation affected some communities more than others. In an enclosure with a petition to the League of Nations, an explanatory note[38] described the rationale behind the new taxation scheme:

The Turkish government collected its share in kind from the land revenue at the rate of 1/10 of the product. This share was collected by the system of Iltizam (contract). That is, the multazim paid the government a fixed sum and then collected the 1/10 share in kind from the cultivators. In order to arrive at an approximate figure, the government used to send a committee to assess the product. In some years when the estimate was low, the Christians themselves took the contract and collected the share from their brothers. When the estimate was high, often the Moslems took up the contract and lost considerably on it, failed to pay the government their money and got themselves into trouble. At present, the share of the government is also 1/10, but this had to be paid in cash only. They have altered the procedure of assessment of taxation by ploughs. That is to say if a man has one acre of land and a plough, he is taxed more than his land and produce are worth together. The ploughs are graded into eight classes and can be taxed at rates from Rs 8 to Rs 120 per plough. The estimators are all Moslems and they have placed high rates on Christian ploughs. Ploughs estimated at Rs 20 before are now estimated at Rs 100 or 120 a plough, despite numerous appeals. By this simple device, the government has got a stranglehold on the Christian cultivators and can exterminate any one of them any time they wish.[39]

Through this appeal, the Christians hoped to obtain assurances from the League of Nations regarding some form of self-administration that would, among other things, allow the rectification of the taxation inequities.[40] However, the British would not engage in a policy that seemed to 'endanger all the work done in the last decade in Iraq'.[41] Thus the main lines of Iraqi government policy regarding economic and administrative centralism and compulsory acculturation were supported by the British and considered as requirements of modern times.[42] The British attitude helped shape a new line of policy towards the Iraqi minorities, one that implied the economic subordination of the provinces to the capital and the relinquishing of cultural distinctiveness by their inhabitants.

This line of policy was not shared by all. King Feisal himself was not totally convinced that the government's hard line towards the inhabitants of the provinces would strengthen the state. He made his position clear even in regard to the controversial Assyrian affair. Feisal believed in the government's ability to cope with manifestations of separatism, alluding to the possibility that Rashid 'Ali was taking advantage of the Assyrian affair in order to assuage internal political tensions and enhance his own political position. This was in part true. The apprehension, dominant in government circles, that any precedent set by the Assyrian case would lead to the establishment of an 'ecclesiastical state of many faiths' certainly contributed to the preservation of a hard-line policy towards the minorities in general.[43] The government's policy should also be understood in the context of a nascent nationalism drawing much of its substance from other national experiences taking place at the same time. In fact, moods and currents that sprang up in Baghdad's political circles in the early 1930s indicated the reinforcement of three trends whose interweaving shaped the texture of Iraq's nationalism: militarism, etatism and Pan-Arabism.

These trends drew from different sources. Etatism and militarism were emulations of the Turkish model, whereas Pan-Arabism was fuelled by the vision of an Arab nation, culturally crystallized and politically unified. These trends could be perceived in the acclamation of the Iraqi army and its commander, General Bakr Sidqi, after the subjugation of the Assyrians. These trends were also personified in the references to Bakr Sidqi, Ataturk and the Crown Prince, Ghazi, during the demonstration that took place in Baghdad. The hailing of these three figures as national heroes pointed to the delineation of a prototype of national hero. Such an image – stored in people's collective memory – re-emerged in different forms and on different occasions, showing once again the great appeal it had for Iraq's Sunni population.

If one were to indulge in generalizations and comparisons, one could say *en passant* that Iraq's divisiveness was reflected in the way in which the different communities related to their heroes. Each community promoted different types of heroes who embodied some of the concepts shaping their community's collective identity.

Who then were the heroes of the other communities, and how did they reflect the country's acceptance of the idea of a single Iraqi identity? The national hero of the Assyrians remained the Mar Sham'un, as he represented continuity and preservation of tradition in the face of modernity endangering the community as a whole. The struggle to retain the Mar Sham'un's temporal authority suggested the Assyrians' unwillingness to accept the idea of secular statehood and their lack of faith in its capacity to reshape the community's belief system altogether.

The leaders of the other Christian communities remained the priests, the patriarch, and other religious authorities. The heroes of the Kurds and the Shi'is were the tribal chiefs and the religious authorities, a fact that will be further explained in the chapters to come. All this leads us to conclude that among the diverse effects of the Assyrian episode on Iraq's political culture was a redefinition of the government's relations with each minority group in particular and with the non-Sunni Arab population in general.

KURDS AND TURKMEN: POLITICS AND CULTURE

The end of the mandate and the signing of the 1930 treaty brought great tension to the northern provinces. This tension was due, as already mentioned, to the lack of any reference in the treaty's text to Britain's commitment to the inhabitants of those districts, among them the Kurds and Turkmen. The absence of any mention of their status in Iraq and their relationship with the Kurdish and Turkish population across the borders was due to Britain's decision to support the Iraqi government's external policy in general and its relations with Turkey in particular.

The lack of reference to the Kurds and Turkmen as defined ethnic/cultural groups sealed their fate in the area formerly referred to as South Kurdistan. This area was delimited by the Great Zab in the north, the Diyala River in the south, the Turco–Persian frontier in the east and an irregular line running from the Great Zab to the Diyala in the west. These borders left the districts of Arbil, Altin Köprü, Kirkuk and Kifri (inhabited mostly by Turkmen) outside the area in which the Kurds predominated. South Kurdistan was the southern part of a larger area, previously defined as Kurdistan, bordered by the Bühtan River in the north, Persia in the east and the Tigris and Jebel Hamrin in the west.[44] Roughly speaking, Kurdistan covered the ancient Ottoman vilayets of Bitlis, Van and Mosul. Bitlis and Van remained in Turkish territory after the First World War, but Mosul became a subject of contention between the Turks and the British, due mainly to the fact that on 3 November, four days after the armistice, the British had occupied the town of Mosul.

British occupation of the whole vilayet of Mosul, in the following weeks, hinted at the possibility of a change in British policy, thus far characterized by indecisiveness regarding Kurdistan as a whole and its southern part in particular. Among the proposals then raised was the creation of a Kurdish emirate, including Mosul, or a central Arab–Kurdish kingdom separate from Syria and Mesopotamia.[45] Such indecisiveness had been dictated by considerations regarding the character and origin of the Kurdish population (western Iranian tribes that had settled around the Zagros Mountains at the time of the Arab conquest)[46] and concern that the Kurds' political fate should not be decided by associating them with the Arabs.

The change in Britain's position once the war was over was due to its decision to remain in Mesopotamia and to the growing awareness that the ruling power in Mosul would 'command the strategic approaches to Mesopotamia and control the water supply to the Eastern effluent of the Tigris on which Mesopotamia's irrigation largely depended'.[47] However, the practical difficulties of administering a heterogeneous population, together with the legal problems deriving from Britain's theoretically illegal presence in Mosul, made the realization of this new approach difficult. These difficulties finally led to the opening of a series of contacts between British political officers and the notables of the vilayet, among them Sheikh Mahmud ibn Haft ibn Kakha of Sulaimaniya, agha of the Barzinji.[48] Sheikh Mahmud's prominence was due to his descent from Kakha Ahmed, one of the leaders of the

Qadiri Sufi order in the area. However, neither the sheikh's position nor his willingness to collaborate with Britain could guarantee his nomination as governor of the district. This nomination needed the approval of the other Kurdish leaders, who were incapable of over-coming personal differences and were reluctant to accept a British presence that could imply their attachment to Baghdad.[49]

Their eventual acceptance of Britain's proposal was due to two main reasons: the Kurds had relinquished the hope of establishing direct links with London, which in their view 'now replaced Constantinople',[50] and they believed that the hoped-for financial aid that would follow the Pax Britannica would help ease the famine and hardship caused by the war.[51]

The further appointment of Sheikh Mahmud 'on behalf of the British government whose orders he undertook to obey'[52] established the principle of indirect rule in the area. An invitation from the British representative in Iraq, Colonel A. T. Wilson, issued in December 1918 to all the tribes from the Great Zab to the Diyala, 'to accept Sheikh Mahmud's authority' allowed those 'unwilling to do so'[53] to abstain from the deal. This formula paved the way for the establishment of the principle of voluntary connection between the Kurds and the British. It also allowed Kifri and Kirkuk to preserve an autonomous position towards Sulaimaniya. Mainly the Kirkuk notables – of Turkish descent – preferred not to accept the invitation.[54] Consequently, Sulaimaniya's authority and administrative system extended only to Köe, Raniya and Rowanduz in the Arbil liwa',[55] where opposition to Sulaimaniya hegemony had not been so firmly expressed. In these areas, Kurdish officials replaced Turkish and Arab ones, giving rise to a wave of contentment and the hope of political self-determination.

The euphoria in Sulaimaniya attained new heights when stories about the rule of the Baban emirs over the semi-autonomous Kurdish principality – which had flourished some decades before – started circulating among the population, rekindling collective memories and hopes of permanent autonomy.[56] These hopes, however, surpassed Britain's initial intentions. Consequently, Sheikh Mahmud's hegemony was disputed, and tribes were removed from his jurisdiction. In retaliation Sheikh Mahmud took control of Sulaimaniya and its treasury, an act which led to the bombardment of Sulaimaniya by the RAF.[57]

The British decision to give short shrift to any prospect of Kurdish autonomy was directly linked to the delineation of a clearer policy for the whole area. The India Office's position regarding the creation of a special administrative zone in the Kurdish districts gradually lost ground to the Colonial Office's position, according to which these districts should in time be attached to Baghdad.[58]

The Colonial Office, however, had to reconsider its stand after Turkey's proclamation in January 1920 of the National Pact, which recognized the secession of the Arab provinces from the empire (if legalized by a popular referendum) but reaffirmed Turkey's rights over the Mosul vilayet, whose population, composed mainly of Kurds and Turkmen but not Arabs, was Muslim.[59] Sunni Arabs were predominant only in the town of Mosul, not in the whole area encompassing the territory of the former vilayet of Mosul. This impasse was further aggravated by the reference in Articles 62 and 64 of the Treaty of Sèvres (August 1920) to the rights of the Kurds in Eastern Anatolia to become autonomous and Mosul's Kurds to join the autonomous Kurdish state.[60]

Although these resolutions did not materialize,[61] their effect on Mosul's population was enormous. Percy Cox, the British Civil Commissioner in Baghdad at the time, issued a communiqué recognizing the legitimacy of the Kurds' aspirations and their right not to be attached to Baghdad against their will.[62] The option offered to the Kurds entailed the creation of a sub-liwa' in Zakho, 'Aqra, Dohuq and 'Amadiya (Mosul liwa'), governed by a Kurdish mutasarif and Kurdish qaimaqams. The same administrative system would be installed in Köe Sanjaq and Rowanduz (Arbil liwa'), while Sulaimaniya would constitute a separate mutasarifliq governed by a local council appointed and advised by the British.[63]

The meaning of this was manifold. Together with the recognition of the need to establish a special regime for the whole area, there was the need to separate administratively the Turkmen from the Kurds. Moreover, this option gave Sulaimaniya's notables the opportunity to counterbalance Sheikh Mahmud's hegemony over the area.

Taking advantage of this opening, Sulaimaniya notables chose to boycott the referendum set up to legalize Feisal's appointment as king of Iraq – as well as his coronation on 23 August 1921. This illustrated their desire to continue nurturing a direct link with Britain,[64] without becoming a part of the new state.

Sulaimaniya's special status was subordinated to Britain's political and military support. However, the possibility of an advance of Turkish forces coupled with the withdrawal of British troops from the area offered Sheikh Mahmud a second chance to make himself the *de facto* authority of the area. Taking the title of King of Kurdistan (November 1922), he attempted this time to give his rule the stamp of legitimacy. Articles published in the local newspaper, *Rhoz-i-Kurdistan*, reiterated this tendency, as did official receptions organized to salute visiting Kurdish leaders, among them Isma'il, 'Simko' agha of the Shikak,[65] the famous Kurdish leader who had fought the Russians, Turks and Armenians during the war and murdered the Mar Sham'un, the temporal and spiritual leader of the Assyrians.

The need to neutralize Sheikh Mahmud's growing prestige brought a joint British–Iraqi declaration in December 1922 in which mention was made of the possibility of installing a Kurdish government in the district. The use of the term 'government' instead of the previously current one of 'administration'[66] represented a breakthrough in the negotiations, as it suggested an equality of status between Kurds and Arabs.

The communiqué meant to circumvent Sheikh Mahmud's prestige by trying to find the message that would strike the right chord and induce the notables to consider alternatives to Sheikh Mahmud's regime.[67] However, the tension generated in the Kurdish areas by the failure to repeat at the Lausanne Conference (February 1923) the political gains obtained at Sèvres prevented the British plan from materializing. Sheikh Mahmud's reaction to this stalemate was to engulf Rowanduz and Kirkuk. The consequent bombing of Sulaimaniya by the RAF temporarily halted the illusion of an autonomous Kurdish territory. Sheikh Mahmud's withdrawal to Surdash did not, however, put an end to the episode, as he continued to publish the *Bang al-Haqq*, a periodical in the Kurdish language, and to collect taxes from the population.[68] This confusing situation, with an exiled leader exerting nominal authority over the area in spite of his expatriation, continued until July 1924, when British and Iraqi troops entered Sulaimaniya and transferred control of the administration to the High Commissioner.[69]

These events illustrate the changes in political positions during the mid-1920s by which Baghdad was confirmed as Britain's main focus of interest in the area. The ensuing description of these events as nationalist contrasted with the minimalist approach exposed in the documents of the period depicting the same events as being merely the result of the personal ambitions of local chieftains.[70]

Other explanations of the Sheikh Mahmud episode see it as a clash between two ethnic communities, the Kurds and the Arabs, generated by the refusal of one to submit politically to the other. Still other explanations see these events as being caused by the resistance of a tribal system to the restrictions imposed by a modern state. A more recent approach even tried to colour these events in Marxist hues by linking the Kurds' resistance to economic reasons. Accordingly Sheikh Mahmud was seen as the representative of the aghawat, whose unwillingness to relinquish the tribesman's taxes (the cultivator's tithe, and the flock owner's *koda*[71]) made them rise against the state.

All these explanations are partially true but not complete, as they do not take into account the fluidity of life in the Kurdish areas, where the passage from a nomadic to a settled life should not be seen as an irrevocable process. There are reports of tribesmen who lost their flocks and settled for a while, then, having restored their fortunes, resumed nomadic life again, causing a shift of focus from one level of opposition to another.[72]

All this leads us to conclude that the only viable explanation is the one that combines and juxtaposes all the above explanations. A more detailed analysis of historic documents demonstrates that the clash between the Kurds and the Arabs was multidimensional – the ethnic factor weighing heavily, underlining the refusal of the Kurds to submit politically to the Arabs, whereas the economic factor found expression in the Kurds' refusal to submit economically to Baghdad mainly in matters such as taxes, awqaf revenues and the marketing of tobacco. But above all, or, perhaps, encapsulating it all, there was a cultural reaction from the Kurds, as a community with deep-rooted religious, cultural and social characteristics.

To clarify this explanation, it is necessary to point out that the term *culture* is employed here in its anthropological dimension and not just as an aspect of human relations determined by language and its derivatives. Although language played an important role in the description of the strife between Arabs and Kurds, *culture* encompasses the clash between these two communities in all its varieties. In this broader sense the term *culture* embraces religion, traditions, symbols and sets of beliefs that mould the structure of a human group and determine the parameters of its members' identities. Religion is accordingly seen as a predominant element in any cultural system. Religious identities are delineated by values, symbols and traditions codified in customs and traditions. Religion is at the basis of a whole social structure, consequently affording a different way to perceive reality. It is again important to remember that religion was the main trait defining a group's identity in Ottoman times.

In this case too reference is made to Islam in its local variants. Even Sunni Islam gains, in the context of Iraq's Arab-Kurds' contention, a multiple dimension, and it would not be wrong to speak of Islam*s* shaped by, and embedded with, local traditions, social references and cultural diversities.[73]

A good example of how religion contributed to the forging of a cultural system and a social structure was the social network created by the mystic orders and the way in which it acquired political significance. The interwoven social links created by the *tariqas* (literally – the way, the path[74]) flourishing at the time in the Kurdish areas supplied many of the motifs of resistance against the Arab state. The organization of life around the Sufi tariqas and the imprint it had on the social and cultural aspects of human hehaviour helped define a distinct kind of identity, one that bridged social differences and economic interests. This was so because the Sufi tariqa operating in the Kurdish areas represented a whole network of social contacts and influences that should be seen as a variant of their *modus operandi* in other areas. Consequently, the prestige bestowed upon the tariqas' sheikh – as the murshid (teacher) of the order's members and at the same time as the agha of the village – was translated into political and social functions that were hardly transferable to outsiders.[75]

The origin of these Sufi orders remains a subject of debate. The current explanation claims that they derive from the influence of Eastern Christianity and from the appeal of the idea of direct communion with God. The word *Sufi* comes from the woollen (*Suf*) clothes of the first followers of the mystic orders.

The spreading of the Sufi orders in the Kurdish areas was facilitated by the closely knit villages, assembled around water sources, and by the already mentioned compatibility of roles bequeathed upon the head of the village.

The two most popular orders in the Kurdish areas were the Naqshabandiyya (founded in the fourteenth century by Muhammad Baha' ad-Din Naqshaband from Bukhara) and the Qadiriyya (founded in the eleventh century by Abd al Qadir al Gailani, whose descendant kept the title Naqib al Ashraf in Baghdad). The orthodox character of these orders in great urban centres contrasted with the almost heretic aspect of their manifestations in rural areas such as the Kurdish provinces. There the followers of the Qadiriyya were called *derwishes*, while the members of the Naqshabandiyya bore the name *Sufis*.

Although the Kurds' attraction to Sufism was attributed to its consonance with their pre-Islamic beliefs,[76] it seems that Sufism related mainly to the Kurds' reaction against instituted Islam in its political manifestation.

In modern times, the opposition of the Kurds to the state and its institutions must be understood also as a cultural reaction rooted in popular Islam that was further translated into political resentment.

The impossibility of separating culture from politics in this kind of resentment – erroneously depicted at this stage as nationalism – can be illustrated with the name of the periodical issued by Sheikh Mahmud at Surdash. For the members of the Naqshabandiyya, *Bang al-Haqq* had more than a strict political connotation, as *haqq* (truth, right) meant in mystical language Divine Reason, or even God Himself.[77]

The cultural dimension of politics in this period can be further illustrated by the aspirations of the other groups to join their cultural matrix and relinquish the advantages that could have derived from their acceptance of Kurdish or Arab hegemony. Effectively the Kirkuk's Turkmen population was culturally and economically driven to Turkey, whereas the Arabs in Mosul were driven to Aleppo and Damascus. The Kurds for their part were driven to their counterparts in Persia, Turkey and Syria.

All of the above indicates the supremacy of cultural/ethnic ties over social and economic convenience as they manifested themselves during the period here studied. Kirkuk's Turkmen notables, the Naftchizadas and the Ya'qubzadas, identified with the Turks across the border more than with the Talabanis,[78] Kirkuk's Kurdish notables who rose at the time to a position of wealth and power similar to that of the Turkmen notables.

Both the Talabanis and the Naftchizadas (as the names of the latter indicate) were given administrative rights over oil wells, a fact that could have brought about a greater identity of interests than in fact occurred.[79]

Another variant of links and associations was the case of the Talabanis, this time in an internal communal context. They wanted to maintain a separate relationship with the British, to whom they owed much of their prestige, and not to be engulfed by the Turkmen or by Sulaimaniya, given their personal rivalry with the Barzinji aghas. Much of this rivalry stemmed from the Talabanis' belonging to the Qadiriyya order, whereas the Barzinji belonged to the Naqshaban-diyya. This is another illustration of the way in which politics was shaped by socio-religious affiliations rather than by economic inter-ests. The effects of these links and associations and, on the other hand, rivalries and dissensions were double-edged. Aware of their complexity, the Iraqi government, backed by the British, was success-ful in driving a wedge between the Turkmen and the Kurds on the one hand and between the Kurds themselves on the other, consequently preventing the formation of a territorial unit.

Constant administrative reorganizations, facilitated by the links and associations along cross-cutting ethnic and cultural lines, contributed to the above. Although the administrative divisions inherited from the Ottomans (liwa's, qadas and nahiyas, administered respectively by mutasarifs, qaimaqams and mudirs) had been maintained all through the 1920s, their boundaries were changed several times in order to fit new political interests.[80]

For the same reasons distinct elements of the population were promoted at the expense of others. This was particularly conspicuous in the early 1920s, when the fate of Mosul had not yet been sealed.

Britain's promotion of the Turkmen (not only the rich landowners and merchants but also the powerful and highly placed administrative officials who had served the Ottomans) was in fact intended to neutralize the growing influence of the Kurds in the liwa'.

A Turkman mutasarif and Turkmen officials were appointed in 1921 to top administrative posts as part of the government's attempt to persuade Kirkuk's notables to participate in the elections for the Constituent Assembly.[81] The purpose of these elections was to formalize the 1922 treaty with Britain and obtain support for the drafting of a constitution and the passing of the 1923 Electoral Law.[82]

These elections had been organized by the British in order to bestow legitimacy upon the new rulers. The rationale was that legitimacy would spill over and legitimize their own presence in the country.

The Kirkuklis, for their part, considered participation in the election as premature, as it hastened a decision they wanted to postpone. On one hand they refrained from an attachment to Baghdad. On the other they considered Kirkuk's official annexation by Sulaimaniya to be a most unappealing option. Here again the main reasons were the cultural/religious factors which enhanced personal rivalries and shaped politics. A good example was the reluctance of Kirkuk's Kurdish leader, Sayyid Ahmad-i-Khanaqah, to see Kirkuk annexed by Sulaimaniya. The reason was his position as a Naqshabandi sheikh, in spite of his belonging to the Barzinji family.[83]

The Kirkuklis made their participation in the electoral process conditional on four provisos: (1) non-interference of the government in the electoral procedures; (2) the preservation of the Turkish character in the liwa's administration; (3) the recognition of Turkish as the liwa's official language; and (4) the appointment of Kirkuklis in all cabinets to be formed in Baghdad thereafter.[84]

In a telegram in Turkish sent in July 1923, the Prime Minister, 'Abd el Muhsin al Sa'dun, confirmed the Council of Ministers' acceptance of conditions two and three, asking the mutasarif to transmit the government's decisions to the *Majlis idara* (the provisional administrative council) formed by Kirkukli notables.[85] This was a *de facto* recognition of their authority and a promise to safeguard Kirkuk's distinct cultural identity, as the non-acceptance of conditions one and four meant non-participation in the decision-making process. Accordingly no Kirkukli representative would be included as a full member in the cabinet, but would rather function as a middleman between the population and the Baghdadi authorities.[86] However, these concessions were not sufficient to induce the notables to register for the elections,[87] underlining their unwillingness to become Iraqis. 'It isn't fair to ask us to choose at this stage',[88] complained the notables, reiterating their desire to be seen as an *idara makhsusa*, and enjoy special administrative rights 'somewhere between the licence given to Sulaimaniya and the central control of the rest'.[89] What all this meant was that they desired to preserve the liwa's cultural and administrative autonomy when considered as part of either an Arab state or a Kurdish-oriented area.

Cecil J. Edmonds, the Acting Political Officer in the northern districts, proposed a solution that would circumvent the problems thus created: as a first stage, a special regime (*idara makhsusa*) would be instituted in Kirkuk and Arbil unconnected, even nominally, to 'Kurdistan'; and, as a second stage, a meeting of delegates from Kirkuk, Arbil and Sulaimaniya would be organized in Baghdad with the aim of forming a federation of the three territories.[90] The relationships that would consequently develop between the 'federated Kurdish state' and Baghdad would not entail the imposition of an 'Arab nominal suzerainty' over the area or the subordination of the Turkmen to the Kurds.[91]

Edmonds' suggestion was shelved as the Baghdadi authorities and the British still tried to induce Kirkuk's and Arbil's notables to participate in the elections. Arbil's special position is worth noting. Although subordinated administratively to Kirkuk, Arbil constituted an almost autonomous sub-liwa', headed by a Kurdish mutasarif, a fact that complicated even more the complex relationship between Kurds, Turkmen and Arabs. Seen in this light, the government's attempt to bring legitimacy upon the state by gaining support from all the factions of this ethnic mosaic was doomed from the outset.

How, in fact, could legitimacy be drawn from the application of the principle of universal suffrage in Iraq of the 1920s? According to the then prevailing electoral regulations, the male adult population constituted the body of primary electors supposed to choose the secondary electors, who would then elect the deputies to Parliament. However, the impossibility of estimating the number of primary electors in a patron–client system led to the overestimation of their numbers.

'While the population of Iraq is estimated as 3,000,000, the number of males for electoral purposes reaches 10,000,000', explained Edmonds in 1923.[92] However, the overblown numbers were not the only factor preventing the democratic process from taking place. Bribery was then a common practice, and even the Electoral Law itself appeared to provide an opportunity for misconduct. The stipulation in Clause 29 of the elector's obligation to define himself as an Iraqi national and to declare his intention to remain an Iraqi on a permanent basis made a *sine qua non* condition for the electors' participation in the process.[93] In other words, Clause 29 disenfranchised voters who did not see themselves as Iraqis, leaving practically the whole electorate out of the process.[94]

The elections provided, however, the legal facade needed by the authorities to annexe the northern districts to Iraq. But administrative changes were more easily undertaken than cultural ones, even if apparently linked. Although the decision to homogenize the area by turning the dialect spoken by the Kurds in these three liwa's, the Sulaimani,[95] into a main category of political reference seemed a step towards Kurdish cultural unification, it proved in fact to be a device for the administrative annexation of Kirkuk and Arbil to Sulaimaniya and the further subordination of the whole area to Baghdad.[96]

The language criterion by itself was not the right one, in this as in other cases. Although Southern Kurdish was subdivided into two principal linguistic groups – the Mukri-Surani and the Sulaimani-Ardelani – there were no clear lines of division. The dialects merged into one another, making not only philologic but also political boundaries difficult to trace.[97]

The attempt to reshape cultural manifestations to suit political needs was doomed, as it was already clear at this early stage that the clash between the Turkmen, the Kurds and the Arabs was a contest for the preservation of identities that for generations had been moulded by culture in its variant dimensions.

This strife meant much more than the apprehensions of tribal groups, Kurdish or other, *vis-à-vis* a modern state. It meant a struggle for cultural continuity in the face of changes that endangered the very essence of their communal existence. It also became an attempt to preserve traditional personal loyalties to the sheikh, the agha and the murshid and not to renounce them for the sake of wider, more complex and not yet fully understood frames of identification. That is why the concepts of national sovereignty and cultural homogeneity implied in the state-building process could affect these ethnic groups only superficially. The possibility of inculcating a sense of overlapping identities (necessary to transport human groups from one stage of social cohesion to another) and further of channelling these new allegiances into more specific national identities remained a difficult task.

This very issue erupted in all its complexity during the dealings over Mosul's future after 1930.

The stalemate at the Lausanne Conference in 1923 resulting from opposed Turkish and British positions led the Turks to suggest the organization of a plebiscite to measure the Mosul population's willingness to be annexed to Iraq. The British opposed this idea, arguing that Mosul had already been legally allotted to the mandate's territory by the resolutions in San Remo in 1920. The British also maintained that Mosul was to be automatically annexed to Iraq once the mandate was over.[90] A League of Nations commission (headed by Colonel A. Paulis, Af Wirsen and Count Paul Teleki) was sent to Mosul in 1925 to determine the population's opinion. 'Those in favour of the continuance of the present government should whisper "Iraq," those who desired the return of the Turks – the word "Turk,"' reported Edmonds, the commission's liaison officer.[99]

However, it didn't take long for the commissioners to understand that objective opinions were almost impossible to obtain, as the 'government's envoys had been caught listening at doors',[100] preventing the population from expressing their views freely. Given these difficulties, Colonel Paulis suggested a solution in which two separate administrative systems would be created within the frame of the Iraqi kingdom, one for the Arabs and one for the Kurds.[101] This solution, if adopted, would help preserve the political frame without subordinating the Kurds or the Turkmen administratively and economically to the Arabs. The commission members were in fact convinced that Mosul, a self-sufficient economic unit, could easily find markets other than Baghdad for its wheat, rice and tobacco. Aleppo would become a suitable market for Mosul's products, whereas Baghdad would have trouble finding supply sources. As one of the commissioners explained, 'If a state had been created that could not support itself economically – *tant pis pour l'Iraq.*'[102]

Above all, commission members were convinced that none of the economic advantages that might accrue to Mosul from its integration into the Iraqi state could compensate for the political impasses that would arise as the state-making process proceeded. What finally led to the decision to annexe Mosul to Iraq was not only a need to counterbalance the Shi'i majority with the Sunni Kurds – nor Mosul's oil (whose commercial potential was confirmed only years later)[103] – but the problem of the Assyrian refugees. The impossibility of repatriating them to Turkey implied that these Christians would remain in Iraq. As the British appeared to be the only mediators capable of neutralizing the tensions between the communities and preventing the

a continuous British presence was to be
ears as stipulated by the treaty. To end the
y the return of the entire district of Mosul
rds, Iraq without Britain was unable to
terior aggression (meaning Turkey) or to
ethnic tensions within its borders.[105] No
le. The only hope was the formulation of a
Kurds, the Christians, and the Yazidis to
bs'.[106]

1926 of the Tripartite Treaty between
sealed the fate of the district. Turkey
Mosul (in exchange for 10 per cent of the
the future). The treaty also established the
een Iraq and Turkey regarding the Kurdish
es.[107]

f the die in the political realm brought a
cultural one, as culture meant identity.
, such as the Yanai-Sarkastan-i-Kurdan

(Kurdish Progress Society) and Jamiati Zanisti Kurdan, flourished in Mosul and Sulaimaniya,[108] offering a clear indication of the context in which culture was thereafter to be grasped. A good example of the cumulative effect of the cultural factor lies in the quantity of petitions to the government and the League of Nations about the educational system to be instituted in the district. These petitions outnumbered previous ones calling for political and economic autonomy.[109] The struggle for the preservation of the Kurdish language reflected a real concern for the Kurds, who equated the threat to their language with cultural erosion and potential obliteration of their collective identity.[110]

This struggle of the Kurds, the Turkmen and the Christians to preserve their identity became even more evident after the implementation of a governmental divide-and-conquer policy in the summer of 1930. The dismissal of a Kurdish mutasarif, Tawfiq al Wahbi,[111] was an additional proof of the changes that had occurred at the time.

Britain's adoption, from 1930 on, of a different policy towards Iraq's internal affairs was decisive in shaping a new relationship between the Kurds and the government after independence. Britain's new political line was deployed during a joint visit to Sulaimaniya by Major H. Young, the Acting High Commissioner, and Ja'far al 'Askari, the Acting Prime Minister, in August 1931.[112] The statement issued on this occasion clearly revealed Britain's blind support of the Iraqi authorities in their dealings with the minorities, including the Kurds. Although administrative measures were to be introduced to give the Kurds some compensation for their annexation to Baghdad, the underlying message was that, as Iraqi citizens, the Kurds were expected to subscribe to the concept of nation moulded in Baghdad's political and cultural circles.

The Kurdish language had, at this point, set new parameters for the relationship between Arabs and Kurds. The acuity of the language issue was illustrated by Major Young's words at Sulaimaniya: 'There is no question of a Kurdish child being compelled to take his first lesson in any other language than his mother tongue – or of any Kurd having to defend himself in court in a language he does not understand.'[113]

The preservation of language and culture became the axis around which all negotiations between the government and the Kurds turned, and since language spelled identity, the government's promises to introduce Kurdish to the educational system and to the administrative one by appointing 'Kurdish-speaking officials' (who were not necessarily Kurds) seemed to the Kurds half measures. They were seen as expressions of tolerance – limited in time and reduced in scope – and not an expression of the full acceptance of a Kurdish identity in all its political dimensions. In other words, these seemed to be measures planned to circumvent the problem and finally subordinate the Kurds culturally and politically to the state. The rationale behind the state-formation process led, effectively, to the appointment of Kurdish-speaking Arabs as administrative authorities in Kurdish areas, as Arab officials were considered more entitled to represent an Arab government vis-à-vis the Kurdish population.[114]

The reactions to the notions of centralism and modernity embedded in the concept of state drew on the deepest layers of tradition and folklore that had sustained the Kurdish culture as a collective experience for generations. The rise of Sheikh Ahmed of the Barzinji is one of the best examples of this type of reaction. Deriving from the Sufi mysticism tightly interwoven in Kurdish culture, Sheikh Ahmed's rise surpassed other cultural manifestations by appealing to the most extreme forms of mysticism which thereafter took on a clear political meaning.[115] Although the Naqshabandiyya, the dominant mystic order in Kurdish areas, was known for the eccentricities and strange rituals effectuated during the majlis,[116] Sheikh Ahmed's eccentricities – among them the order to his followers to eat pork – pushed the whole chain of cultural reactions to an extreme. Such a heresy to Islam reflected a reaction not only against modernity, but also against an institutionalized Islam embedded in the idea of a Sunni Arab state.

Sheikh Ahmed's refusal to give in to the Iraqi authorities and his surrender only to the Turks further delineated the parameters of this kind of cultural resentment. But more than anything else, the Sheikh Ahmed episode reflects the tight weaving of the spiritual and political threads in the role of the Kurdish leaders at that time. Their complementary functions as aghas and Sufi sheikhs reinforced the double effect of the physical and spiritual ties linking the members of a village. Such ties determined the nature of the community, indicating why outsiders – men or ideas – found it difficult to break through the protective layers of the communal group and to alter the internal order of its social network.

This network was determined, among other factors, by the physical and spiritual links – embodied in the double role of the sheikh/agha – that characterized a self-sufficient cultural system whose signs of communication and ways of behaviour remained resistant to ideas and doctrines drawing on different sets of associations. That is why the idea of an Iraqi state – modern, Sunni and Arab – could not appeal to the Kurds as individuals or as a collective. More than just ethnic – but not yet national – the Kurds' reaction to the state was at this stage social and cultural.

Translating these reactions into political terms would mean forming an autonomous Kurdish area in Mosul, recognizing Kurdish as the official language in education and administration, appointing Kurdish officials in the area and in the government, forming military forces under Kurdish officers, and instituting a Kurdish court of appeal in Baghdad – everything that spelled the preservation of a separate social code inside the Arab state. This trend found expression in an attempt by the Kurds to be annexed to Iran rather than to Iraq.[117] Seen in this light, Edmonds's recognition of the need to integrate the Kurds into Iraq 'qua Kurds' and not as 'semi-Arabized provincials' acquires an even deeper meaning.

Britain's increased support of the government and its endorsement of the new administrative measures implemented after Iraq's independence[118] only reinforced the resentment in the northern provinces. Parliament's approval in 1931 of a new version of the Local Language Law, one that retained very little of its former spirit, fuelled this resentment. According to this new version, Kurdish would remain the official language in the courts in 'Amadiya, Zakho, Ziba, 'Aqra (Mosul liwa'), Köe, Raniya and Rowanduz (Arbil liwa'), Gil, Chemchemal (Kirkuk liwa'), Sulaimaniya, and Halabja (Sulaimaniya liwa'). However, Arabic, not Kurdish, was to become the language of technical services – Post, Telegraph and Health Departments – the main services utilized by the population.[119] The new version of the Language Law also instituted the use of Arabic in the official correspondence of judicial courts in Dohuk and Sheikha (Mosul liwa'), Arbil and Makmur (Arbil liwa'), Kirkuk and Kifri (Kirkuk liwa').[120] Exceptions were made in the use of Kurdish or Turkish during the hearings because of the differences in dialects spoken in these areas. The introduction of this proviso in the original text of the Language Law was a clear attempt to prevent the standardization of the Kurdish language – a process already launched by the Kurds themselves. The adoption by the Kurds of the Sulaimani dialect as the official one did not prevent Iraqi authorities from encouraging the population in the different liwa's to use their own dialects. 'This is indeed a subtle poison', wrote an air officer in November 1931, as it prevented the standardization of the Kurdish language and attempted to weaken the Kurds politically.[121]

'The secret aim of the Iraqi government is to debase official Kurdish into an Arabic dialect. This is easier than it sounds. The Kurds have no standard literature or grammar and attempts to meet this need have been short circuited', explained the same air officer in his report.[122] All attempts to institute a practical scheme for writing Kurdish in Latin characters – as proposed by C. J. Edmonds – or in modified Arabic script – as proposed by Kurdish intellectuals – were debarred by the authorities. For them the only viable solution was the writing of Kurdish in Arabic characters. The same fate awaited a Kurdish grammar book, published in 1929 by Tawfiq al Wahbi.[123]

'The only Kurdish newspaper published at present is *Zhian*, a government controlled weekly, printed in Sulaimaniya. This paper is written in a style which can be fairly described as a string of Arabic words interlarded with a few single Kurdish phrases – without a knowledge of Arabic, it is impossible to understand it',[124] explained a local observer.

The introduction after independence of Arabic as the first language in all secondary and even in some primary schools[125] was thereafter presented as an indispensable measure to allow the enrolment of Kurdish students in the state's higher education network located in Baghdad.[126]

Arabic also became the official language in the Awqaf Department's correspondence. 'The Awqaf are a religious institution and Arabic is the language of religion', explained Nuri al Sa'id to the Kurdish notables.[127] However, Arabization of the administrative and educational systems implied the introduction of a curriculum that made no mention of Kurdish history, culture and tradition.[128] This step brought widespread reaction from Kurdish students. These reactions must also be understood in the context of a campaign launched by the Ministry of Education to promote a version of the history of modern Iraq that enhanced the Arab Sunni character of the Iraqi identity. These reactions, which took place in the urban areas, were easily stifled by the Iraqi government.

The Kurds' resentment on the cultural level was exacerbated by a sense of misrepresentation on the political one, due to the gradual absorption of their representatives in the political game in the capital. Attracted by the 'fruits of office', the Kurdish representatives gradually prolonged their stay in Baghdad, alienating themselves from the population in the provinces. All this exacerbated the population's estrangement from the state and its political apparatus.[129]

An indication of this was a protest visit by a delegation of forty aghas to Baghdad in 1935. They raised the same issues that had characterized the very early stage of their political strife. Among these issues were the reappointment of dismissed Kurdish officials as administrators of Kurdish areas, the unification of the language and the curricula in the primary schools, and the opening of secondary schools in the Kurdish areas, to permit the students to remain in their home districts and not move to Baghdad.[130] The aghas' demands also included the establishment of a system of technical education in the Kurdish areas, in order to form a technically skilled generation that would contribute to the development of an industrial and technical infrastructure in these provinces. The Baghdadi authorities' refusal to extend the secondary education network to the northern districts proved the political dimensions acquired by the struggle over education.

During the years that followed, the Kurds remained hostile to the state and its institutions. Strangely enough, and defying all logic of those not familiar with the complexities of the Middle East, the Kurds aligned themselves in mid-1936 with the government and against the Shi'is. The element that struck the right chord was Islam – the defence of Sunni Islam against Shi'a. However, this *ad hoc* union could hardly be seen as a sign of shared interests, shifting allegiances or complementary identities.

3

The Southern Provinces in the 1920s and 1930s

LAND TENURE AND STATE-FORMATION

The mid-thirties were characterized by rebellions among the Shi'i tribes of the Middle Euphrates. Stemming from cultural dissonances and political antagonisms separating a tribal system from the state, these rebellions also revealed the economic and social aspects of the Sunni–Shi'i strife.

Among the problems that surfaced at this time were the maladministration of the agricultural countryside and the unsolved issues of land ownership, some of which dated from Ottoman times. In order to put the economic aspects of this confrontation in perspective, a digression is necessary.

In early Ottoman times, land was occupied communally. Difficult conditions dictated a collaborative system among the cultivators, who helped maintain an elaborate scheme of irrigation and a joint time-table of planting and harvesting. Such a close interaction was also dictated by the collective ownership of the *dira*, tribal land committed to the tribal sheikh. In the dira, the tribesmen moved from plot to plot according to need.[1] Linked by tight social and economic ties, the tribesmen were also bound by an unwritten code of law and mores stemming from long-established customs and traditions.[2]

In the seventeenth and eighteenth centuries, the Ottoman government introduced changes that affected the social structure of the agricultural areas of the empire. These changes were linked to the introduction of a new system of taxation – the *iltizam*, a contract between the *multazim* and the government, appointing the former as the collector of taxes from cultivators.[3] These taxes supposedly covered the sum formerly paid by the multazim to the government and were collected in kind. In the areas bordering the Euphrates, as in other areas difficult to reach and control, the multazim managed to increase his gains by taking advantage of the system's failures.[4]

In order to redress this situation and to tighten governmental control over remote provinces, a new land code was introduced in 1858. Its main purposes were to centralize tax collection and to ensure maximum revenue to the government. The Land Code – part of a broader system of administrative reforms known as the Tanzimat – was introduced in Iraq in 1868 by Midhat Pasha. It contained a more clearly defined land policy, designed to balance the power of rising tribal sheikhs who threatened governmental authority. Accordingly, the fellah was given the right to register the parcel he and his family cultivated, thus becoming the parcel's legal owner. The purpose of this policy of formalizing private ownership of land by means of the *tapu sanads*[5] was to establish a new class of small landholders who would accept – more easily than the large-estate holders – the taxes and obligations deriving from the centralization of the system. However, the tribal sheikhs managed to register much of the land in their name, since the fellahin failed to present themselves at the local branch of the Tapu Department for fear of being conscripted.[6] The outcome was the registration of the sheikhs as the owners of very large estates. At the same time, different types of land tenure were created, reflecting the intermediary stages in the process of land privatization.

When the British arrived in Iraq after the First World War they found a complex situation regulated by impracticable laws. Understanding how vital it was to define the situation before outlining their own land policy, they set up a commission to unravel the complex web of rights and claims over land.

Their point of departure was the adoption of the Ottoman system of land registry as the code to be used to settle clashes between cultivators and tapu holders. This was not an easy choice, given the system's many shortcomings and its failure to take into account a variety of situations in different areas. Hundreds of claims were awaiting investigation, while the information contained in the title deeds – the tapu sanads – could hardly be translated into operative terms.

'Crisscross boundaries', together with poorly defined rights, made the delineation of a clear revenue policy difficult.[7] The principles established during Ottoman times, based on traditional customs and on the Quranic law, had been elaborated into a system of sharing based on the decimal system. Accordingly the state's share of unirrigated lands was one tenth.

If water was supplied by flow, a second tenth was demanded in return for the water. Where water was obtained by lift, no charge was made for it and the land was treated for assessment purposes as if it were unirrigated.[8]

In Mesopotamia, lands were usually irrigated by flow, and the term *khums al-miri* (the government's fifth) became the general term for the state's profits.[9] This tax policy showed some understanding of the fellah's revenues and took into consideration uncertainties such as weather conditions, failures in the irrigation system and natural catastrophes like locusts.[10]

Tax rates were also determined by the cultivator's position in relation to his original tribe. This was an important factor, given the fellah's greater or lesser vulnerability, depending on his status in the tribe and on the stage of the tribe's transition from nomadic to settled life.

The situation became even more complex when members of one section of a tribe became full-time cultivators while another section remained nomads, pasturing their flocks in the desert during wintertime. Other variations were found in the marshes, where tribesmen became as 'amphibious as their own buffaloes, living by fishing and weaving reed mats'.[11]

In other areas, such as land stretching from the Persian Gulf to Qurna, a town on the left side of the Tigris, the tribal system was deteriorating and traditional tribal cohesion seemed almost non-existent. In these areas, the links between the fellahin working in the date gardens were too loose to indicate former membership in the tribes subordinated to the Sheikh of Mohammara.[12]

In the area stretching from Qurna to Baghdad, the indexes of tribal cohesion varied, making characterization of tribal divisions along social lines difficult. The Albu Muhammad, the Banu Lam, the Banu Rabi'a, the Khaza'il, the Zubaid, the Dulaim and the 'Ubaid found themselves at different stages on the continuum from nomadic existence to permanent settlement. The socio-economic relations inside each tribe were in no small measure determined by the type of land tenure prevalent in their territories and the effects it had on the sheikh–tribesman relationship.

In many of these areas, the prevalent type of land tenure was the *lazma*, by which the right of occupancy and cultivation (*Haqq al sukna wa'al zira'a*) of governmental lands was accorded to the titleholder.[13] In some of these parcels, the fellah was merely the lessee of the titleholder,[14] whereas in others a more complex relationship existed.[15] Generally, there was a lessor–lessee relationship where tribesmen were only vaguely affiliated with their original tribes, such as in the areas bordering towns and cities like Hilla. In other areas, such as in the Muntafiq, Diwaniya, 'Amara and Kut, tribal cohesion was tight. The land was allotted to tribal sheikhs.[16] In these areas, no land was ever transferred to the cultivator, and the few lazma parcels and their fellahin were subordinated to the tribal sheikh.[17] In areas close to towns where it was possible to ensure effective possession of land, a great number of titleholders were town dwellers.[18]

Among the officials who had acquired land was the Sultan himself. Abdul Hamid owned some of the most fertile parcels near Karbala', Hilla, Diwaniya, Najaf and Basra.[19] The Sultan's lands – the Sanniyya – were administered directly from Istanbul until 1908, when Abdul Hamid was deposed. Under the Young Turks, the Sanniyya lands became the property of the state, acquiring the name of *mudawwara* (the converted).[20] Although these lands continued to be administered separately from other miri lands, their management was transferred to the local daftardar.[21] In the Sanniyya lands, the fellah enjoyed certain privileges, such as exemption from military service and attenuations in taxation.[22] This was not the case in other areas, where the fellah's inability to cope with heavy taxation gradually led to permanent instability.

In an attempt to redress this situation, two laws were passed, in 1906 and 1913 respectively, which suspended land title grants and emphasized state authority over miri lands.[23] Without formally changing the five basic categories (mulk, miri, waqf, mawat and matruka), some subcategories were introduced to meet new needs.[24] These laws failed, however, to alleviate the growing tension caused by rivalries among sheikhs, sirkals (the chiefs of a tribe's section) and fellahin over land rights.[25]

After the creation of the state, the British launched a new land policy. Its principles were described in two memoranda, written in 1926 and 1928 by Henry Dobbs, the High Commissioner. Drawing from his experience in India,[26] Dobbs attempted to centralize the system by bestowing the rights and duties of collecting revenue upon a few tribal sheikhs. Thus Dobbs indirectly brought about the expansion of the sheikhs' properties, since they were entitled to engulf parcels while compensating the fellah with the retention of occupancy rights.[27] This approach, intended to slow the process of tribal disintegration, led in fact to the concentration of great power in the hands of a small group of sheikhs, who became the backbone of the British presence in the area.

This interference in the country's customs distorted relationships

53

between sheikhs and tribesmen, as it affected the mutual dependence that for generations had characterized the links between them. Thus Britain's interference and the support it gave the sheikhs whenever a dispute with their cultivators arose[28] changed the parameters of the process without slowing down its outcome.

This policy was criticized by Sir Ernest Dowson, former financial adviser to Egypt, who was brought to Iraq in 1929 by Dobbs's successor, Gilbert Clayton. Dowson's conclusions, published in his Report on Land Tenure Practices, were described in more detail in a secret letter to Francis Humphrys, who became High Commissioner and later Britain's ambassador in independent Iraq. In this letter, Dowson called for radical changes in the British approach, suggesting a system of direct relations with all types of landholders – big or small.[29]

Dowson's main argument pointed to the undesirability of artificially creating an 'agricultural hierarchy' in southern Iraq.[30] In his view, Dobbs's policy of simplifying the administrative apparatus would in the end bring instability, not the stability so looked for by the British. However, Dowson's attempt to deal with land tenure from a strictly administrative angle was doomed to failure, as the mandatory policies in the area were dictated mainly by political and strategic considerations.

Dowson's recommendations were elaborated in his *Inquiry into Land Tenure and Related Questions*, which led to the setting up of committees to deal with the problems from a purely administrative viewpoint. However, it soon became apparent that the committee members were unable to overcome the personal influences and political manoeuvres[31] of the landowners, among them powerful sheikhs – allies of Britain.

Theoretically, the British purpose was to protect tribal customs and traditions from possible assaults on the system by the Iraqi government before and after independence.[32] However, Dowson was unable to prevent the misreading of his recommendations or their distortion when put into practice. The recommendations were translated into two laws passed in 1932, the Land Settlement Law, No. 50, and the Lazma Law, No. 51. Although recognizing *lazma* as a legal form of land tenure, these laws fell short of providing a viable solution to the fellah's difficulties, which included the inability to prove the land's continuous productivity – a *sine qua non* condition for the enforcement of his rights over the parcel.[33]

In fact, instead of improving the fellah's situation, both laws, when analysed in the full context of developments in the southern districts before and after independence, seem rather to have reinforced existing inequities. Thus the two laws could hardly redress the situation created by the Pump-Owners Law of 1928, which granted full owner-ship to those able to install a pump on former governmental lands. Designed to enhance the land's productivity, the 1928 law helped create a new class of landowners and permitted the intrusion of Baghdadi politicians and entrepreneurs into the Shi'i countryside.[34] Simply by erecting a pump, the new landlords circumvented the lazma holder's claims over the parcel, turning him and his fellah into mere labour suppliers.[35] The ensuing antagonism was multidimensional, as the new landlords were not only considered outsiders, alien to agri-culture in general and to the fellah's needs in particular, but were also seen as Sunni effendis, culturally distinct and politically opposed to their Shi'i cultivators.

The impoverishment of the fellahin, and the sirkals who followed in the process, aggravated the vicious circle, as more tapu sanad (rights over the land) were transferred to town dwellers as part of payment for outstanding debts.

> The indebtedness of sirkals to money lenders in the qada of Shatra had increased out of all proportion during the past two years. Nearly all sirkals borrow their seeds at sowing times from town merchants and repay them at very large interest at harvest times. By this improvident method, the small sirkal loses nearly all the profit that he should derive from his crops.[36]

And, further,

> None of the debts contracted at the time of sowing could be repaid at harvest. As a result, most of the moneylenders gave the sirkals another year's grace and took from them sanads, promising repayment of a very much larger sum a year later. The moneylenders appear usually to have extracted anything from 50 to 100 per cent interest for the year's delay.[37]

Both quotations point to the economic subordination of the Shi'i countryside to the capital, as the impoverished sirkal surrendered *sirkala* (his rights over the land and the crops) to money lenders, who were mostly town merchants.[38] In other cases the sirkal, 'in order to satisfy his creditor, borrowed money from yet another merchant at still higher interest',[39] contributing further to the vicious circle.

This state of affairs could not but shake the social structure of whole areas, as in the Shatt al Gharraf, where a class of town merchants managed to subdue economically the most powerful tribes.[40] '[T]he sirkals are ignorant and the educated money lender [can] easily drag them into signing almost anything by threatening them with a complaint in the courts [that would] result in their arrest and imprisonment.'[41] Thus the government's agricultural policy resulted in the town dwellers' control of great parcels of agricultural lands.

These post-independence developments shattered the structure of the countryside even more than the changes that had taken place during the decades preceding independence, whereby land was accumulated in the hands of the tribal sheikhs.

The last blow to the status of the fellah was the famous Law Governing the Rights and Duties of Cultivators, issued in June 1933.[42] This law made the fellah dependent on the landlord for traditional activities, such as sowing, irrigating and harvesting. It also confined the fellah to the land, since it prevented him from moving from the parcel when in debt.[43] This final blow further alienated the fellah not just from the landlord but also from the state and its institutions. The disruption in the countryside's structure led to violent reactions, such as the ones that occurred in 1933 in Rumaitha, 'where a mudir was seized and beaten by the tribesmen'.[44]

Protests against the authorities' indifference to the fellah's predicament had become commonplace. The first serious manifestation occurred in 1927 after the introduction of a new method of estimating crops – the *tathlith*.[45] According to this method, the government's share in the three years to come was based on an average of the three previous crops. While guaranteeing the government's share, the tathlith failed to take into consideration the many difficulties that the fellah might encounter in the years to come,[46] an obvious contrast with the khums al-miri of Ottoman times.

The sectarian factor thus added to the fellah–landlord equation was enhanced by the tightening of connections between Sunni absentee landlords and Baghdadi political circles. It was not long before the members of the Baghdadi political elite started acquiring agricultural lands.[47]

This sectarian factor introduced in the socio-economic reality of the southern provinces was not a totally new phenomenon. Already in Ottoman times personal connections with the Ottoman authorities were at the basis of concessions of parcels of land to Sunni landlords.

This was a situation that had developed in the Muntafiq from the end of the nineteenth century.[48] There, a long-standing conflict between Sunni landlords of the Sa'dun family and their Shi'i cultivators, members of the Mayyah tribe, grew with the passing of the years. This conflict reached its apex when the new Sunni authorities established their position in Baghdad.

This conflict was further aggravated in the late 1920s when the government refused to cancel the *mallakiyya*, the land tax normally paid to the mallak (the landlord). This step was seen by the fellahin as an act of support for the Sa'dun, support that would not be so readily accorded to a Shi'i landlord.[49]

The reason for this was that the Sunni landlord was much better connected than the tribal sheikh, more familiar with the system, and could take greater advantage of an administrative apparatus whose echelons were manned entirely by Sunni officials. The fellah's protests that he was now forced to pay the mallakiyya to 'two masters', fell on deaf ears, as the government continued to retain its share. The government's decision to support the Sa'dun can be explained by the personal connections between 'Abdal Muhsin Sa'dun, then Prime Minister, and the Sa'dun mallaks of Shatra and Qal'at Sikkar, his relatives.[50]

By turning the Sa'dun–Mayyah conflict into a test case of the government's own authority in the provinces, it revealed its intention of gradually subordinating the Shi'i countryside to landlords related to and supported by a Sunni administrative apparatus. Officials for the southern provinces, such as the qaimaqam and the civil judges, were appointed by Baghdad[51] and provided a supportive network for the new landlords.

All these developments lead to important conclusions, namely that the status of the tribal sheikh as a big landlord was maintained by British support during the 1920s.

However, as the process of state-building proceeded, there was a change of gear, and an assertive Sunni government, backed by the British, arose as the axis of a new configuration. The alliance of the Sunni government with the landlords was determined mainly by the attempt to reinforce the state's dominance over the countryside.

Once set in motion, the state machinery erased any apparent similarity between the Sunni town dwellers, the Shi'i sheikhs and the Kurdish aghas. No equality of wealth – erroneously characterized as lying at the basis of a newly formed 'intersectarian social status'[52] – blurred the lines of sectarian and ethnic divisions. Given the dissimilarity of their social functions, the Shi'i sheikh, the Kurdish agha and the Sunni absentee landlord cannot be categorized simply as landlords – a categorization that implies cross-sectarian interests and positions.

As I have tried to demonstrate, the complex reality in the Shi'i agrarian provinces does not lend itself to a simplistic definition of roles or to a two-dimensional categorization. The introduction of a sectarian dimension to the fellah–landlord equation changed the course of events by preventing a natural evolution towards detribalization and possible parcelling of the land.

The analysis of economic realities in the Shi'i provinces helps to describe the conditions in which the Shi'i community in Iraq evolved. It does not, however, offer a full explanation of the reasons that led the Shi'i tribesmen to rebel; nor does it indicate the full range of subtleties involved in the definition of loyalties and solidarities.

Thus the economic factors defining mallak–fellahin relations run as a subtext in the study of Iraq's southern provinces but fall short of altering their inhabitants' perceptions of themselves or of their community as an entity *per se*.

STATE-FORMATION AND POLITICAL/CULTURAL REACTIONS

Two obstacles prevented the Shi'is at this early stage from totally identifying with the Iraqi state: first, the traditional Sunni–Shi'i contention, anchored in centuries of religious animosity that stems, as mentioned before, from a primordial dispute about the Caliphate and the right method for selecting a successor to the Prophet, and, second, the political and social aspects of a confrontation between a tribal and an urban society.

The difficulty of measuring the effects and implications of each of these factors, given their interrelatedness, is due to the difficulty of separating out the sectarian aspect. It is also important to note, at this early stage of the discussion, that the Iraqi Shi'is were not opposed to the concept of an Iraqi state, but to its translation in terms of Sunni hegemony.

I shall focus on the tribe-versus-state aspect of the conflict first, because it played a decisive role in the earlier stages of the Sunni–Shi'i confrontation in Iraq. The dichotomy between tribes and state was then characterized by the disharmony between two socio-cultural systems having specific and opposite approaches to key socio-political determinants, such as authority, autonomy and solidarity.

The idea of authority implied in the model of nation-state could not but clash with the tendency towards rebellion and autonomy typical of a tribal society. By the same token, the idea of modern citizenship runs counter to the basic set of loyalties characteristic of a tribal society. For the state to gradually win over the loyalties of a tribal society (characterized *a priori* by a set of behavioural codes distinct from those of an urban one), an extension of loyalties and a redefinition of identities must occur. Identities are, however, difficult to define, as is the estimation of their components. This difficulty appears even more complex in the case of the Iraqi Shi'is.

Although the Shi'is and the Sunnis derive their identities from a single cultural system whose main components are the Arab language and history, the social structure of Shi'ism, and the historical conditions in which it developed, helped shape a variant. This variant was also determined by its confrontation in Iraq, as in other places, with other identities (the Sunni in particular). In both cases, symbols, rituals and customs helped to define the members' collective identity.

Although in Iraq's case the ethnic common origins serve as a palliative, allowing the Shi'is full identification with the Arab dimension of a nascent Iraqi identity, it is important to emphasize that their divergences from their Sunni counterparts cannot just be defined as a contention over 'fruits of office'. In reality, the Shi'i differences from the Sunnis, during the period studied, encompassed much more: a due share in the shaping of an Iraqi identity which would allow it to also draw from the Shi'i cultural reservoir.

Given the difficulties encountered by the Shi'is during the decades here in focus, one could ask whether the principles of modern citizenship and a national doctrine embedded with values drawn from a Sunni cultural reservoir could serve as a continuing source of appeal.

As the answer to this question is not clearcut, a short historical digression is needed. The origin of the Iraqi Shi'i tribes – Bedouin who began emigrating from the Hijaz to southern Iraq in the seventeenth and eighteen centuries – is thought to be the major reason preventing their adoption of Shi'ism in its structured form. Theirs was a popularized version of Shi'ism, and their conversion was accomplished in stages.

When the state's foundations were laid, large segments of the Shi'i tribal population were newly converted. Even some of the leading tribes and confederations, such as the Zubaid, had been converted as late as the nineteenth century. Other tribes, such as the Dulaim and the 'Ubaid, based outside the radius of the holy cities of Najaf and Karbala', had not fully subscribed to Shi'ism at the time.[53] Conversion was also conditional on the tribe's location in the settlement process: the nomads were more prone to the lingering effects of their Sunni origins, whereas the cultivators were more open to the influence of the predominant religious cultural system in their area.

The cultivators were more easily persuaded by the mu'mins, the

Shi'i itinerant preachers, or by the local mujtahids, whose religious and social position was also translated into political influence.[54] The process was still in flux, as important tribal leaders, such as the sheikhs of Suhaiyim and Shurafa' and some of the Sa'dun, who were 'ashraf akin to the Sherif of Mecca and of the purest Sunni stock',[55] converted to Shi'ism just before the First World War.

What could the appeal of the Shi'i mujtahids consist of? Much of it was linked to the need to belong to the area's dominant social and religious culture. Moreover, the traditional Shi'i motifs had great appeal for tribesmen experiencing increasing hardship. Among these motifs were grief, resistance to oppression and an inclination to stand up to temporal authorities. This inclination was linked to one of the dogmas of Shi'ism, namely that any temporal ruler was *a priori* a usurper of the Hidden Imam's political rights.[56] While the struggle for political legitimacy inherent in Shi'ism (inlaid in the original disagreements over the Caliphate) appealed to the Shi'i community as a group, the classical motifs of martyrdom (*shahada*), occultation (*ghaiba*) and combat (*jihad*) appealed to the Shi'i tribesmen as individuals. As members of a community in a state of constant protest, the Shi'is rebelled against the Sunni authorities, be they Ottoman Turks or Baghdadi Arabs. Their protest grew in proportion to the government's pressure and became, as the situation evolved, directly related to the enforcement of administrative cultural measures in their area. The transfer of the polemic from the realm of religion to that of daily politics further reinforced the line dividing the rulers from the ruled.

This was the situation in the area before the arrival of the British and the setting up of the state's structures.

Immediately after their landing in Basra in 1916, the British began to contact tribal leaders and heads of confederations even before they had defined their political aims in the area. In fact the purposes of these first contacts were mainly the collection of intelligence.

With the advance of British troops towards Baghdad and the delineation of the main lines of Britain's policy in Iraq, contacts with the Shi'i leaders increased. This was mainly due to Britain's growing need to create a network of support in the area. The rationale was that the British should draw support from the traditional leadership and should try – as far as possible – not to disturb the status quo in the countryside. This was, however, an illusion, as their mere presence stirred antagonism among the Shi'i tribesmen.

The antagonism has to be understood in the context of the historical circumstances and the Sherifian officers' (Feisal's followers) constant attempts to return to their native areas.

Some first contacts were then established between the representatives of the Sherifians and the Shi'i tribal leaders, opening a Sunni–Shi'i front against Britain which further led to the 1920 rebellion.[57]

In order to understand the two parties' positions in the 1920 rebellion, it is important to refer to two main factors: the tribesmen's traditional resistance to the *kuffar* (infidels) and their traditional resentment of authority. The first factor emerges when tracing a parallel between the 1920 rebellion and the 1915–16 jihad against the invading British forces declared by Sayyid Mirza Mahdi al Shirazi, Sayyid Muhammad Shar'a al Isfahani and Sayyid Muhammad al Khalisi, the main divines of Samarra, Najaf and Kazimiya.

The second factor relates to the traditional tribal opposition to authority, apparent in the role played by tribal leaders such as 'Abd al Wahid al Hajj al Sikkar, Muhsin Abu Tabikh and Sha'lan al 'Atiyya in the 1920 rebellion and other uprisings against authorities. These uprisings became the very expression of the tribesmen's political and social discontent and of their resistance to all kinds of control.

It is also important to underline a third factor – the Shi'i urban sector, personified at this stage by two Shi'i politicians: Ja'far abu Timman and Muhammad Sadr. Their party, the Haras al Istiqlal, accorded a political dimension to the 1920 rebellion that could not have been obtained otherwise. It was the Shi'i urban sector that conferred a wider territorial scope on the episode – and a sense of common Shi'i–Sunni political interests.[58]

The 1920 rebellion was thereafter depicted as the starting point in the process of forging a national Iraqi identity, in spite of the fact that this temporary alliance dissolved as soon as divergent interests re-emerged. Quarrels about the role each party played in the rebellion and their future weight in the political arena erupted as soon as the rebellion was quashed. It is therefore difficult to accord to the Sunni–Shi'i alliance a national dimension at that point. It was national only in the sense of its being directed against a foreign presence; it cannot yet be seen as a reflection of a nascent national unity.

National unity would entail the maintenance of a united Sunni–Shi'i front that would bestow upon the country the legitimacy of a cross-sectarian political leadership.[59] However, the tension and the power games that followed revealed deep and profound differences between the two groups.

The power games that developed between the parties were due mainly to the Shi'is' bitterness at not getting their proper share in the country's administration. However, as time passed, the Shi'i complaints started to reflect a profound protest against the implications of

Sunni political and cultural hegemony. The Shi'is' protests grew in intensity after independence and shed a different light on the 1920 rebellion.

'[Have] the Shi'is sacrificed their men, orphaned their children and widowed their wives in order to set up governmental chairs for the Sunnis on the skulls of their martyrs?' asked a Shi'i student in November 1931.[60]

If they were not to be masters of the country, as was due to them according to their numbers in the population (almost 60 per cent), the Shi'is wanted to be considered the Sunnis' equal partners in the political and administrative domains. This was reflected in the debates that ensued, where each party attempted to win a monopoly on legitimacy and the lion's share of political power. The Shi'is described the Sunnis as 'political upstarts', while the Sunnis qualified the Shi'is as 'non-Arabs', depicting their participation in the rebellion as dictated by an attempt to 'replace the British by a Persian occupation'.[61]

The recurrent theme of the Shi'is' disloyalty to the state and the Sunnis' monopoly of Arab values emerged at every political impasse. As late as June 1933, this theme was launched almost officially in the book *Al 'Uruba fi-l-Mizan* (Arabism in the Balance), published by the Sunni writer 'Abd al Razzaq al Hasan, whose connections with the Sunni political establishment were apparent.[62] Demonstrations took place in the Shi'i areas of Kufa and Diwaniya and in the holy cities of Najaf, Karbala' and Kazimiya, as the Shi'is believed there was an attempt to discredit them politically.

The protests of the Shi'is took various forms during the years in review – from a blunt refusal to participate in the elections for the Constituent Assembly of 1924 (elections that legalized the British–Sunni alliance and formalized the Sunnis' control over the country)[63] to pressures for a return to Turkish rule in the mid- and late 1920s.[64]

The cultural/ideological aspect of the Sunni–Shi'i dissension became thereafter a struggle over the principles guiding the country's identity. Deeper and wider than simple demands for a more equitable distribution of political posts, the conflict between the two parties evolved over the years into an open discussion on the essence of *Arabism*, or, in its wider political version, *Pan-Arabism*, its ethnic dimensions and its cultural and ideological implications.

The main feature in the Shi'is' resistance was their refusal to relinquish their code of cultural values and accept the idea that to be Arab meant being a Sunni. Feeling no less Arab than their Sunni counterparts, and being more numerous and better armed, the Shi'is rejected the idea that the longing for a united Arab nation – Sunni in essence – was enough to bestow upon the Sunnis (inside Iraqi borders) the right to political hegemony. Aware of the practical reasons for the formation of political Pan-Arabism – namely the bestowal of legitimacy upon a Sunni minority to rule over a Shi'i majority – the Shi'is still believed in the late 1920s that a political turnabout permitting them to rise to a position of equal footing with the Sunnis would be possible.[65]

A Shi'i–British alliance modelled on the existing Sunni–British one was then proposed by the Shi'is.[66] Although briefly tempted to consider such an alliance, the British soon abandoned the idea. Their refusal stemmed from the belief that a pact with the Shi'is could not be easily circumvented, given the Shi'is greater likehood of becoming Iraq's legitimate rulers.[67] Counting on the dependence of the Sunnis on Britain's support and on their indisputable interest in keeping an informal British presence in the country, the British rejected the Shi'i offer, sealing Iraq's political fate.

Unable to secure Britain's support on a national scale, the Shi'is then tried to preserve it on a regional one. A return to direct British administration was considered preferable to full Sunni hegemony.[68] This solution involved separating the southern provinces from Baghdad and defining them as an independent Shi'i state. The second possibility was to create an autonomous Shi'i territory administered and protected by Britain.[69] A petition that circulated at the time calling for the 'appointment of British officials also in the Holy Cities'[70] represented a stunning and unprecedented change of attitude and a transgression of the Shi'is traditional refusal to open the very heart of their communal and religious life – the holy cities of Najaf and Karbala' – to foreigners. Their preference of infidels over Sunni Muslims indicates the extent of apprehension registered at the time in the Shi'i provinces. These apprehensions were directly linked to the behaviour of the new authorities. Sunni officials 'threatening the tribesmen with the dispatch of British aeroplanes'[71] aroused great resentment among the tribal and religious leaders.

The use of the RAF was the only way to impose Baghdad's writ on the southern provinces. No Iraqi forces were then able to bring the Shi'i tribesman to submit militarily to the Sunni government. Viewed in this light, the Shi'is consequent refusal to submit to the 'go-between', preferring to deal directly with the owners of the aircraft, seems understandable.

The possibility of a Shi'i–British alliance vanished in 1927 when Britain decided to end the mandate earlier than planned. Realizing that an autonomous area under British (or Turkish) protection was not possible at this stage, the Shi'is delineated the conditions that would constitute the basis of their integration into the state:

(1) Fifty per cent of parliamentary and administrative posts would be given to the Shi'is.

(2) The administration of Shi'i provinces would be assigned to Shi'i officials, who would fill positions as high as mutasarif, qaimaqam and mudir.

(3) Shi'i religious courts would be established all over the country, modelled on the Jewish and Christian courts inherited from Ottoman times. The establishment of Shi'i courts was meant to address a bias stemming from Ottoman times by which the Shi'is (Muslims and therefore not recognized as a distinct millet) were not entitled to hold separate courts. The Shi'is also rejected the division of the judicial system into two branches – *mahakim shar'iyya* (religious courts covering strictly personal matters, drawing from the precepts of the Hanefi school of jurisprudence) and *mahakim nizamiyya* (civil courts based on the Majalla, the Western-inspired Ottoman code established in 1869).

The Shi'is wanted a unified judiciary system that would legitimize the Ja'fari school of jurisprudence and turn its principles into practice. This new system would reinstate the Ja'fari school section at the Shari'a Court of Appeal in Baghdad (first created by the British in 1918) and consequently prevent a *de facto* and *de jure* control of the judicial apparatus by Sunni judges.

(4) The control of the awqaf funds collected in Shi'i areas would be handed over to the Shi'i community and used in the development of their communal territory. This condition was particularly important at a time when the large fees paid for burial in the holy cities – traditionally collected and administered by Shi'i mutawalis – began to be transferred to the Awqaf Department in Baghdad, administered entirely by Sunni officials. This condition was also important at a time when the initial hopes for the creation of a separate Shi'i section in the Awqaf Department faded.

(5) A radical reorganization of the land taxation system would be undertaken, preventing the inequalities arising from the exemption of payment by absentee landlords, among them not only rich Baghdadis connected to political circles, but also ministers and government officials.

(6) Education would be promoted in Shi'i provinces based on a curriculum that would draw from Shi'i religion and culture.

To ensure all the above the Shi'is reiterated the need to maintain an active British presence in the country, if not in the form of a mandatory power, then at least in the form of a tight network of adviser-ship. That is, the Shi'is requested the retention of British officials at the very time when the issue of advisership became the greatest point of friction between Britain and the Sunni government in Baghdad.[72]

The Shi'is protests against the establishment of a state that was Sunni both in essence and in form became a constant. Violent reactions erupted in Nasiriya and Suq al Shuyukh on the occasion of census preparation. Fear that the census-taking would lead to the implementation of widespread conscription induced the Shi'is to rebel. The riots were barely controlled by the authorities. Not even the politicians' usual bribes to the tribal leaders forming their personal clientele could stop the protests.

Conscription, as a way of creating an all-embracing national army, was considered by Shi'i leaders to be a means of perpetuating Sunni domination and as a clear attempt to undermine their position as the heads of their community. Aware of their lack of experience in the administration of a modern state or a modern army, the Shi'i leaders turned once more to the British, asking them to freeze the process that would assign them a secondary role in the management of the country's affairs. Although opposed to the implementation of draft measures, given their effect on the equilibrium between the com-munities, the British were unable to persuade the government to abandon the idea altogether. In fact, Baghdad authorities accused the British of trying to prevent the formation of a national army in order to retain their own armed forces in Iraq.[73]

Growing apprehensions in Shi'i areas finally induced the 'ulama' (known for their traditional opposition to Westerners) to give verbal support to the tribesmen's position, reiterating that it would be preferable 'to return to the days of absolute British control than to be under the heel of an entirely Sunni administration'.[74]

This statement caused unprecedented agitation, an agitation that must be analysed in the context of the 'ulama's previous disapproval of the Shi'is' propensity to engage in politics.

An example of the 'ulama's reluctance to mingle in politics was their refusal to endorse the programme of the Nahda Party, headed by two Shi'i politicians, Amin al Charchafchi and Ja'far abu Timman, there-by preventing the party from becoming the mouthpiece for Shi'is all over the country. The 'ulama's position in this, as in other cases, stemmed from their distrust of the rules of a political game in which rigged elections and patron–client connections turned against the Shi'is themselves.

Lacking the support of the 'ulama', the Nahda Party was dissolved.

Its inability to represent a united tribal–urban Shi'i front, in which both sectors could find equal expression, led to its failure.[75]

Parallel to the organization of the Nahda Party in Baghdad, the Hizb al 'Ashura was created with the aim of representing the Shi'i population in rural areas. Assembled after the army's attacks on the 1927 Muharram processions in Kazimiya and Basra, the 'Ashura Party had a larger tribal base than its urban counterpart. Having its headquarters in Rumaitha, one of the centres of the rural Shi'i sector, Hizb al 'Ashura could not but focus on the problems of the Shi'i countryside. However, precisely because of its rural constituency, the party was characterized by personal rivalries and internal divisions typical of the tribal sector. Although its members tried at first to rise above the cliques inspired by Baghdad politicians, it did not take long for them to succumb to the prevailing pattern of divisiveness. Thus Muhsin Abu Tabikh and 'Abd al Wahid al Hajj al Sikkar were excluded from the party ranks because of their connection with Yasin al Hashimi. Their exclusion pointed to Nuri al Sa'id's influence on their opponents.

Parallel to the activities of the Nahda and the Hizb al 'Ashura, another current started taking shape, focusing on emerging republican tendencies. This movement was stirred up by Yasin al Hashimi, Muzahim Beg al Pachachi and Ja'far abu Timman and included some of the most important rural leaders, such as the heads of the Fatla and the Albu Sultan confederations. Its aim was to create a national assembly along the lines of the new Turkish parliament; although a secular republic, Turkey continued to serve as a model. Adherence to the movement was influenced mainly by the belief that a republican system offered possibilities for a more equitable Shi'i political representation and opportunities to determine the country's identity. Iraq's identity should be forged by local traditions and not by external ('Syrian', to quote the Shi'is) political forms and ideology.

The republican movement remained active after independence, its activities increasing in proportion to the government's assertiveness.[76] Republican ideas grew in shape and substance after Feisal's death in September 1933,[77] as if it were seen as the disappearance of the only centralizing factor that could personify the state in the eyes of the Shi'is. The closing of the channel of communication with the Shi'i tribes opened in the early days of Feisal's reign further alienated the Shi'is from the state.

The advent of Ghazi, young, inexperienced and not as familiar as his father with the rules and mentality of tribal life, contributed to the strengthening of the Sunnis and the obliteration of the Shi'is. Educated in England and at the Military Academy in Baghdad, Ghazi was less inclined to engage in dialogue with the tribal leaders. In his time, the political game at the capital attained new parameters, as the young King was more inclined to concentrate on his hobbies than on affairs of state.[78] This political game can be illustrated by the contention between Rashid 'Ali al Gailani and Nuri al Sa'id for total control of Parliament – a contention that finally brought the appointment of 'Ali Jawdat al Ayyubi as Prime Minister in August 1934.

'Ali Jawdat's past position as secretary of the Royal Diwan under both Feisal and Ghazi and his close connection with the young King helped him obtain permission to call for elections, a move that permitted him to fill the chamber with his personal nominees.[79] This chamber was further seen as the embodiment of a *de facto* Sunni rule over the country.

The exclusion of the Shi'i representatives of Diwaniya and the Muntafiq from Parliament led to the organization of a movement against the government, headed by Sayyid Muhsin Abu Tabikh, an important Shi'i landowner.[80] This movement needed, however, a wide popular basis in order to win some influence in the capital. Popular support could only be obtained by convincing the Shi'i 'ulama' to support the movement. However, the efforts of the tribal leaders to win the support of the 'ulama' were not successful, as the 'ulama' continued to refuse to take sides in a conflict that failed to reflect the community's general interests. The splitting of Shi'i tribal leaders into groups controlled by Baghdadi politicians was seen by the 'ulama' as an attempt to undermine their potential political weight and a manoeuvre to postpone the search for genuine solutions to the community's problems.[81]

This was in fact true, but the Shi'i tribal leaders were much more impatient and given to a more radical and short-sighted style of action than the Shi'i religious leaders.

The escalation of tension in the southern provinces, culminating with an attack by 'Abd al Wahid al Hajj al Sikkar and Sha'lan al 'Atiyya and their followers from the Fatla and 'Aqra tribes on government posts and irrigation pumps in Hilla and Abu Sukhair, caused the downfall of 'Ali Jawdat's cabinet some months later.[82] Two explanations were given at the time for the army's lukewarm reaction to the prospect of stifling the rebellion. The first reason was that Taha al Hashimi (then Chief of the General Staff) hesitated to open fire on the tribesmen, as they were being used by his brother, Yasin al Hashimi, as a means to pressure the Prime Minister, Jamil al Midfa'i; and the second was Shi'i soldiers' refusal to open fire on their Shi'i counterparts.[83]

These two reasons are significant because they indicate important developments taking place at the time. The first reason points to the first signs of the army officers' intervention in affairs of state (or deliberate non-intervention, which is the same). And the second reason points to the difficulty of bringing the Shi'i rank and file to identify with the army's higher echelons and their view of the country's interests, and, in a wider context, the difficulty of turning a conscript army into a melting-pot.

In either case, the fact is that the army's non-intervention brought about the fall of Jamil al Midfa'i's cabinet. Not sure of the army's support and reluctant to enter into an open confrontation with the Shi'i tribes (incited to rebellion by Rashid 'Ali and Yasin al Hashimi), Jamil al Midfa'i resigned on 15 March. After his resignation the king appointed Yasin al Hashimi to organize the new elections.[84]

The next cabinet, headed obviously by Yasin al Hashimi, included figures as politically opposed as Nuri al Sa'id and Rashid 'Ali al Gailani. The appointment of two Shi'i ministers – Muhammad Rida al Shabibi, Minister of Education, and Ra'uf al Bahrani, Minister of Finance – politically affiliated with the Ikha Party broke the traditional pattern of a single Shi'i minister in an overwhelmingly Sunni cabinet. Their appointment was presented by 'Abd al Wahid and Sha'lan al 'Atiyya as a political victory.

Delegations of Shi'i tribesmen headed by the two leaders reached Baghdad 'to remind the new authorities whom they owed their position to'. Official receptions organized by the government gave the tribesmen the temporary illusion that they had become a decisive factor in Iraq's internal politics.[85] However, the Shi'i delegates (as well as the Kurdish ones assembled at the capital by the government in order to counterbalance the Shi'is massive presence) realized that they had been instrumental in the personal rivalries at the capital.

The minor concessions made to the Kurds and the Shi'is in return for their active support in deposing the former cabinet confirmed their growing suspicions. The nomination of a greater number of Shi'i deputies after the elections in the summer of 1935 did not represent a real change in the parliament's composition. An expanded parliament (increased from 80 to 108 representatives) in fact proportionally preserved the Shi'is', Sunnis' and Kurds' former shares.[86]

A further centralization of power in the Prime Minister's hands brought the resignation of the Shi'i Minister of Finance, Ra'uf al Bahrani, and dissipated the Shi'is' remaining illusions of improving their political position.[87] Factionalism continued to divide the Shi'i ranks, as the government promoted 'Abd al Wahid's faction by granting it extra quotas of irrigation water and by reducing the taxes on its lands.[88] The government's divide-and-conquer policy proved effective for a while, as it prevented 'Abd al Wahid from subscribing to the People's Charter (Mithaq al Sha'b), issued by the Shi'i tribal leaders and supported by Sayyid Muhammad Kashif al Ghita', the most important Shi'i 'alim.

This document is worth analysing at some length, as it sets out a clear and far-reaching programme that included the following points:

(1) An amendment of the 1923 electoral law preventing government interference in the electoral process.

(2) An exemption from taxes for all cultivated lands (leading to inequality between the government's supporters and the other landlords), and a more equitable distribution of irrigation water among the different factions and groups. The creation of an agricultural bank as protection against urban moneylenders.

(3) A curtailment of the salaries of governmental officials, whose number had increased disproportionately after independence and whose presence in the Shi'i areas provoked great resentment among the Shi'i leaders.

(4) Reforms in the judicial system based on Article 77 of Iraq's constitution, stipulating the nomination of judges from among the majority of the inhabitants of the area. Accordingly, Shi'i judges would be appointed in the southern provinces. In parallel, a course on the principles of the Ja'fari school of jurisprudence would be instituted at the Law School in Baghdad. This measure was meant to put Shi'i doctrine and its juridical practice on an equal footing with the Sunni Hanafite school predominant in Baghdad.[89]

(5) The abolition of the Tribal Criminal and Civil Disputes Regulation (TCCDR), introduced by the British in 1919. Drawn originally from tribal customs and usages while providing instructions for settling disputes in rural areas, the TCCDR became an instrument of mismanagement and oppression in the hands of the new authorities.[90]

The Mithaq al Sha'b is a most important document, as it reflects the claims of the majority of the population in the southern provinces, notwithstanding the differences between its two main factions: the hukumiyyun and the mutamarridun (the pro- and anti-government groups respectively).

However, the common interests of the community – vital as they were – did not serve as an underlying thread linking the factions together. Divisiveness remained one of the characteristics of tribal societal life, further explored by the Baghdadi politicians.

The schism in the Shi'i camp could not help affecting the Shi'is ability to stand up against the Sunni administration. This finally led Sheikh Muhammad Kashif al Ghita' to issue a statement warning the Shi'is to 'beware of parties, as parties are a remedy in the West and a disease in the East'. The claim also warned the Shi'is to remain united: 'If [you are] united, any government will listen to you, but if [you are] divided, no benefit whatsoever will derive from it.'[91]

The government, for its part, continued to fuel as much dissension as possible in the Shi'i ranks by bribing the hukumiun. Land grants became even more frequent than before; 'a grant of 25,000 acres was accorded to Sheikh Sha'lan al 'Atiyya',[92] and the miri lands of Sha'lan al Salman (head of the Khaza'il) were transferred to Muhsin abu Tabikh, one of the leaders of the hukumiun. Even more serious was the transfer of miri lands pertaining to Khawwam al 'Abbas, the leader of the Bani Zuraij, to Saddiq Shanshul, a Sunni politician and supporter of the government of the day.[93]

These measures exacerbated the tension in Shi'i areas. The already eroded social structure offered the authorities a further opportunity to advance their policies. Sirkals, tribesmen, and sheikhs became allies or were driven apart for different and sometimes controversial reasons, while Baghdad's politicians pulled strings behind the scenes, benefiting personally and politically from the deteriorating situation.[94]

Driven by personal interest, Nuri al Sa'id incited Khawwam al 'Abbas (of the mutamarridun) to actively rebel against the government. Khawwam assembled the Dawalim and the Bani Hasan and, in May 1935, attacked the railway station at Rumaitha and the government's posts at Suq al Shuyukh. The discontent among the mutamarridun was further fuelled by numerous cases of land eviction, by the appointment of non-representative figures (affiliated with the hukumiyyun) to parliament, and by the increasing hardship resulting from the government's mismanagement of affairs in the provinces.[95]

All the above did not, however, bring the tribesmen to rebellion. Affronting as they were, these developments did not evoke as much resentment as the measures taken later on, measures that were seen by the Shi'i as a real menace to their communal existence and an offence to their values.

The first signs of the implementation of conscription measures (officialized some months earlier in 1934 with the approval by the parliament of the National Defence Law) finally induced the whole Shi'i sector to rebel. Threatened politically by the long-term implications of a Sunni-dominated army, and hurt in their religious feelings by the imposition of secular measures (such as the use of the occidental, or 'Pahlavi', hat, the abolition of the veil for women and the banning of certain ceremonies at the 'Ashura procession), the Shi'i tribesmen rebelled again in the spring of 1936. This time the rebellion spread from Nasiriya to Rumaitha and Daghara, provoking violent reactions from the army: crops were burned, entire villages destroyed and tribesmen executed without trial.[96]

A new phase in relations between the government and the Shi'i tribesmen began, followed by a radical reorganization of the administrative apparatus in the provinces. This included the creation of a new Department of Tribal Affairs that permitted much closer governmental supervision of tribal areas.[97] The military and political subjection of the Shi'i tribes to the state seemed now to have been accomplished.

The next step would be an attempt to win them culturally by instituting a unifying system of education designed to foster a new – all-embracing – national identity.

4

Contexts, Textures and Nationalism

It is a complex matter to pinpoint the elements forging collective identities. It is, however, clear that, as in the case of the Kurds and the Shi'is, Islam is a definite component of the Arab Sunni collective identity in Iraq. Sunni Islam is the religious cultural ground upon which a whole social and cultural structure was moulded. In Ottoman times, Sunni Islam also defined the essence of links between the Sunni elites in the Arab provinces and the institutions of the Empire. These links encompassing the idea of Umma Islamiyya (the all-embracing Islamic community) were basically a-national. Nationalism did not become a widespread idea in the Middle East until after the First World War, nor was it a movement with a real political impact until then. Although the first signs of cultural consciousness had developed in the Arab provinces of the Empire at the end of the nineteenth century,[1] it is highly debatable whether these first demonstrations of cultural distinctiveness had already become a current trend.

Before the First World War, Beirut, more open to Western influences than other Arab centres, took the lead in what has been further defined as the first signals of the Nahda, the revival of a cultural and secular current later equated with nationalism in its modern versions. In contrast, Baghdad, even more than Damascus, was an essentially Arab centre, far less open to Western cultural influence. Baghdad's social structure was formed by an interaction of different groups among which the Sunni Arabs were politically predominant. The main communities forming the population – Christians, Jews, Sunni Arabs – intertwined socially and economically, but these interactions did not blur the lines dividing one community from another.

Among these communities, the Arab Sunni community was the leading one, as manifested, for example, in personal links with the Empire's nobility. The Sunnis' leading position resulted from two main factors: their belonging to the official current in Islam and their status as retainers of key posts in the administrative apparatus in the provinces. The community's internal divisions comprised traditional families of notables, from which the local bureaucracy was drawn, and the religious authorities headed by the Naqib al Ashraf.[2] The position of these notables as intermediaries with Istanbul further enhanced their authority inside their own community, and these links with the institutions of the Empire also contributed to the Sunnis' political and social ascendancy over the other communities. The circularity of this interaction underscored Sunnism as the dominant trait in the community's collective identity. All this reinforces the impression that in Iraq, as in other parts of the Empire, reference could be made to Islams, or to the distinct imprints of Islam in its local variations on the forging of cultural life on the spot.

The close relationship developed over centuries between the Sunni aristocracy in the provinces and the bureaucracy and military elite in Istanbul continued to exist until the last decades of the nineteenth century. The changes in self-perception that began with the first cracks in the imperial structure highlighted the differences between the Turks and the Arabs. The ethnic factor – overlooked until then – began to emerge as a cultural and political determinant. However, as changes in self-perception do not occur overnight, time was needed for these changes to be translated into social realities. These changes were, in fact, part of a process in which continuities continued to interact, on some occasions more conspicuously than on others. Although the cracks in the Empire's structure enhanced the differences between the different ethnic groups forming its population, the patterns of communication were not so easily eradicated, continuing to shape much of the social interaction between the different communities and the capital in spite of the administrative reforms introduced with the Tanzimat. Their preservation was due not only to the system's structural legacies but also to people's tendencies, inclinations and convenience.

Reversing the effects of a centralistic policy implemented by Istanbul from the second part of the nineteenth century, the British sought at first to restore the power of the traditional leadership, as the preservation of the traditional social structure seemed to be in the best interest of the new British administrators. These measures were not taken only for the sake of reviving old traditions, but also as a means of preserving order and better administering the countryside. In the towns, the British had planned at first to follow the same kind of policy. However, their action in bringing in a king, the Emir Feisal from the Hijaz, and installing him in power changed these premises. The takeover of key military and governmental positions by his followers, the former Sherifian officers, exacerbated the antagonism of the Sunni elite towards the newcomers. The British were not unaware of their unpopularity, as a report of the time indicates: 'There is no royalist feeling in the country and the King, only too conscious that he has no roots in the soil, intrigues recklessly now with the extremists, now with the 'ulama' in order to make himself a party.'[3] Feisal's presence in the country could be justified only in the name of Arabism, the doctrine that had laid the grounds for the political separation of the Arabs from the Turks and delineated the ideological frame for their possible political unity in the future. In the interim, while waiting for this ideal to materialize, the British hoped that the act of bringing to Iraq the leader of the Arab revolt against the Turks would, by itself, legitimize their own presence on Iraq's soil. An Arab king would – so the British hoped – counterbalance lingering allegiances to the Ottoman Sultan. As mentioned above, the choice of Feisal was, however, not the expression of popular views in Iraq, but rather the result of pressure from Sherifian officers on the British officials on the spot, and from Colonel T. E. Lawrence on his connections in London political circles.

Feisal's difficulties in imposing himself as the ruler of Iraq persisted throughout the 1920s.[4] A note from C. J. Edmonds, then the assistant to Cornwallis, the adviser to Iraq's Minister of the Interior and the British political officer best acquainted with Iraq's internal situation, confirms Feisal's difficulties. Other British officials concurred with Edmonds's views but believed that the King's possible abdication or his giving in to the pressures of the local population would not serve Britain's interests at that point.[5] The apprehension that Feisal's abdication could lead to the loss of Britain's control over the country and over the nascent Iraqi army prevented the British from manoeuvring the King in this direction.[6] Moreover, it was thought that Feisal's dependence on Britain would prevent him from standing up to Britain's presence in Iraq. This dependence was not confined only to the political level. The King's personal difficulties also led him to turn to Britain for financial assistance: '... the King has no private means to ensure a retirement', reported Henry Dobbs, the British High Commissioner, to his superiors in 1928. This situation reinforced the vicious cycle of dependency between Britain and Iraq's King.

In his struggle to impose himself as the sovereign ruler of the country, Feisal also tried to neutralize other focuses of power which might threaten his own position. This was the background for his standing up to the Suwaidi brothers when they gained control of key political and financial posts in the capital. Tawfiq al Suwaidi's appointment as Prime Minister, Naji al Suwaid's as head of the Finance Committee in parliament, and Yusuf al Suwaidi's as President of the Senate amounted to a combination the King could not easily tolerate. His further efforts to topple the Suwaidis' position by exploiting rumours linking their names to speculative dealings in sugar and alcohol[8] finally brought about the fall of the cabinet. This incident serves as an example of the struggle for political power going on in the capital at the time and, on the other hand, of the irrelevance of arguments raised by the British concerning the unconstitutional character of the King's moves, in particular, and of Iraq's political system in general. Britain's attempts to build a state on the basis of Western models of constitutionalism, parliamentarism and political order could hardly succeed. The different kind of logic underlining events and developments in the Middle East proved that recommendations of the League of Nations drawn from political realities in Europe could hardly find an echo in a country where different codes of political behaviour were still predominant.

Another example of the above is the stratagem resorted to by the King and Nuri al Sa'id on the occasion of the signing of the 1930 Treaty. In view of the agitation provoked by the terms of the treaty, seen by many as too favourable to the British, the two men employed a scheme well-known in the history of the area. The mutasarifs, the representatives of the Sunni government in the provinces, were invited to Baghdad to greet the King upon his return from a trip to Italy. Once in the capital, all of the mutasarifs were arrested in order to prevent their opposition to the treaty.[9] By putting them in prison for the period of time needed to pass the treaty, Feisal and Nuri al Sa'id ensured the treaty's ratification by parliament. All this is to say that local political traditions hardly corresponded to the ideas of parliamentarism Britain wanted to inculcate in Iraq's political system. The mutasarifs, in this case, were all opposed to the treaty, considering it an opening for a continuous British presence in the country. These mutasarifs had been appointed by Yasin al Hashimi, the strong man in the former cabinet. Yasin was known to be anti-British and firmly opposed to the extension of Britain's influence in Iraq after independence. Feisal and Nuri understood his attempt to take advantage of the mutasarifs' influence in the provinces in order to jeopardize the treaty, arrested the mutasarifs and prevented any active opposition.

The polarization of the political system between Nuri al Sa'id and

Ja'far al 'Askari on the one hand and Yasin al Hashimi and Rashid 'Ali al Gailani on the other underlined the discussion going on in Iraq's political circles in the early 1930s, over the right method of substantiating Iraq's formal struggle for independence. While Nuri al Sa'id and Ja'far al 'Askari believed in the pragmatic need to collaborate with Britain and to construct the country's political and military system on the basis of the British model, Rashid 'Ali al Gailani and Yasin al Hashimi rejected both the pattern and the pragmatic message behind it, and rejected the idea of compromising with Britain in order to speed up the process leading to independence. For them, the model was inadequate and the compromise it involved – unbearable.

These two variations elaborated on the very essence of Iraq's nationalism and on the texture of its contents. This confrontation also reflected the fact that, at this early stage in the history of modern Iraq, the very texture of Iraq's nationalism was not well defined. If textures are defined by the interweaving of cultural and historical threads, the threads of Iraqi nationalism were not yet tightly interwoven. History was still in the making.

The confrontation between the two tendencies was not just theoretical; it also found expression in the way in which the political system functioned. Not only did interventions in the electoral system become current practice, but bribes, intrigues and constant threats to the country's stability were used for the sake of advancing political positions. A common stratagem was the periodic incitement of the tribes of the Middle Euphrates as a means of pressuring the government of the day. This was part of a new variant in the system of patron–client relationship in which Baghdadian politicians developed webs of alliances with the heads of the main tribal confederations, taking advantage of these alliances to further their own interests. A good illustration of this was the involvement of the Shi'i tribes, in the summer of 1931, in the general strike organized by the trade unions in Baghdad. Yasin al Hashimi and Rashid 'Ali al Gailani incited the Shi'i tribes in order to remove Nuri al Sa'id from power, or at least make him revise the government's new taxation policy. The two politicians, using the popular motto of sectarian discrimination, provoked the Shi'i tribes to rise against the government on the anniversary of the Prophet's death – a propitious date for expressing resentment. The rebellion, however, exceeded the limits set by the politicians, and the tribes were subdued only by the threat of British aerial bombardment.[10]

This incident, apart from proving the ability of the armed Shi'i tribes to shake the new state's foundations, offered, on the other hand, an additional illustration of Britain's basic commitment to the preservation of Sunni hegemony over the country. Accordingly, the Air Officer Commanding on the occasion did not bother to measure the amount of 'misgovernment' that would justify Britain's air action against the tribes. British airplanes were used against the tribes while reference was made to Article 40 of the Tribal Criminal and Civil Disputes Regulation (TCCDR), indicating the code's instrumentality in the control of tribal areas.[11] The pattern that developed from this type of intervention became thereafter a constant in Iraq's political life.

The manipulation of the tribes by Baghdadi politicians and Britain's support of the Sunnis' internal security became dominant features and contributed to the establishment of the former Sherifians as the political elite of the country. Their leading political position also brought about the improvement of their economic situation. Even the King learned to cope with his financial problems in a way not very different from that employed by other Iraqi politicians; he simply expropriated an extensive tract of land at Khanaqin on the outskirts of Baghdad, giving the owner a very meagre sum of compensation.[12]

It is, however, important to note that once Feisal was established in power his identification with Iraq, its inhabitants and their problems grew immensely, turning him into the major figure (albeit not the strongest one) in the country's political arena. He became the very embodiment of Iraq's political unification and emerged as a monarch who spared no efforts to shape a modern Iraqi identity. By the same token Feisal did not spare any effort to restrain the politicians and reconcile the different factions in Iraq's population.

This was particularly true in the case of his relations with the Shi'i tribes. Realizing that the support of the majority of the population was needed in order to make Iraq a sovereign state, and aware of the latent political strength of the southern tribes, Feisal developed a pattern of relations with the Shi'is that was not repeated by any other Iraqi ruler. In fact, his awareness of the dimension of the Shi'i factor preceded his appointment as the ruler of the country. Contacts with Shi'i tribal and religious leaders were established even before his own arrival in Baghdad in 1921. The task of these envoys was to arouse the sentiment of common interests between the two parties as a *sine qua non* condition for the attainment of independence. After his installation in power, his earlier conviction that the Shi'is' contribution to the forging of a modern Iraqi identity was essential grew even stronger. His sudden death in September 1933 changed the course of Iraqi politics and contributed to the delineation of a different policy regarding the means to be used for this endeavour.

After Feisal's death, two main interpretations of nationalism – as the process leading to the crystallization of an Iraqi national identity – were delineated. *A priori*, the main idea underlying both currents was the need to get rid of the British.

However, as mentioned before, the contention between the two currents centred at this stage on the most effective way to ensure independence, while extending Baghdad's authority to the provinces; in other words, the contention centred on the means to be used in order to preserve the country's integrity.

While Feisal and Nuri's tacit acceptance of the maintenance of British air bases on Iraq's territory after independence could be attributed to reasons of *Realpolitik*, Yasin al Hashimi's and Rashid 'Ali's opposition to the presence of the RAF on Iraq's soil after 1930 derived mainly from their belief in the ability of the Iraqi army to maintain order in the countryside.

More generally, the main figures in both currents believed that the army would also be instrumental in the forging of national cohesiveness and in accelerating the process of national integration.

The differences between the currents as they evolved in the late 1920s and early 1930s were more a matter of emphasis than of substance.

It is apparent from the memoirs of the main figures in Iraq's political circles at the time[13] that all attention was then focused on forming and equipping Iraq's nascent army and turning it into the very embodiment of Iraq's sovereignty.

Only after independence were the leaders of both currents compelled to come to terms with the question of how to define the parameters of Iraq's nationalism and characterize the components of the country's collective identity. This second stage was, however, more complex than was at first imagined. One of the reasons for this resided in the fact that both stages were interconnected, so that the process was not a sequential one. Another reason was the confusion underlying some of the concepts directly related to the process. Although complementary, these concepts were not identical or analogous. It is important to note that the differences between them can be more easily grasped nowadays than at the time of their creation. *Nationality*, for instance, implying among others the notion of modern citizenship, was not yet a fully grasped idea at the time when the transfer of the former allegiances to the newly formed state was not so easily accomplished. This transfer implied the passage from a traditional and multidimensional type of loyalty (encompassing the loyalty to the Sultan-Caliph and the more immediate loyalties to the community, the village, the town) to a modern, exclusive type of loyalty which sharply clashed with the traditional and immediate ones. This was not an easy passage, nor could the rationale behind it be easily assimilated. An even harder notion to grasp at the time was the idea of a national identity.

National identity, in its modern sense, should be seen as the idea pervading the national experience and determining the nation's character. National identity is seen as the result of collective cultural traits which imbue the nation with a particular meaning and provide the basis for a viable and stable polity. It also implies social cohesion and political unity. In other words, the modern concept of national identity overrrides all other forms of loyalty, without, however, necessarily implying their total eradication. National identity is also often seen as an extension or by-product of nationalism and as an inevitable outcome of the process of national formation. The idea itself encompasses a rediscovery of the nation's past and tends to emphasize the common ethnic origins of its population.

In Iraq's case, the very thought of aspiring to such a goal implied enormous difficulties. Iraq was a new state, without common myths of ancestral territory to rely on or common historical memories to appeal to. There was no single past to be reappropriated by the different groups forming Iraq's population, nor a widespread yearning for collective political redemption. Each group, even when subscribing to the idea of an Iraqi state, retained distinct collective memories and a distinct vision of the nation's collective future. This is why the process of national formation at its very beginning could hardly pass the litmus test of a wide-scale popular response to the appeals of a national leadership.

Together with the struggle for legitimation, the new Iraqi leadership also grappled with the question of how to define a national identity that would be politically instrumental and culturally attractive, providing at the same time the socio-cultural framework for a modern pluralistic society. This was not an easy task to accomplish. This dilemma was finally defined in terms of a choice between a 'territorial' and an 'ethnic' type of nationalism.

The ethnic type of nationalism – implying more emphasis on ethnic homogeneity – hardly corresponded to the reality on the spot, whereas the territorial type of nationalism – implying the recognition of cultural/ethnic diversities in a given territory – seemed to correspond better to Iraq's specific conditions.[14] However, the choice of the territorial type of nationalism implied a totally different ideological background from the one in which the new Iraqi leadership grew and developed. Their version of ethnic nationalism was Arab nationalism in its outward-looking version, namely Pan-Arabism, and not an inward-looking version of it. Their choice further hampered the adherence of non-Arab elements (Kurds, Yazidis, Turkmen, among others) to their vision of Iraqi nationalism, and the predominance of the Sunni elements in the doctrine posed difficulties for the Shi'is to identity fully with it.

Particularly in the case of the Shi'is, the question of defining Iraq's national identity arose in all its complexity. Although totally identified with the idea of an Iraqi state, the Shi'is wanted to mould a national identity that would evoke resonances and elicit commitments even among the illiterate sectors of the Shi'i rural population, less attuned to the secular expressions of Arab nationalism than the urban, educated sector. This could be achieved only by the interweaving of Shi'is cultural/religious motifs into the texture of Iraq's nationalism. The result would be the creation of an Iraqi national identity embedded with different local traditions, beliefs, myths and designs – a nationalism that would be territorial in essence as well as in focus.

This was not, however, the theoretical approach of those in charge of shaping Iraq's national image, namely the Sunni authorities, whose focus transcended the territorial borders encompassing the idea of an Arab nation in which the Sunni Arabs were politically and culturally predominant. The circularity of this argument redefined their mission and bestowed upon them the legitimacy otherwise lacking.[15]

The Shi'is' reaction to these definitions embodied in the process of national integration, reinforced after independence, did not stem solely from the centuries-old dispute over the election of the Prophet's successor. The Shi'is' difficulties in framing the idea of an Iraqi identity stemmed from their undermined political position and from their reaction to the cultural and political expressions of Iraq's nationalism.

Deep-rooted associations of betrayal and unfairness pervading the community's collective memories helped shape the emotional environment in which cultural and political reaction took shape, pointing to the fact that the Shi'is' difficulties in accepting the type of nationalism sought by Iraq's leaders did not arise from their lack of identification with the ethnic dimension of Pan-Arabism, but from their lack of identification with the predominant Sunni elements in its texture. This is why attempts to simplify the Sunni–Shi'i conflicts in the context of Iraq's formative years, by defining it just in terms of educating the Shi'i rural population, or subordinating tribes to the state,[16] overlook the real nature of the problem.

The advance of the national process was also conditioned by the choice of nation to be emulated. During the first stage of state-formation, Britain was the model to be emulated, mainly in regard to the modernization of the administrative and political systems and the organization of the army. With time, resentment against Britain grew, pointing to the need for new models of emulation. This need was enhanced by growing awareness of the inadequacy of a British-inspired parliamentary regime in a country still dominated by contradictory loyalties, allegiances and interests. In the eyes of the nationalists, a centralist regime seemed more appropriate to the realities of the country and more instrumental in the forging of cultural homogeneity.

A growing infatuation with the fascist model further deepened the gap dividing the Iraqi leadership into two main camps. From the mid-1930s on, Rashid 'Ali's faction openly expressed a leaning toward's Germany and Italy, while Nuri al Sa'id's group still believed in the need to collaborate with Britain and respect the commitments laid down in the 1930 Treaty and its annexes.

This aspiration for new models of political and social order led finally to the army's entry into politics and to the emergence of a third current in Iraq's political stream: a version of Iraqi nationalism that challenged the compatibility of the German or the British models of nation with Iraq's realities.

THE 1936 *COUP D'ÉTAT* AND ITS IMPLICATIONS

Early on the morning of 29 October 1936, 11 military aircraft flew over Baghdad dropping leaflets appealing to King Ghazi to dismiss Yasin al Hashimi's cabinet and to set up a new administration under Hikmat Sulaiman.[17] All officials were called upon to leave their posts until the new cabinet was formed. It was suggested that the army might be compelled to take forcible measures if the government were not dismissed at once. The pamphlets were signed by General Bakr Sidqi as the 'Commander of the National Forces of Reform'.[18]

The movement appeared to have been carefully planned and put into effect without raising any suspicions on the part of the authorities. Two battalions of the army gathered at Qaraghan for annual manoeuvres under General Bakr Sidqi, and two others were gathered, one in Mosul and the other in the Euphrates area, leaving the capital, which was normally teeming with troops, open and defenceless.[19]

All of this happened when the Chief of Staff, General Taha al Hashimi, was in Ankara. The command of the forces was in the hands of the Acting Chief of Staff, General Bakr Sidqi, who gathered around himself the officers of the two divisions upon whom he could rely, while the rest of the army was left in ignorance as to what was going on.[20] Bakr Sidqi also managed to neutralize any possible interference from his opponents by sending a telegram to Taha al Hashimi, demanding that he should stay in Turkey.[21]

The entire Iraqi Air Force had also been neutralized before the *coup* when it was ordered out of Baghdad for combined manoeuvres with ground forces[22] and the RAF on the Iranian frontier.[23] The British Ambassador was called to the palace by the King, who was in a 'highly nervous state'[24] after receiving a letter brought by Hikmat Sulaiman and written by Bakr Sidqi and 'Abd al Latif Nur, the generals commanding the two divisions engaged in the manoeuvres. This letter reiterated the demands made in the leaflets to relieve Iraq of a government indifferent to the country's difficulties.[25] The ultimatum put forward was that if Yasin's cabinet did not resign within three hours, Baghdad would be bombed from the air.[26]

The King promptly dismissed the feasibility of any resistance. When reports about the advance of military forces towards Baghdad arrived at the palace and some bombs were dropped in the vicinity of the Serai, Yasin al Hashimi decided to resign.[27] All of those present at the palace, with the exception of Nuri al Sa'id, were in favour of immediately complying with the plotters' demands to set up a government headed by Hikmat Sulaiman.[28]

Thus far, the sources describe the events as they appear in other well-known accounts, leaving many questions open. According to American reports, the British were caught by surprise, given the small number of Iraqi officers involved in the conspiracy.[29] The element of surprise also pervades the reports in the official files of the Foreign Office. However, Edmonds, in his private papers, points out that Hikmat Sulaiman tried to get in touch with him before the *coup*.[30] This meeting did not take place, but it indicates the rebels' intention to secure Britain's support for their move.[31] Edmonds's letter also throws light on Nuri al Sa'id's position in the affair. Counting on his adherents among the officers, Nuri believed they could induce their colleagues to abandon the movement.[32] Nuri's attempt proves how rife dissension and factionalism already were within the ranks of the officers at this stage.[33]

The involvement of the King in the preparations for the *coup* remains a controversial point. Edmonds maintains that the officers close to Ghazi, in particular the commandant of the Iraqi Air Force, 'Ali Jawad, warned the King of the rebels' intentions.[34] Edmonds also maintains that the King's animosity to Yasin al Hashimi and his jealousy of Nuri al Sa'id were behind his prompt submission to the army.[35]

The British decision not to intervene[36] introduced new norms into Iraq's political life,[37] reinforcing the impression that the only question preoccupying the British was the future status of the RAF bases, since no provisions had been made in the treaty for the contingency of an unfriendly regime installed in Baghdad. By the same token no sufficient guarantees were given to preserve the immunities and privileges of the British forces inside and outside these bases.[38] Although British troops in Egypt were placed on stand-by,[39] the fear of possible detrimental effects in their relations with the Iraqi authorities led the British to abstain from sending these troops to Iraq. This decision was taken in order to prevent a clash with the new Baghdad military and political circles. Since their prestige had already been damaged by the murder of Ja'far al 'Askari[40] the British tried not to push the anti-British movement any further.

Ja'far al 'Askari was murdered as he tried to dissuade the commanders of the two battalions from advancing on Baghdad and appealed to those officers who still recognized him as one of the founding fathers of the Iraqi army. His messages to personal adherents among the officers were, however, intercepted by Bakr Sidqi. Fearing Ja'far's influence, Sidqi sent two of his men – Isma'il Tohalla, the man behind the massacre at Simmel, and Akram Mustapha of the Iraqi Air Force – to get rid of him.[41] Ja'far al 'Askari's murder was considered an open challenge to the 'old order' and an illustration of Bakr Sidqi's determination to assume control over the army as a first stage to gaining control over the country.[42] With the flight of Nuri al Sa'id to Cairo[43] and of Rashid 'Ali and Yasin al Hashimi to Beirut and Istanbul, the first stage of the *coup* came to a successful end.

The new rulers claimed to have been moved by their revulsion against corruption, pointing to the wealth acquired by the politicians during their term of office. Yasin al Hashimi's acquisition of large estates of agricultural land, while taking advantage of the system of land tenure, was one of the main charges raised by the new rulers.[44] Yasin was also accused of having suggested the creation of an Agricultural Credit Bank, not in response to the Shi'i cultivators' demands for loans and grants, but as a means to mobilize capital to be invested in his own estates.[45] The second figure harshly attacked by the new rulers was Rashid 'Ali al Gailani, who had seized many plots of land under fictitious names.[46] Yasin's nomination in 1935 as trustee of the Qadiriyya waqf, after the death of Sayyid Muhammad, the Naqib al Ashraf, was also considered by the leaders of the *coup* as an open abuse of authority.[47]

It is important to note here that the Qadiriyya waqf consisted of miri land endowed by the Sultan to one of the members of the Gailani family. This was a ghair-sahih waqf owned by the state, the revenues of which were alloted to the family and were used for pious purposes.[48] In the early 1920s, the Gailani family pressed for the appointment of Sayyid Muhammad Efendi al Gailani (Sheikh of the Qadiriyya order and Naqib al Ashraf) to the post of mutawali, or trustee, of the waqf. Rashid 'Ali, 'an illegitimate child held in contempt by the Gailani family',[49] then saw an opportunity to avenge himself. After gaining control over the Muradiyya mosque waqf by his marriage to one of the daughters of Murad Beg (Hikmat Sulaiman's brother), Rashid 'Ali attempted to seize control of the Gailani waqf, claiming for himself the post of trustee. Compelled to give up his projects in 1924, while he was Minister of Justice in Yasin al Hashimi's cabinet, Rashid 'Ali was finally able to attain his objective in 1935, when serving as Minister of the Interior. He appointed his brother 'Asim as Naqib al Ashraf, neutralizing any possible intervention on the part of the Gailanis[50] and of the official authorities.[51] He then proceeded to the Diyala liwa' with a number of armoured cars in order to collect awqaf dues dating back to the time of Sayyid 'Abd al Rahman al Naqib. Within a space of less than four months, a total of over Rs 80,000 was collected, apart from the monies taken by his agents as bribes. By leasing the awqaf properties in the liwa's of Hilla and Diyala for a sum of about Rs 60,000 payable in advance, Rashid 'Ali collected an aggregate sum of approximately Rs 170,000.[52]

Nuri al Sa'id was the third figure attacked by the perpetrators of the 1936 *coup*. Nuri had not acquired land, but had used public funds for private purposes and built a palace with the monies received from the British Oil Development Company in exchange for a concession to extract oil from Iraqi soil. According to British sources the buying of oil concessions through personal connections was a common feature in Iraq's political circles during the old regime.[53]

The three principal figures of the former regime were also criticized by the new rulers for the signing in 1935 of the Railway Agreement that 'bound Iraq hand and foot to the British'.[54] Thus the message the newcomers wanted to transmit was one of new political and social priorities and non-interference by the army in the affairs of state.[55]

The cabinet's programme reflected the latent influence of the members of the Ahali group. Their ideas, at first revealed in the newspaper of the same name, were expressed in the cabinet's pro- gramme, which included a more liberal approach to the press and changes in the administrative apparatus, whose representatives in the provinces (mainly urban effendis) were considered the epitome of the faulty political system.[56]

According to British sources, the Ahali group's role in the *coup* itself was more limited than appeared at first, as was their ability to organize themselves into a regular political party, the Association of People's Reforms.[57] According to these sources, rather the opposite took place. The extremist positions taken while in office by Kamil al Chadirchi, the Minister of Economics and Communication, and Yusuf 'Izz al Din, the Minister of Education,[58] as well as their pressure on Hikmat Sulaiman to recognize the Association as the official ruling party, finally led Hikmat to change his favourable attitude towards the group's ideas.

Fearing he might lose the support of the public, Hikmat Sulaiman withdrew his former proposal regarding the absorption of the Association into a less radical movement that would more easily appeal to the masses.[59] Effectively, the growing agitation in the labour sector and the strikes of December 1936 and January 1937, organized by Muhammad Salih al Qazzaz, president of the Workers Union,[60] induced Hikmat to dissociate himself from his former partners and their radical political positions. Some of the cabinet's decisions were simply abandoned, while others lost their effectiveness, as happened with the Labour Law of May 1937. In fact the Labour Law could not, by itself, change the situation in the labour sector: small enterprises continued to evade the law, while large ones complied only under pressure. The absence of an effective system of control made the enterprise even more difficult to accomplish.[61]

Hikmat's main preoccupation was the reforms in the agrarian areas. There an oligarchy emerged by taking advantage of the system's failures, mainly by getting hold of lazma titles provided through personal connections. The new cabinet's land policy aimed, there- fore, at eliminating lazma titles, making possible the distribution of those lands to cultivators.[62] Hikmat's policy met with strong opposi- tion from the tribal sheikhs. They were apprehensive about the confiscation of lands and losing control over the peasants.[63] The sheikhs accused the government of adopting a policy designed to break their authority and destroy the tribal structure in the country- side.[64] Their fears were not totally unfounded. Hikmat Sulaiman's policy was, in effect, designed to weaken the tribal sheikhs' position, by significantly reducing the financial subsidies accorded to them by previous governments in exchange for their support.

However, Hikmat's plans to split up the large estates and distribute the land to the tribesmen were not put into practice. This was, once more, attributed to the ineffectiveness of the administrative apparatus and its inability to implement the government's suggestions.[65] The truth was that the tribal structure was so deeply rooted and the sheikhs' authority still so decisive (in spite of the eroding of their position) that the government's attempt at reforms was easily neutralized by the sheikhs' claims that the government's real intentions were not to introduce agrarian reforms but to register peasants for conscription.[66]

The problem of the southern provinces continued unsolved, and renewed interference brought two well-known figures – 'Abd al Wahid al Hajj al Sikkar and Sayyid Muhsin Abu Tabikh – back on the scene at the head of the previous regime's adherents. Their opponents rallied around Khawwam al 'Abbas, the banished sheikh from the Bani Zuraij whose properties had been transferred to his rival Shanshul.[67] The quarrel between the hukumiun and the mutamarridun was thus reopened,[68] although the affiliation between the two camps was less clear than before. In view of this escalation in the situation, Hikmat Sulaiman finally resorted to the traditional means of imposing order in the tribal areas: air action. Thus the government whose main priority was to implement structural reforms in the agrarian areas quickly found itself compelled to take coercive action in the provinces in order to retain control over the capital.

The campaigns against the tribes were exposed as the main reason behind the resignation of four ministers from the cabinet.[69] To what extent their resignation was the result of political positions or the outcome of personal differences with Hikmat Sulaiman remains an open question. Kamil al Chadirchi, Yusuf 'Izz al Din, Saleh Jabr and Ja'far Abu Timman, all former members of the Ahali group, claimed that they had been induced to resign by the events in the south.[70] In any case, the vacuum left by their collective resignation was promptly filled by Bakr Sidqi, who emerged as the strong man in the internal arena.

Bakr Sidqi was an intriguing figure, determined and tenacious.[71] He was born either in 'Askar, a Kurdish village, or in Baghdad, to a family of Kurdish origin. The mystery surrounding his birth and origins was exploited by him according to political necessities. He rose rapidly in the army and in 1934 was already described by the British as the 'best commander in the Iraqi army and the most efficient one'. He served as an intelligence agent of the British military forces in 1919–20[72] and was recommended by the British General Staff to officership in the Iraqi army in January 1921.[73] Bakr Sidqi's ambition was to become Chief of the General Staff, planning to use the army as an instrument to further his own political aims.[74] His enemies, among them Taha al Hashimi, accused him of being a 'Kurdish upstart' and of favouring a 'pro-Kurdish' policy[75] as many Kurds were awarded promotions and grants in the army at the time and sent to subdue the Shi'i tribes in the south.[76] Bakr Sidqi reacted to these accusations by emphasizing his half-Arab origin, claiming not only that he came from the same village as Ja'far al 'Askari but also that he was Ja'far's relative, signing some of his orders as 'Bakr Sidqi al 'Askari'.[77] He also paid lip service to Pan-Arabism whenever necessary. However, even when doing so, his attention was turned inward: 'I keenly sympathize with the Arab cause; however, I feel compelled to establish my own country first on a firm footing.[78] In this interview, Bakr Sidqi formulated his 'Iraq first' doctrine in which priority was to be given to the different ethnic, linguistic and religious groups,[79] and not to the Pan-Arab orientation of Iraq's former cabinets.

This orientation towards the minority groups became the new government's main focus of attention. Yazidi properties confiscated by Yasin al Hashimi after disorders in the Sinjar area in the summer of 1935 were restored to their former owners, and the mutasarif of Mosul who had criticized Bakr Sidqi's 'pro-Kurdish policy' was dismissed, opening the way for a more comprehensive policy towards the Kurdish population.[80] Everything seemed to indicate a breakthrough in the former official position. However, all these new theoretical approaches could not blur the fact that the real force behind the new regime was the Iraqi army.[81]

The British were concerned about the changes such a shift of orientation could bring about: '... Bakr Sidqi may try to buy Turkish support by some kind of concession in the north which might be at the expense of the Christian minority ...'[82] In fact, Bakr Sidqi's, and mainly Hikmat Sulaiman's, inclination towards Turkey, due in part to Hikmat's family links with the Turkish elite[83] and his declared admiration for modern Turkish methods and Kemalist political lines,[84] led British observers, such as the former ambassador, Sir Francis Humphrys, to express their apprehension about a possible infringement of the whole status quo. The British mainly feared a renewal of the dispute over Mosul and the reversal of the situation in the northern provinces.[85]

As the faction in the army headed by Bakr Sidqi started taking control over the country, Bakr Sidqi appointed personal adherents to key political and military posts: 'Abd al Latif Nur was appointed Minister of Defence and Muhammad 'Ali Jawad became head of the Iraqi Air Force.[86] Bakr Sidqi also started interfering in cabinet meetings, threatening the primacy of the Prime Minister himself.[87] Hikmat Sulaiman's intention to push the army 'back into its proper place'[88] appeared at that point to be completely cut off from reality.

Bakr Sidqi's growing interference in political affairs aroused increasing hostility from different sectors in the country. Two incidents illustrated the atmosphere of terror then prevailing in the capital: the murder in Baghdad of a Mosul notable, Diya' Yunis, secretary of the cabinet during Yasin al Hashimi's term of office,[89] and the attempted murder of Mawlud Mukhlis, President of the Chamber, known for his sympathy towards Pan-Arab ideas.[90]

Hikmat Sulaiman's and Bakr Sidqi's lack of faith in 'Pan-Arab schemes'[91] and their challenging of the special place of Pan-Arabism in Iraq's national message aroused great opposition from Pan-Arab circles, whose influence in Baghdad at the time was in the ascendant. Given the atmosphere, Hikmat Sulaiman found himself compelled more than once to pay lip service to the political and military circles championing the idea.[92] Disturbances in Syria and Palestine were being widely covered by the Baghdad press, intensifying the pressure on the government to change its policy of non-active involvement in Pan-Arab schemes. 'At one of my early talks with the new Prime Minister, he said that he did not want to see Iraq busying herself with the interests of sister Arab states, she had too much to do at home,' reported the British Ambassador to London, 'but as the days passed, I fancy that he shifted his ground a bit ...'[93]

Bakr Sidqi's dissociation from Pan-Arabism, in addition to the increasing criticism of his personal conduct, led to his murder in Mosul on 10 August 1937. En route to Turkey in order to attend the army's autumn manoeuvres, he was shot in the garden of one of the Air Force bases, together with Muhammad 'Ali Jawad, the officer commanding the RIAF.[94]

There were some points of similarity between October 1936 and August 1937, and between the murders of Ja'far al 'Askari and of Bakr Sidqi.[95] However, this time the incident was accompanied by a general public calm, the press merely printing a brief official communique.[96]

'Hated and feared by all, the general appears to have been loved by few,'[97] reported O. Scott, from the Residency to London. '... After

Sidqi's murder – only a house on the outskirts of Baghdad, usually dark and silent, was gaily illuminated, streams of people came in and out, while sounds of revelry and song were heard from the outside ... Mme Ja'far was celebrating the death of her husband's murderer ...'[98]

Who was behind Bakr Sidqi's murder is still an open question. Rumours at the time implicated Nuri al Sa'id and the British.[99] It seems, however, that those behind the murder were the officers dismissed by Bakr Sidqi when he promoted his own adherents to key posts in the army.[100] Seven officers were in the plot, among them 'Aziz Yamulki, Muhammad Khurshid, Mahmud al Hindi and Fahmi Sa'id.[101] The conspiracy and Bakr Sidqi's murder marked the culminating point in the struggle between the principal factions in the army and the beginning of a new period in Iraq's history.[102]

The course of events after Bakr Sidqi's murder is worth mentioning as an illustration of the new trends then growing in importance in Iraq's political and military circles. The most significant trend was the army's increased assertiveness. This could be illustrated by an un-precedented step on the part of Amin al 'Umari, the officer command-ing the Mosul forces: the refusal to hand over Sidqi's murderers to Baghdad, declaring that he would no longer obey orders from the cabinet.[103] The sources described Amin al 'Umari as the 'champion of the Pan-Arab faction in the army that was pushed aside by Bakr Sidqi.'[104] Amin al 'Umari's move reflected the reaction of the Pan-Arab officers pressing for the removal of Bakr's adherents from top political posts.

Hikmat Sulaiman's own position became very precarious after Bakr Sidqi's murder. There was growing opposition to the cabinet in the parliament[105] which finally led to Sulaiman's resignation. A cabinet headed by Jamil al Midfa'i was set up in August. Midfa'i's declared intentions were 'to keep the army out of politics and to eradicate all traces of the 1936 *coup d'état*'.[106] All attempts at reforms made by the previous cabinet were quickly pushed aside and the strongest memory left by the previous rulers seemed to be Hikmat Sulaiman's mistake in having associated himself with Bakr Sidqi.[107]

The return of Nuri al Sa'id to Baghdad from his exile in Cairo symbolized a closing of the circle and the reinstatement of the previous status quo. Indeed, well-known figures returned to fill key positions: Taha al Hashimi became Minister of Defence, Naji Shaw-kat, Minister of the Interior, and Rustum Haidar, Minister of Finance.[108] Nuri al Sa'id's comeback was supported by the Pan-Arab faction among the army's officers.

There were those officers who were grouped around Husain

Fawzi, those who supported Amin al 'Umari, a group who were friends of Nuri's, and others tired of the political intrigues of their seniors. Then there were the Kurdish officers, disgruntled because they were made to feel that they were foreigners by the persistent efforts to give the government and administration an exclusively Arab character ...[109]

explained Hikmat Sulaiman to the British Ambassador in January 1938.

The 'Iraq first' orientation of the Hikmat–Sidqi cabinet – which secured Iraq's place in the immediate regional context (Turkey and, in a lesser measure, Iran) and focused on the pluralistic nature of Iraq's population – could, if persistently pursued, have become a new texture from which a new version of Iraqi nationalism could have evolved. Instead, the 'Iraq first' version had to leave the political scene and make way for a triumphant return of Pan-Arabism. A stillborn option, the 'Iraq first' version could not cope with the changing times.

NATIONALISM, OFFICERS, SOLDIERS

Nuri al Sa'id came back to the Baghdadi political scene supported by army officers. Bakr Sidqi entered the political arena after having drawn power from his control over the army. What was this army like, having acquired, in just a few years, the ability to dominate the power play in Baghdad?

The Iraqi army had been currently described as the force preventing the politicians' misconduct. It was considered the vanguard of modernization, the first element to absorb modern Western technology and modern patterns of thinking. Similarities were traced between the founders of the Iraqi army and the Young Turk officers, both products of the military academy in Istanbul.[110] The reality appears, however, to be more complex, as a study of contemporary documents indicates.

The creation of a national army as the symbol of national sovereignty was the aspiration of Feisal and the Sherifians from their earlier days in Iraq. Britain's opposition to the creation of a large, conscripted army is widely considered to have been the main obstacle on the nationalists' way towards full independence and national integration. However, the difficulties encountered by the Iraqi leaders in accomplishing this goal were not the result of obstacles put in their way by the mandatory power, but stemmed from the absence of a national spirit, without which the development of links between the soldiers and their officers became difficult. The lack of homogeneity among the recruited soldiers, drawn from racially and ethnically diverse backgrounds, led a previous author to observe that 'non-identification with the state naturally resulted in the unwillingness to defend it ...'[111] Here, in fact, lies the most significant explanation of the basic problems concerning the army in the context of the period under discussion.

This problem remained a constant during the 1930s, as no changes in the relationship between the bulk of the population and the army were recorded after independence or after the implementation of the National Service Law in 1934 imposing conscription. This was true even when some changes were introduced in the original text in order to avoid reactions from the population in the provinces. In fact, when the law was finally submitted to parliament in November 1933, Article 38 made possible the postponement of its implementation in any area where its application could raise inopportune reactions.[112] This article in fact provided a loophole for evading its execution in problematic areas such as the northern and southern tribal provinces.[113] In these areas, where the taking of a census was prevented by the population, a 'nisbi' (proportional) system was applied. Article 38 made it possible to partly satisfy the requirements of the law by calling up a small fixed quota through the mediation of the local chiefs without formally conscripting all men eligible for service. This measure attempted to neutralize tribal resistance, but in fact increased the power of the tribal sheikhs.[114]

It is important to note that not only the Kurds and Shi'is were opposed to conscription. Other smaller minority groups, such as the Yazidis, considered it another violation of their religious and political rights, leading them to ponder an 'en masse migration' to Syria.[115] In fact, sections of the Samaqa tribe crossed into Syria in 1936 after the implementation of conscription measures, and in 1938 and 1939 families from the Hababa, Qiran and Dikhliya tribes crossed the frontier for the same reason.[116] Among the violations complained of by the Yazidis were the government's attempts to 'obtain rights of ownership over their properties and to register Yazidi religious shrines as Moslem waqfs'.[117]

The Yazidis' resistance to conscription grew in spite of halfway solutions suggested by the authorities, such as the creation of special Yazidi units in the army, or the application in the Sinjar, as in other areas, of the 'badal' system, by which exemption from military service was made possible by payment of an annual tax.

In spite of these attempts to circumvent opposition from the minority groups, the essence of the problem remained the same. In the Sinjar, as in other areas, although the ranks of the army increased from 11,500 recruited soldiers in 1933 to double that number by the end of 1936,[118] the recruits came from among the tribesmen, while the overwhelming majority of the officers were Sunni town dwellers. This affiliation of the officers with the political establishment led them to demand a larger share in the control of the affairs of the state after independence.

'It is in fact doubtful whether the army is as strong a factor as it considers itself. Its total number at present is 800 officers and 19,500 men, a proportion of those being raw conscripts whose fighting qualities are doubtful if opposed by any resistance ...',[119] wrote J. G. Ward in 1936, expressing a different opinion from the one in vogue in government circles at the time.

In fact, the government seemed to have achieved its objective as the Iraqi army emerged as a factor to be reckoned with. The resistance to conscription faded over the years as a result of the weakened resistance to the government after it crushed the Shi'i rebellions in the mid-thirties. The result was an army able to achieve what was unthinkable some years earlier without the massive help of the RAF and the Levies: the imposition of the government's dominance over the provinces. However, 'loyalty within the armed forces was not based on either national or professional grounds, as soldiers and officers continue to carry their class, ethnic, and cultural differences with them in the army ...'[120]

Hence the picture that emerges is one of an army divided and torn by the polarization between the soldiers and the officers, as well as by the rivalries in the officer corps itself. The politicians in the early 1930s took great advantage of these rivalries, gathering as many personal adherents among the officers as they could. As time passed the officers learned to manoeuvre among the politicians in order to get key posts, personal advantage and still more influence both inside the army and outside it. The movement, then, was in both directions. In the late 1930s, the army officers became the very embodiment of Iraqi nationalism. And the army – its symbols and models – provided the main motifs thereafter interwoven into the texture from which a new version of nationalism took its colours.

It was not only the money spent by Dr Fritz Grobba, the German minister in Baghdad, that nurtured trends towards a growing infatuation with Germany and all it represented. A predisposition to 'emotional germanophilia'[121] in the mid-thirties had its roots in the image of Germany that had developed during the nineteenth century and the years preceding the First World War. Then German influence was felt especially in the Ottoman army and in the Ottoman military academies, where the officers surrounding Feisal received their military education.[122] The Sherifians transported to Baghdad pro-German sympathies that spilled over into many domains, especially the army and the educational system,[123] and became one of the key elements in the image of an authentic nationalism.

Slogans such as 'the army should be the school for the nation' inspired military circles in Iraq.[124] Youth-oriented propaganda flowed from Berlin to Baghdad, prompting youth delegations, mainly members of the Futuwwa (the Iraqi youth movement officially modelled on the Hitler Youth Movement), to visit Germany on several occasions, most notably during the Nuremberg Games in 1938.[125] The British, in order to counter this move, planned to invite Iraqi scouts to a Boy Scout Jamboree, but could not cover the expenses. All attempts to persuade the Iraqi Petroleum Company (IPC) and the British banks to pay for the project proved useless. The Germans won one more battle in their general struggle to win over the Iraqi youth.

A delegation headed by Fadel al Jamali was then sent to Berlin to study German pedagogical methods.[126] Cultural ties between the two countries were tightened; schools and institutes promoted the German language and culture; and clubs such as the Muthanna Club and the Palestine Defence Society were formed, subsidized largely by the Germans.[127] Citizens and leading military and political figures such as Taha al Hashimi and Bakr Sidqi became Dr Grobba's close friends.[128]

Co-operation on the military level also flourished, as orders for weapons and spare parts to be supplied to the army and the Iraqi air force increased in direct proportion to Britain's difficulties in providing them.[129] The escalating situation in Europe paralysed Britain's chances and reinforced Germany's position in Iraqi political circles.

Such first-rank figures as Bakr Sidqi established secret liaisons with the German army,[130] lending weight to former conjectures that the 1936 *coup* had been perpetrated by direct German interference.[131]

A wide-scale information system was established, sponsored by the German Ministry of Propaganda, and the Iraqi press became Germany's mouthpiece in the Middle East. Personal links between leading army officers, such as Taha al Hashimi, and German armaments dealers, such as Major Steffen, became frequent. 'This friendship brought the Ministry of Defence to order a further 18 anti-aircraft tank guns for the Iraqi army through Major Steffen, at a considerable profit,' reported an air officer to his superiors at Habbaniya.[132]

The same attitude prevailed in the civil sector. German industrial penetration was so heavily subsidized by the German government that 'it was possible to find German machinery cheaper in Iraq than in Germany'.[133] German firms such as I. G. Farben, Siemens and Ferrostal found their way into the Iraqi market by 'placing some bribes and douceurs' among officials and army officers.[134] Dr Grobba actively promoted these exchanges, causing growing concern among the British. His command of Arabic and Turkish and his deep knowledge of the affairs in the area contributed to his increasing popularity. Other German figures played a role in the tightening of these relations, the most important being Dr Jordan, a representative of the Nazi Party who held the official position of Archaeological Attaché at the German legation. However, it was Dr Grobba who 'pulled the strings' behind the scenes by setting up a network of agents among the Baghdadis.[135]

Among the most active of these were the two Shawkat brothers, both physicians. Dr Sa'ib Shawkat was the principal of the Royal Hospital in Baghdad, and Dr Sami Shawkat became Director General of Education. Both men were directly involved in the activities of the Palestine Defence Society and the Muthanna Club[136] (named after Muthanna bin Haritha, leader of the Muslim conquest of Iraq in the seventh century). Both had graduated from the University of Istanbul at a time when the influence of German doctors at the medical school there was enormous, and their infatuation with Germany continued over the years; one of the brothers was reported to have brought back from Germany 'a complete Nazi uniform'.[137] A third physician, Dr Amin Ruwaiha, served as middleman in Grobba's contacts with Nuri al Sa'id. 'Free passages to Sabah, Nuri's son, and his wife to Germany have been accepted by Nuri's family', reported an air officer to his superiors at Habbaniya. 'It will be hard for Nuri to refuse Dr Grobba a favour in return.'[138] What had started as admiring glances towards Germany in the military and civil academies in Istanbul thus turned, in the late 1930s, into a most serious commitment.

The place Germany occupied in Iraqi affairs reflected the sharp decline of Britain's influence in Iraq, to the point where even King Ghazi's death in a car accident in April 1939 was used to attack the British. In leaflets distributed by the Young Muslim Society, subsidized by the Germans and organized by Saddiq Shanshul, author of a booklet entitled *How to Form an Arab Empire*, the British and then Prime Minister Nuri al Sa'id were accused of engineering the accident as part of a plot against the King.[139] The consequent murder of British consul Monck Mason in Mosul in a violent anti-British demonstration forced Britain to reconsider its role in Iraq.[140]

This retrospective was long overdue, as the terms of the alliance established in the 1930 Treaty and its annexes were being contested by such politicians as Taha al Hashimi and Rashid 'Ali al Gailani, who pushed the cabinet to adopt a neutral stance towards the crisis in Europe.[141] In order to neutralize the two ministers, Nuri al Sa'id announced in a broadcast on 1 September 1939 that Iraqi troops would not be employed outside Iraqi territory,[142] a measure considered by the British to be a violation of the terms of the treaty. In the same broadcast Nuri refrained from declaring war against Germany.[143] Although some measures were taken against the Germans (German representatives were deported from Baghdad, and the Iraqi newspapers subsidized by Germany were closed), the government was far from demonstrating a clear alignment on the side of Britain, as expected from an ally.[144]

On a more direct level, Nuri al Sa'id made some moves, such as the restoration of the Gailani waqf administration to Rashid 'Ali's supervision (suspended in 1937 during Hikmat Sulaiman's regime). However, these moves, calculated to win the allegiance of the two ministers, could not prevent the situation from deteriorating.[145] The impasse deepened following the assassination in January 1940 of Rustum Haidar, the Shi'i Minister of Finances. His murder contributed to the polarization of the Shi'is and the Sunnis, both inside and outside the parliament, enhancing the difficulties of the less extremist among the nationalists in imposing their views and avoiding a growing alignment of the population on the side of the Axis powers.[146]

These difficulties, together with tension in the armed forces and Nuri's inability to win the support of the faction headed by Chief of Staff Husain Fawzi and General Officer Commander of the First Division Amir al-Liwa Amin al 'Umari,[147] finally induced him to rely on the Golden Square, four militantly Pan-Arab and anti-British army officers – Salah al Din al Sabbagh, Kamil Shabib, Fahmi Sa'id and Mahmud Salman. Feeling himself bound hand and foot by these officers, who had been pushed to the forefront of politics largely by his own actions[148] and by the general atmosphere of instability and political power games in both the army and the political arena,[149] Nuri resigned.

The alignment of Iraqi politicians along pro-Axis and anti-Axis lines and the appointment of Rashid 'Ali al Gailani as Prime Minister and Taha al Hashimi as Minister of Defence indicated the direction that mainstream Iraqi politicians had taken.[150]

The British found themselves in a delicate situation. On one hand, Rashid 'Ali's appointment signified the strengthening of the anti-

British faction in the government. On the other hand, a direct intervention in Iraqi internal affairs was unthinkable. The British wanted to believe that Rashid 'Ali's cabinet would fall on its own, avoiding possible accusations of British pressures or threats to Iraq's sovereignty.[151] Rashid 'Ali, for his part, grasped the complexity of the situation and declared his willingness to retain the 'spirit of the Treaty'.[152] However, the strengthening of the pro-German faction in the army by the final alignment of the Four Colonels[153] along their lines rendered Rashid 'Ali's declared intentions ineffective.

After the collapse of France and Italy's entry into the war, the Iraqi press, supported by the government, spread the view that Iraq had aligned herself with the losing side, and the British had no chance of winning the war. In June 1939 reports appeared concerning the increasingly large sums of money being paid to newspaper representatives by the Germans. These payments were made through local figures affiliated with the Muthanna Club. Among the newspapers were *Al Yawm, Al 'Alam al 'Arabi, Al Nahar* and *Al Istiqlal*.[154] In spite of constant warnings, the government did nothing to moderate the daily picture presented by the press. Rashid 'Ali continued to pay lip service to the British while supporting the press in its campaign.[155]

Rashid 'Ali refrained from intervening in the activities of Hajj Amin al Huseini, the famous Mufti of Jerusalem exiled in Baghdad, in spite of Britain's continuing appeals in this direction. The Mufti's growing influence among political circles in Baghdad had turned him into an 'arbiter', the traditional role played for decades by the British Ambassador himself.[156] The Mufti formed a sort of mini-government, supported by 5,000 followers, and was the guest of honour at all state functions. He also indirectly controlled a great part of the governmental system by placing his men, usually Palestinians and Syrians, in key posts in education and in the administrative apparatus. The Mufti received direct grants from Iraqi officials and intervened in internal and external political issues. He also exerted great pressure on official circles to continue diplomatic relations with Italy after it entered the war, openly challenging Britain's warnings and increasing the escalating tension.[157]

By the same token the cabinet's consequent refusal to sever diplomatic relations with Italy and Germany as late as October 1940 increased Britain's reluctance to meet Iraq's requests for supplies of arms and ammunition.[158] The vicious cycle thus perpetuated doubled the complexity of a situation already complicated from the outset: according to Article 5 of the treaty annex, Britain was required to provide weapons and equipment to the Iraqi army, while the Iraqis, according to Article 6 of the same annex, were to preserve the same type of armaments in the army as those used by the British forces.[159] The motive behind these stipulations was clear: they safeguarded the possibility of joint British–Iraqi action in time of war. However, in such a politically charged atmosphere, the army officers reacted to Britain's reluctance to respond promptly to their demands by calling for a clear and official alignment with the Axis powers.[160] Thus the officers' initial neutrality in the European crisis turned into an unequivocal anti-British position.

Initial contacts with Germany had already been established by Nuri al Sa'id himself during an official visit to Turkey in July 1940 (when Naji Shawkat, a member of his entourage, delivered to Von Papen, the German minister in Istanbul, a letter from the Mufti asking for assistance),[161] but the contacts between Rashid 'Ali and the Axis powers became almost official. In August 1941 the text of a secret pact between Rashid 'Ali and the Italian Ambassador in Baghdad, allegedly signed on 25 April 1941, was forwarded to the Eastern Department of the Foreign Office by a former British consul at Nice, Major Dodds. The document had been obtained by Dodds from the Italian Armistice Commission in Marseilles. Its authenticity has not been totally proven, but a quick glance at its text reveals both sides' intentions. According to this document, the Axis powers acknowledged the legitimacy of Rashid 'Ali's government and undertook to promote a fusion between Iraq and Syria, opening the way for the creation of a United Arab State. Germany and Italy also committed themselves to supporting Iraq's government in the event of a break in the Alliance Treaty with Britain. Financial support (including a personal grant of one million Italian liras to Rashid 'Ali) was to precede the transfer of weapons, heavy armaments and airplanes to Baghdad. In exchange, the government was required to (1) nationalize Iraq's oil and appoint a board of directors controlled by the Axis powers; (2) lease to Germany and Italy three ports on the Syrian–Lebanese littoral; and (3) transfer to the Axis powers the sponsorship of the Christian minorities in the Syrio–Iraqi kingdom to be created.[162]

The document caused great concern in British circles. Worried by the advance of the Soviets towards Persia and Afghanistan, the British decided to reinforce their military presence in Iraq.[163] At this point, however, they were still reluctant to engage in a direct confrontation with the Iraqi government.[164]

Britain's indecision strengthened the Iraqi officers and pro-German politicians, who continued negotiations with the Axis powers with little fear of reprisal. The British bargaining position grew so weak that the Iraqi government even considered the opening of diplomatic relations with Germany, clearly challenging the terms of the treaty with Britain.[165] The British then sought to bring about the downfall of Rashid 'Ali's cabinet by pressing Nuri al Sa'id, then Foreign Minister, to resign. Nuri in fact resigned, but the cabinet fell only weeks later.[166]

In the meantime Rashid 'Ali's position remained as strong as before, in contrast to the seriously damaged prestige of the Palace.[167] The tension between Rashid 'Ali and the Palace epitomized the polarization between the old and the new forces in the fight for control over Iraq's political destiny. In this struggle, the old forces were compelled to withdraw, even if only temporarily. Prince 'Abd al Ilah, who succeeded to the throne after King Ghazi's death, fled from Baghdad to Habbaniya in order to escape the pressure of Rashid 'Ali's allies among the army officers. The Golden Square reinstalled Rashid 'Ali in power after a short period in which Taha al Hashimi fulfilled the functions of Prime Minister. Taha al Hashimi's removal from office is also proof of the army officers' increased power: it was linked to his abortive attempt to break their political influence by transferring two of them from their posts near Baghdad to divisions in the northern and southern provinces.[168]

As Britain considered Rashid 'Ali's regime to be unconstitutional, the Regent was installed in a British warship in the Shatt al 'Arab and allowed to organize resistance to the regime.[169] Rashid 'Ali retaliated by inducing the parliament to depose Prince 'Abd al Ilah and to appoint as regent Sharif Sharaf, a distant member of the royal family. The new regent, for his part, reappointed *ipso facto* Rashid 'Ali as Prime Minister, giving his regime the much-needed constitutional stamp of legitimacy. The move, perfectly planned, left Britain facing a deadlock.

Britain's decision in April 1941 to send troops to Basra in spite of the anti-British upheavals in Baghdad was linked to the need to secure its position in the area after Germany's military victories in Libya and Greece and to protect the oil pipeline from Kirkuk to Turkey.[170] When British troops finally landed on 17 and 18 April 1941,[171] Rashid 'Ali made his acceptance of the landing conditional on Britain's recognizing the legitimacy of his regime. The British, on their side, demanded the landing of additional troops, as stipulated in the 1930 treaty, as a *sine qua non* condition for further dialogue with Rashid "Ali without wanting to compromise any further.[172]

When these additional troops arrived in Basra, Rashid 'Ali, incited by the officers, made their landing conditional on the departure of the former troops, claiming that the presence of the new troops violated Iraq's sovereignty.[173] Both sides based their arguments on Article 4 of the 1930 treaty, which stipulated that in case of war 'all the facilities in Iraqi territory such as railways, river ports, aerodromes, and other means of communication' would be put at the service of British troops, and Article 5, which authorized the maintenance of British forces at air bases in Basra and west of the Euphrates.[174] In other words, these articles covered the passage of British troops through Iraq's territory without legalizing their maintenance in unlimited numbers for an unlimited period of time.

On his side, Rashid 'Ali questioned the binding character of the secret correspondence exchanged before independence between Nuri al Sa'id and Sir Francis Humphrys (30 June and 15 July 1930), in which Nuri had accepted Britain's control over the forces assigned to protect British bases and Humphrys had further agreed that RAF units, with 'ancillary services', would be maintained in Iraq 'providing the achievement of a special arrangement with [Iraq's] government'.[175] Eleven years later the debate centred on whether these additional troops fitted the description of 'ancillary services,' and as such were entitled to remain on Iraq's soil.

The nature of these troops of 'special guards', established under Article 4 of the treaty annex, had been in question throughout the years following independence. The Iraqi rulers wanted these troops to consist of Iraqi army units, ignoring Nuri's secret commitments, while the British, for obvious reasons, wanted to preserve the Levies or, alternatively, replace them with British ground forces. Both sides interpreted differently the terms of the secret correspondence between Nuri and Humphrys without, however, having to escalate their divergences into open clashes. That situation changed in 1941 when an open confrontation obliged both sides to come to terms with the 1930 correspondence. Rashid 'Ali refuted the British position by quoting Article 7 of the treaty annex, which referred to Britain giving 'prior notification' of its plans to land troops on Iraq's soil. As it had not been specified in the correspondence how far in advance such notification should be given, no outlet to the impasse was found. In fact, this very impasse proved that the treaty, its annexes and the secret correspondence had failed to provide what Britain most expected: a safe corridor for its troops in time of war.

And, as usually happens, pressure from one side reinforced assertiveness from the other. Iraqi troops sent by Rashid 'Ali threatened Habbaniya and prevented the RAF's planes from taking off, while another sector of the army surrounded the British Embassy in Baghdad. This action constituted a near declaration of war. British troops landed in Basra and proceeded to Baghdad. Forces under the command of General J. G. W. Clark occupied the capital, forcing the Iraqi government to surrender. The armistice, signed on 30 May 1941 by the Mayor of Baghdad, Arshad al 'Umari (the remaining local authority after Rashid 'Ali and the colonels had fled the capital), officially restored Britain's control over Habbaniya and Basra. The retention of British forces in the aerodromes 'in times of peace' and Britain's control over all means of communication 'in times of war' were thereby reconfirmed.[176]

The return of the Regent, 'Abd al Ilah, and Nuri al Sa'id to Baghdad on 1 June 1941 signalled to many the re-establishment of the *status quo ante*, and to the British the return of the legitimate Iraqi government.

However, radical changes had occurred in the realm of perceptions, and the situation could hardly be restored to an earlier stage. Although disappointed at the ineffectiveness of much-needed German assistance, Iraqi officers and politicians continued to admire Germany and fascist ideology and values. The reasons for this were many, but hatred for Britain and the West on the one hand and frustration with the country's local difficulties on the other should be counted as the primary factors. Hatred, frustration and anger were also at the basis of the attacks perpetrated on the Jewish minority in Baghdad by members of the pro-German youth movements. This anger was further exacerbated by the escalation of events in Palestine and by the feeling that the British were backing the Jews in their conflict with the Arabs. The Farhud – a pogrom in which hundreds of Jews were murdered and their properties looted – represented the ultimate expression of this anger.[177] It sealed a period in Iraq's history that can be compared to the first upheavals of adolescence – upheavals that would continue to disrupt Iraq's normal and steady evolution towards political maturity.

Seen in this light, the purges in the army, the education system and the administration that followed the installation of Jamil al Midfa'i as Prime Minister could hardly restore the *status quo ante*.[178] The British Ambassador, Kinahan Cornwallis, understood the situation well:

> It should not be assumed that this event will bring an end to our political difficulties in the country. People of all classes have been worked up into a state of bitterness and hatred towards Britain and it will take time for passions to cool down.[179]

After attempting to build a political structure based on reason, the

British finally realized that in the Middle East passions could scarcely be tamed by clauses and treaties.

The conclusions to be drawn from this formative period in Iraq's history are various. They are intertwined with motifs rooted in the late 1920s that continued to stir mixed reactions during the 1930s and 1940s. These motifs seemed to correspond with themes prevalent at the time in other countries in the Middle East. Although developing in parallel, these motifs differed, as they were fuelled by local events and coloured by perceptions based on each country's cultural environment.

The process of political assertiveness that took place in the area during these years, generated by the reaction against Western domination, is usually attributed to the national feelings which reached an apex in the late 1930s. In Iraq, as in other Arab countries, a 'chamelon-like' nationalism took its colours from a context[180] in which the idea of *istiqlal tam* (total independence) appeared as the Ariadne thread.[181] Many believed then that istiqlal tam could be obtained more quickly by an alignment with the Axis powers than by the preservation of Iraq's links with Britain. Inspired by motifs of Risorgimento from Italy and Germany, many Sunni leaders considered those countries' versions of national assertiveness the natural option to adopt.

This tendency was not a new one, even when analysed in the context of modern Iraq. Infatuation with German culture and political doctrines had already been expressed by King Feisal after a visit to Italy in 1931. However, the translation of infatuation into economic and political commitments was a novelty of the mid-1930s. This change in orientation stemmed not only from external causes, such as the decline of Britain's political and economic influence, but also from internal ones, namely the self-perception of the Sunni population as the leading political community. Much less dependent on the RAF from the mid-1930s on, the Sunni leadership saw an alignment with Germany as the opportunity to liberate themselves from a forced dependency on Britain. Although this new trend had been nurtured by 'the bribes and douceurs' distributed by Dr Grobba, it also reflected the change in mood that had gradually infiltrated Iraq's Sunni population. The catalyst of this change in mood was the youth educated in the government's schools and seminars. The translation of their ideas into daily politics became a constant, characterizing Iraq's political culture in the decades to come.

Another feature of Iraqi political culture that has its roots in this period in history is the constant preoccupation with territorial continuity and integrity. This preoccupation was fuelled over generations by the lingering effects of the trauma of the British landing in April 1941. Preoccupation with territorial continuity was also nurtured by collective memories of former claims over Kuwait. These claims, registered in the early 1920s and in King Ghazi's speeches in the late 1930s, cannot be seen as mere slogans, as they reflect deep-rooted references to historical and geographical continuity. Basing their claims on Kuwait's previous attachment to Basra and on the former status of Kuwait's ruler as an Ottoman official (recognized in the Anglo-Ottoman Convention in 1913), Iraqi politicians continued to see Kuwait as part of Iraq's territory. In their eyes, the 1899 agreement between the al-Sabah family and the British was illegitimate,[182] given Iraq's status as *de jure* inheritor of the rights of the Ottomans in the area.

Britain's argument that Turkey's 1923 renunciation of its claim over Kuwait also applied to Iraq, was rejected and seen as a compromise of the Kemalist government not to be reckoned with. Iraq's claim over Kuwait, although interlaced with economic and strategic considerations,[183] remains, therefore, ideological in its essence and must also be seen as part of the context from which Iraqi nationalism derives its colours.

The belief that 'national bounds are the strongest among all other social commitments'[184] became a constant in the political rationale of the Iraqi leadership.[185] The language–race–territory equation[186] forming the basis of the German and Italian national experience infiltrated into Iraq's national education system, further contributing to the shaping of the context from which Iraqi nationalism took its colours. However, this context, focused as it was on territorial unity and cultural homogeneity,[187] would not appeal to the non-Arab or non-Sunni elements in Iraq's population. National education could not change the context determining the Kurds' and the Shi'is' collective experience.

The success of national education in Iraq could only be proven by its ability to neutralize the unresolved tension between cohesiveness and divisiveness persisting in Iraq's politics. Although it is still early to jump to conclusions, it is possible to point out that divisiveness continued to play a role in Iraqi politics in the decades to come. A tendency to divisiveness appears in Britain's furtive attempt in 1941 to revive a shelved 'five vilayet scheme' in which a more equitable distribution of powers between the different communities was envisaged in order to tame an assertive Iraqi nationalism.[188] Divisiveness and cohesiveness also pervade the attempts of the two nationalistic tendencies at the time – the British-oriented and the German-oriented ones – to come to terms with Iraq's political destiny. A similar concern is also present in the stillborn attempt to give official recognition to a third current drawing upon the 1936 'Iraq first' option, which could have changed the trends in Iraq's history and brought about a new search for a pluralistic, inward-oriented Iraqi national identity.

Part II

5

The Search for a National Identity

The lines dividing the Iraqi population in the state-formation stage were vertical, as they separated first and foremost community from community. By vertical I mean inter-communal lines perpendicular to cross-communal – horizontal – lines. That is to say that, although inter-communal divisions were affected by the state-building process, they retained their primacy in the majority of social and political relationships during the years here in focus. The shifting associations inside the communal groups were also vertical, composed of temporary alliances and associations between tribes and confederations. Short-lived, cross-communal connections were also vertically characterized by shifting associations of Shi'i tribes and confederations with Baghdadi politicians. These temporary associations, although weakening the community internally and undermining its potential influence on the country's politics, did not make the axis rotate definitively to a horizontal position.

The Kurdish community, although less susceptible to outside influences (a result of the Kurds' strong consciousness of their distinct cultural/ethnic identity), was not less prone than the Shi'is to internal divisions. But in this case too, the basic lines of division remained vertical, separating clans and tribes from each other, as well as the rural enclaves from the urban population.

These alliances rarely cut across the lines dividing the different communities. In the case of the Shi'is, the fact that these alliances were dominated by Sunni politicians reinforced their ephemeral character. To this one should add the effects of the musical-chairs game at the capital where politicians moved from the government benches to the opposition ones. These temporary associations, although creating the illusion of common causes and interests, proved after a while the difficulty of radically transcending communal boundaries.

Moreover, a historical analysis of Iraq's formative years shows that the economic advantages bestowed on the elements in the communities temporarily associated with Baghdad's various political factions were not translated into lasting political alliances. The Shi'i tribesmen and the Sunni politicians stuck to their basic interests and positions in spite of the transient effects of cross-sectarian connections. Even if temporarily debilitated by Baghdad's interference in its traditional structure,[1] the Shi'i community reacted as a collective when its identity seemed to be in danger. On these occasions, the religious authorities emerged as the guardians of the community's collective identity.

During the 1920s and the 1930s, the roles of the 'ulama' in the Shi'i provinces, the Naqshabandi and Qadiri sheikhs in the Kurdish areas, the patriarchs in the Christian communities, and the chief rabbi in the Jewish one were not just religious. Their multi-dimensional role was a natural extension of their role in Ottoman times. These religious authorities were the guardians of the collective identities of their communities and part of their cultural heritage. They also shaped the parameters of collective consciousness which affected the way in which the communities faced the government, the state or modernity in a wider sense.

At the same time, the typology of social/religious organization inside each community determined the parameters of their members' political activity. These same parameters further affected the way in which communal leaders confronted the government in defence of the community's collective values.

The various occasions when Shi'i religious leaders took the lead in the community's resistance to the state revealed the dimension of their social function and the differences between their role and that of the tribal sheikhs. These differences resulted from the fact that the tribal sheikh saw the conflict with the Iraqi authorities as a conflict between a tribal society and a modern administration whose representatives usurped their traditional rights, whereas the Shi'i ālim focused mainly on the cultural/religious dimensions of the Sunni–Shi'i contention and the way it found expression in daily politics.[2] This distinction of roles and political function between the tribal sheikh and the ālim in the southern provinces helps to explain the relative ease with which Baghdad's politicians were able to drive wedges between different tribal factions and create temporary alliances. It also explains the 'ulama's importance in preserving the community's identity in the decades to come.

In the northern provinces, this dichotomy was less conspicious. There, the traditional temporal functions fulfilled by the religious leaders of the various communities (the Turkmen, the Jews and the different Christian sects) made it difficult for the government to interfere and to split each community into factions supporting or opposing the government. This was partially true in the case of the Kurds. The Kurdish agha's combined role of temporal and religious authority fostered a greater and more constant awareness of the cultural threat implied in the state-building process, preventing rival factions from searching for external connections. The threat to the community's collective identity deriving from these alliances affected the Kurdish agha twice: in his role as a tribal leader and as the head of a religious order.

The Kurdish agha's radical reaction to the cultural homogeneity imposed by the state stemmed from the apprehension that the violation of the community's cultural identity would lead to the disturbance of his own position and to the weakening of the community's internal cohesion. In the case of the Shi'i sheikh, by contrast, the reaction stemmed mainly from the threat to his individual position, economic interests and personal power. For the Shi'is, there was no threat to the most immediate manifestation of cultural identity: the language. The Shi'i leaders' reaction to the state centred mainly on the administrative and religious levels. This was not so in the case of the Kurds. The linguistic factor became primordial in the delineation of the parameters of their conflict with the Arab government.

The meshing of the ethnic, religious and cultural elements in the Kurds' collective awareness strengthened their reaction to cultural amalgamation, whereas overlapping criteria, such as a common ethnic descent and linguistic unity, made the distinction between the frames of reference of the Sunnis and the Shi'is more difficult. This is why the Kurdish aghas reacted to the government's educational policy as if their collective cultural identity was threatened at its very core, whereas the Shi'i tribal sheikh seemed to concentrate on the economic and social aspects of his community's conflict with the state.

This distinction also explains why state-oriented education *per se* was not perceived as a threat by the Shi'is but became the very essence of the Kurds' conflict with the state. All the above brings us to the question why the contention between the communities was concentrated on the educational level.

In more general terms, education spelled literacy, the acquisition of technical skills and of the ability to cope with the prerequisites of modern society. For the Shi'is it also meant the acquisition of tools that would permit their further association in the state's administration on an equal footing with the Sunnis. In their case there was also the acceptance of the message contained in the state-building process, as well as identification with the media of transmission: the Arab language.

For the Kurds, the idea of modernity encompassed in the notion of state clashed with the desire to secure autonomous administration for the Kurdish areas. By the same token, the idea of modernity could be appealing only if transmitted in the Kurdish language.

For both the Shi'is and the Kurds, however, acceptance of the message advanced through the spreading of state education was not achieved as easily as envisaged by the theoreticians of Iraq's official educational doctrine.

Sati' al Husri, the man responsible for conceptualizing an all-embracing, identity-forging educational policy and 'the father of Iraq's public education',[3] was a well-known public figure who had played key roles in the Ottoman education system and served as Director of Education during Feisal's short administration of Syria.

Without dwelling on biographical details or scanning the sources of Sati' al Husri's ideological formation,[4] this chapter will focus on the practical applications of his education policy, which promoted unity of language and history, and the effects of this policy on the different communities.

Drawing upon the principles of secular nationalism tinged with the romantic ideas of Herder and Fichte, al Husri's aim was to create the conditions for the cultural flourishing of the Arab nation and pave the way for the creation of a united – borderless – Arab state encompassing all the Arab provinces of the former Ottoman Empire. These conditions demanded unity of language, of values and of economic interests.

The first step on the way to cultural unification was the establishment of a curriculum that would educate the new generations to Pan-Arabism. Its main principles were the consolidation of the cultural links between the Arab peoples through the reinforcement of the Arab language heritage. The tools were discipline and readiness to subordinate personal and regional interests to national goals.[5]

The underlying message in the more specific Iraqi context was the promotion of the idea of an Iraqi nation that was part of a wider Pan-Arab one. It also meant the acceptance of new frames of reference by the different groups forming Iraq's population.

Drawing from the French and German theoretical models of nationalism, Sati' al Husri's promotion of the concept of a common language as the basis for a nationwide unified system of reference meant uprooting the younger generation in the provinces from the influences of its immediate surroundings.[6] The uniformization of language, establishing unity of thought, was seen by al Husri as the tool for converting youth to the values of modern nationalism. Moreover, a unifying and compulsory educational system was meant to make the school the instrument of social change that would modify the customs and attitudes of the new generation in the provinces. Above all the new education system was designed to cut across local and communal loyalties by inculcating a modern sense of political and cultural affiliation to the modern state.

Sati' al Husri's position in the Iraqi education system, as Director General in the years 1921–27, as a professor at the Higher Teachers' Training College, and as Dean of the Law College during the 1930s, was very powerful. It neutralized the influence of educational authorities such as Jerome Farrell and Lionel Smith, British advisers to the Department of Education during the 1920s, and circumvented the authority of successive Shi'i ministers of education after independence.

The Shi'i ministers' criticism of al Husri's policy grew with the realization that education meant in fact the subordination of Shi'i traditional religious and cultural values to foreign concepts of modern citizenship. Their position was conditioned by the fact that their own appointment as ministers of education was an attempt to frame their contention with the Sunnis in terms of unequal educational levels, a problem that could easily be resolved by the spreading of modern education to the Shi'i countryside.

The problem was, however, more complex. As the Sunni authorities perceived it, education was meant to help the new generations of Iraqis to assimilate, articulate and disseminate the values of modern nationalism. Its tool was a primary-school curriculum based on a nineteenth-century French syllabus which praised uniformity in approach and methodology.[7] This curriculum was meant to be instrumental in bringing youngsters in the provinces to a greater identification with the state and developing their feelings for the nation's language and history.

A totally different line of thought characterized the authorities' approach to secondary education. The development of secondary education in the provinces was not seen as a natural continuation of the primary level but was rather considered as a double-edged sword.

Although framed by the 'quantity vs. quality' parameters, according to which the concentration of institutions of secondary and higher education[8] in the capital would provide for a higher level of education in the country in general, the authorities' position was also due to the belief that the spreading of secondary schools to the provinces could jeopardize their own efforts to impose Baghdad's cultural and technical hegemony over them.

Sati' al Husri explained his position in the following terms:

> [T]he spreading of secondary schools and teacher training institutions to the provinces would place national unity in great jeopardy ... for naturally the majority of the pupils in these schools in Mosul would be sons of Christians [while] in Hilla [they would be] sons of Ja'farites. This would lead to the strengthening of sectarianism.[9]

The idea that preserving cultural particularism could help forge a multifaceted and all-embracing new identity was not popular at the time. Instead, a code of cultural and linguistic conformity was seen as nation-forging and identity-shaping. The promotion of uniformity as a barometer of nationalism became a key expression of al Husri's method.

The whole issue was complex, and a study of it, including the authorities' viewpoint, highlights the dilemma of nation-building in multi-ethnic societies.

From the authorities' viewpoint, the main aims were to prepare the population for the standardized needs of modern administration and to inculcate in the different communities the notion of a politically and culturally focused Arabism.

The specificity of Iraq's case was not fully understood either by the Iraqi or the British authorities. Some basic errors had already been committed in the mid- and late 1920s. The British intended to build an educational system based on the British one; encouraged by the apparently good results they had obtained in Egypt,[10] they aimed above all to bring the Iraqi population closer to their own Western perceptions of progress and modernity.

However, conditions in Iraq were different from the Egyptian situation: the scarcity of educational institutions and the low level of the existing ones were evidence of Baghdad's former status as a mere province of the Ottoman Empire. This fact was particularly conspicuous in the case of secondary education.

According to Sati' al Husri, only four secondary state schools functioned in the main centres (Baghdad, Kirkuk, Mosul and Basra) before the First World War, and the number of students did not exceed 350.[11] A teachers' seminar, a Faculty of Law (250 students) and a Technological School (70 students) completed the picture.[12]

Many communal schools functioned at that time without interference from the state authorities, among them the Shi'i secular seminar in Baghdad and the religious seminars in Najaf and Karbala'. There was a Jewish school of the Alliance Israelite Universelle network in Baghdad, and the different Christian minorities operated a number of Christian schools in Basra and Mosul. Most institutions had separate divisions for boys and girls.[13]

After the creation of the Iraqi Department of Education, the new authorities started to tackle a situation that seemed to them incompatible with the state's new needs. The situation was considered unacceptable for three main reasons: (1) the outnumbering of Muslim students by non-Muslim; (2) the communal leaders' freedom to determine the curriculum in the communal schools; and (3) the special financial arrangements accorded to the communal schools. These arrangements, inherited from Ottoman times, were preserved by the British by means of a special agreement with the communal leaders, the 'Concordatto'.[14]

Semi-official institutions (the nisf-hukumiyya schools) also enjoyed special financial arrangements (supported by funds from France, Britain and the United States). These institutions were administered jointly by the Department of Education and the different communal leaders. The new Iraqi authorities rejected the policies of Jerome Farrell and Lionel Smith and considered British attempts to preserve the former conditions as part of a plan to perpetuate Britain's presence in the Mosul area.[15]

From 1926 on, following Mosul's annexation to Iraq, new directives concerning the communal schools' budget were introduced. The former advantages were linked to new criteria such as the school's level, the number of classes and of teachers, and the school authorities' readiness to integrate in the official system. Another point of reference was the success of the school's students in the official exams.[16]

Other centralizing measures in questions related to the spreading of the official curriculum and reforms in the schools' administration became official from the mid-1920s on as the British authorities gradually disengaged themselves from direct inteference in educational matters. This trend was reinforced with Sati' al Husri's nomination as head of the commission for implementation and improvement of the curriculum in 1929.[17]

It was also at this time that Pan-Arabism became a conspicuous element in Iraq's official education policy. Special attention was then given to the ideological, conceptual and intellectual links existing among the Arab peoples.[18]

Iraq's pioneering role in the revival of the Arab nation (as the first Arab country to attain independence) became one of the mottos pervading official ideology in general and one of its manifestations on the educational level in particular.[19]

Sati' al Husri's infatuation with the Arab language – as the higher expression of Arab culture and heritage and as a channel of communication among the Arab peoples – contributed immensely to its acquiring a pivotal role in the dissemination of the Pan-Arab ideology.

This was one of the reasons why the dispute over language – and its role in the forging of an Iraqi identity – became a major issue in Iraq at the time. This was also the reason why after independence Arabic became the *de facto* official language in the Kurdish areas despite the passage in 1931 of the Local Language Law establishing Kurdish as the *de jure* vernacular in these areas. It was also the rationale for introducing Arabic characters in Kurdish textbooks.[20]

The importance attached to the implementation of standardized Arabic also held true in matters affecting the Shi'i provinces. There, a new method of teaching Arabic was introduced; the whole-word method – more open to local variations and dialectal expressions – was replaced by a new system in which the Baghdadi dialect appeared as the official one.

The Shi'is resented these measures because they implied official recognition of Baghdad as the country's cultural centre. Considering themselves no less guardians of the Arab language and culture, the Shi'is often directed open criticism against the Sunni elite who spoke Turkish and had been educated in Ottoman institutions.[21] In fact, the network of education in the Shi'i centres of Najaf, Karbala' and Kazimiya – although religious – proved with time to have been most instrumental in the training of Shi'i students in Arab literature and philology and in creating a local elite of literate young Shi'is ready to adopt the Arab dimension of Iraq's modern national message.[22]

Distinction must, however, be made between the Shi'i literate elite and the masses of illiterate Shi'i peasants. For the peasants, religion carried the greatest weight as a constituent of identity. Theirs was a more popular version of Shi'ism than the one officially taught in the Shi'i seminars in Najaf and Karbala'. This was Shi'ism as promulgated by the local mujtahidun, encompassing local beliefs and practices and assimilated in accordance with their special social circumstances.

This does not mean that these Shi'is' frame of reference was distinct from that of their erudite counterparts. It only means that religion and tribal customs (or their lingering effects) influenced them at this stage more than the feelings evoked by the Arab language and literature.

One of the parameters of their identity – the colloquial Arabic spoken in the southern provinces – became a target of the centralist measures of language unification. As a result the large majority of the Shi'i tribesmen became less receptive than their erudite counterparts to the message of secular nationalism.

On the level of language and culture, theirs was not a reaction to Arabic or to Arab culture (primordial elements in their own collective identity) but – again – a reaction to the Sunnis' interpretation of secularism and to the sudden priority accorded by the authorities to the Baghdadi dialect.

The debate over education also encompassed such methodological issues as the implementation of scientific pedagogical methods in the system in general and the finding of the right channel to the Shi'i population in particular.[23]

The public debate over the best method to follow in order to inculcate nationalist feelings in all echelons of the Shi'i population finally cost al Husri his post as Director of the Department of Education. A young Western-educated Shi'i intellectual, Muhammad Fadel al Jamali, ousted him from the centre of Iraq's educational arena, and became Iraq's Director of Education in 1934.

Born in Kazimiya in 1903 to an important Shi'i family, Fadel al Jamali had received his religious and secular education at the elementary theological schools of Najaf and the American University of Beirut, and had a PhD from the Teachers' College at Columbia University in New York.[24] The clash between this young representative of the post-war, American-educated generation and the old, European-oriented, Turkish-educated former Ottoman official underscored one of the classic dilemmas in the nation-building process, whether to use or reject local sources of cultural heritage.

When surveying the pedagogical and theoretical aspects of this dilemma, it becomes apparent that the confrontation between the two educators stemmed from their different backgrounds and different approaches to pedagogic methods envisaging the expansion of literacy, the implementation of education in tribal sectors and the opening of a technical school and special establishments for girls.[25]

The confrontation between the two finally focused on the conclusions of the Paul Monroe Educational Commission, brought to Iraq in 1932. One of the commission's main concerns was the educational problems among tribal populations, the subject of Fadel al Jamali's thesis at Columbia under Paul Monroe's supervision. A detailed analysis of the commission's conclusions is timely, as it gives valuable insights into the cultural contest between the capital and the provinces[26] in spite of the controversy surrounding the issue.

115

Although an inclusive term, 'tribal population' refers in the report mainly to the Shi'i population of the southern provinces. According to the commission, the Shi'i population's illiteracy stemmed from the tribal sheikhs' denial of the validity of an urban-oriented school system.[27] After independence, this denial focused on the incompatibility between modern education and the needs of a tribal society. However, there were more general reasons for the estrangement of the entire Shi'i community (tribesmen and town dwellers alike) from modern education. In Ottoman times this estrangement sprang from resentment of compulsory Sunni religious instruction and the disinclination to study Turkish. The motives behind the Shi'is' resentment towards institutionalized Sunnism were obvious, as they were anchored in the apprehension of Sunni influence. On the other hand the Shi'is were reluctant to study Turkish because they did not believe in the likelihood of ever being integrated into the Ottoman public administration.

The establishment by the British of Arabic as the official language in Iraq's education system during the mandate did not radically change the Shi'is attitude. By the same token, a rigid curriculum planned to meet the needs of an urban population could hardly appeal to the Shi'i rural community.

According to the report, modern education could appeal to the Shi'is only if three major changes were introduced, namely:

(1) The implementation of an educational programme that drew from the tribesmen's daily lives and was structured to meet the needs of a rural community. This curriculum would centre on ways to modernize outdated agricultural methods and on modern marketing procedures.

(2) The training of teachers belonging to and interested in the tribal sector.

(3) The preservation of some of the 'native ways and methods' worth preserving, taking care not to arouse the tribesmen's resentment by attacking sensitive issues such as tribal social institutions and beliefs.[28] Fadel al Jamali, the promoter of the report's recommendations, also believed that 'like-mindedness bringing national cohesion and unity'[29] could be obtained only by promoting an education system compatible with the tribesmen's lifestyle and their social and cultural values. His main failure lay in undermining the religious side of the equation by setting the problem only in terms of tribesmen vs. town dwellers.

The other chapters of the Monroe Report focused on two controversial issues:

(1) The fostering of secondary education, considered by the Iraqi authorities as an indispensable step towards political and cultural autonomy when implemented in the capital and an obstacle to national integration when implemented in the provinces. While pondering the contribution of secondary education to the training of the country's future leadership, the Monroe Commission accepted the former British position, namely the instability concealed in the surplus of academics, given the scarcity of suitable administrative and governmental positions.[30]

(2) The determination of the role of communal schools in the process of state-formation. The Monroe Commission did not question the need to impose a uniform curriculum promoting the study of the language, history and geography of the dominant community. However, it stated the purpose of education as the creation of 'Iraqi citizens, [and] not the making of Arabs or Muslims'.[31] The translation of these recommendations into practical terms meant instruction in the minority's language and teaching the minority's religion. The study of Arabic language, history and geography should not be made compulsory, 'as to do so would defeat its own purpose'.[32] This clause also referred to the government's indirect monitoring of the Christian and Jewish communal schools by granting financial aid 'in accordance to the proportion of the school's service to public education', meaning the 'closeness with which the minoritary school followed the government's syllabus'.[33]

Following the publication of the Monroe Report, Sati' al Husri and Fadel al Jamali clashed over the need to replace the Director and the Inspector General with an advisory council representing the rural areas and the minorities.[34] Sati' al Husri's reactions to the commission's recommendations were published in a booklet entitled *Naqd Tahrir Lajnat Monroe* (A Critique of Monroe's Commission Report), in which he challenged the right of foreigners to evaluate Iraq's educational system.[35]

The real discussion, however, evolved around the need to centralize education, or alternatively to decentralize it in order to reduce tension between communities.[36] Husri's favouring of political fermentation, which was implied in the process of developing a culturally uniform identity, appeared to Jamali as incompatible with the principles of modern management and pedagogy.[37]

The discussion between the two educators therefore centred on questions of form and methodology and not of content, as Jamali himself defined the problem as stemming mainly from temporary and surmountable contradictions between two sectors – rural and urban – of the same population.[38]

117

Husri's resignation in 1935 from his second term as Director of the Department of Public Education left Jamali in control of the system. Jamali's main concerns were the improvement of rural education by appointing additional Directors of Education in Shi'i provinces and by establishing secondary schools in Najaf staffed by Christian and American University of Beirut graduates.[39]

However, these measures did not change the nature of the problem, which was also characterized by the concentration of funds and educational institutions in the Baghdad area and a growing subordination of the communal school system in the capital to the state.[40]

Another important aspect overlooked by commission members in general and by al Jamali in particular was the permanent tension in Kurdish areas, stemming from the unsolved problem of the preservation of a Kurdish identity. Although some school books were translated into the Kurdish dialect of Sulaimaniya and Kurdish teachers were appointed to Kurdish primary schools,[41] the tension between the Kurdish community and the government persisted, given the government's policy of preventing the institutionalization of the Kurdish language and culture.

The Kurds reiterated their previous claims while introducing new requests, among them the creation of a 'Kurdish educational area' with a uniform system of education. The artificial annexation of Arbil to Mosul and the inclusion of Sulaimaniya and Kirkuk in the area administered by Baghdad's education authorities were at the basis of these requests. The re-establishment of a Kurdish educational area, consisting of Kirkuk, Sulaimaniya and Arbil, to be administered jointly by a single Kurdish official, became a *sine qua non* condition for the integration of the Kurdish areas in Iraq.[42] Another request was the establishment of full secondary schools in Arbil and Sulaimaniya.[43]

After the publication of the commission's report Sati' al Husri accused its members of producing a contradictory and inconsequential piece of misinformation which concentrated on problems already solved or on solutions that were basically incompatible with Iraq's special conditions.[44]

Adding to al Husri's resentment of the commission was the fact that its report had been written without consulting him – in spite of his standing at the head of the Department of Education in the crucial, formative years.[45]

Al Husri published (from June to September 1932) twelve responses to the report (later collected into the booklet mentioned above). These letters centred mainly on issues related to the curriculum, to the government's policy towards communal schools, to the principle of centralism and uniformity, to the spreading of secondary education in the provinces and to the formation of a local leadership.[46]

Among issues receiving special attention were the government's plans to create new institutions of higher education, among them a university, as a means of forging a national leadership – this in spite of the commission's conclusion that no human or financial resources were available to this end.[47]

Once again Sati' al Husri reiterated the need to create a united society through the inculcation of common values in the cities and the countryside and by abolishing the privileges enjoyed by the sons of tribal leaders during Ottoman times.[48]

According to al Husri this principle also applied to the government's decision to reduce the scope and number of optional subjects in the high schools. The Iraqi pupils' greater need of basic instruction required more directives than were given to their American counterparts. Al Husri referred to the German curriculum, in which the number of optional subjects and their scope was reduced to a minimum.[49]

Two other issues gained al Husri's special attention. The first centred on the government's refusal to accept the existence of communal schools after independence, because they were seen as reminiscent of colonial times.[50] Al Husri also tried to solve the problem of secondary education in the provinces by suggesting a half-way solution in the form of the *madaris mutawasita*[51] schools which would engulf two years of the primary programme (to be reduced from six to four years) and prepare the student for two more years on the secondary level. In fact, this represented an interim solution by which education in the provinces would be reduced from ten to eight years.

Sati' al Husri's observations did not, however, go beyond the realm of mere suggestions, as his own position in government circles was not as strong as before. Despite the decline in his official powers, the spirit of his message continued to guide the education authorities in the years to come.

In spite of the tension between the different communities and the government, very few changes were introduced in official policy. Attempts to Arabize non-Arab communities and to implement a uniform curriculum in communal schools became a daily occurrence. Very few secondary schools were opened in the provinces, and strict controls were imposed on private schools.[52] This state of affairs was pushed to an extreme in the late 1930s, and a new law, passed in 1940, extended direct government control over all private schools, stipulating that only Arab teachers approved by the Ministry of Education could teach Arabic history, geography and civics. Article 5 forbade injury to national unity, and Article 31 allowed the authorities to close private and foreign schools whose activities were seen as a contravention of Article 5.[53] Article 32 forbade private schools to accept financial aid from foreign sources without the approval of the Ministry of Education. Article 34 prohibited the use of books that were incompatible with the spirit of Article 5.[54]

However, the paragraph that caused the most turmoil was Article 36, prohibiting Iraqis from attending foreign primary schools.[55] In spite of a statement by Nuri al Sa'id (then Prime Minister) that Article 36 referred only to Iranian schools (whose appeal to Shi'i youngsters seemed to have increased in the late 1930s),[56] the Iraqi press included Christian and Jewish schools[57] in the definition.

The discussion of the character and aims of national education led finally to the subordination of the education system to the army. The appointment of Taha al Hashimi, former Chief of the General Staff, as Director General of Education in 1927 after Husri's first dismissal from the post and Taha's resumption of both posts in the mid-thirties underscored the high priority assigned to the army's needs in those years.

The co-operation between the Ministry of Education and the Ministry of Defence led to the establishment of paramilitary youth movements, such as Jaish al Futuwwa (the Youth Army), inspired by German and Italian youth organization.[58] These movements developed after Dr Sami Shawkat, the former Director General of Health and founder of the Muthanna Club, became Director General of Education in 1937. Students' parades and meetings, modelled on similar gatherings taking place in Germany and Italy, became frequent. Students were classified by military rank (juveniles, rovers and futuwwa) and wore corresponding chevrons and badges. They formed the background of Sami Shawkat's speeches, among them the famous 'Speech on the Profession of Death':

> I hereafter shall permit no one to make any propaganda for peace and shall oppose anyone who advocates peace. We want war. We should shed our blood for the sake of Arabism. We should die for our national cause ... it is our duty to perfect the profession of Death, the profession of the army, the sacred military profession.[59]

Although Shawkat's speech was criticized by the more moderate sectors in the population, as well as by al Husri himself, who denounced the dangers inherent in Shawkat's excesses, the principle of individual sacrifice for the sake of national salvation remained a valid one.[60]

The same held true for the more moderate elements in Baghdad's political circles, whose influence at the time was at its lowest. The dominant tendency was the one prevailing among the Iraqi youngsters imbued with the sense of involvement in a historical mission aiming at 'a total renovation and restoration of the Arab society'.[61] A whole political culture was built on their role as a 'national vanguard'[62] ready to redeem the 'corrupt interests' and 'inclinations for compromise'[63] which supposedly characterized the older generation's philosophy.

This generation gap added to the al Husri–Jamali debate, focusing in the late 1930s on Jamali's growing admiration for Fascism and on his suggestions to include the subject in the curriculum.[64]

This infatuation with Fascism was a reflection of the increasing disillusion with Britain and its capacity to meet Iraq's needs. The anti-British feelings which characterized the mid- and late 1930s remained a constant in Iraqi politics after 1941 when the British reinforced their influence in the country and introduced reforms in Iraq's education system. These lingering anti-British feelings, rooted in years of resentment against the former colonial power, were fuelled by the escalation of the situation in Palestine and the belief that Britain was conducting an anti-Arab policy there.

Although of supreme importance to the Sunnis, the nationalist mottos could not carry the same appeal for the youth of other communities. Shi'is and Kurds did not respond with the same enthusiam as their Sunni counterparts to themes such as 'shedding blood for the sake of Arabism' or even 'combat for the sake of Palestine', a recurrent motif in the late 1930s.

The lukewarm reaction of the Shi'is and Kurds to the appeals of extreme nationalism leads us to the conclusion that the Pan-Arab orientation of the curriculum (monopolized in the late 1930s by Syrian and Palestinian teachers), together with the Sunnization of the army's higher echelons, prevented these two classic tools in any nationalist endeavour – education and army – from becoming instrumental in the forging of a new Iraqi identity.

6

The Northern Provinces in the 1940s

The events preceding and following the 1941 watershed speeded up the process of polarization and highlighted the differences within each community.

In the Kurdish camp, the division between the traditional leadership (formed by the aghas and the ashraf) and the younger leaders (comprising young intellectuals and middle-rank officers serving in the Iraqi army) grew wider. This division focused mainly on opposing viewpoints on the realignment of the community as it faced the changes caused by the war. The older generation was naturally inclined to stick to old alliances and to more traditional methods of political protest, whereas the younger leaders sought more effective alliances and radical practices. Accordingly, the ashraf and the aghas chose either to preserve the old set of relations with Britain or to rebel occasionally. The younger generation pressed for more systematic policies. They had come to the conclusion that because the Kurds did not fit into the British imperial scheme as the Arabs had, they should seek the protection of another great power; Germany or Russia seemed more able to provide the support that had not materialized during the Kurds' long and unfruitful alignment with Britain.

These differences took a new turn in May 1941, when Rashid 'Ali's confrontation with the British at Habbaniya seemed to signal that radical changes were in the offing. The irredentists among the older leaders gathered around Sheikh Mahmud and supported his call for open rebellion. The Pizhdar, the Jaf and the Arbil tribes planned to occupy Köe, Surdash, Chamchemal and, at a later stage, Sulaimaniya. This was to be another spontaneous uprising, like those led in the past by Sheikh Mahmud. Its ability to bring radical political changes, however, was in doubt.

The younger leaders' preferred tactic was to synchronize an open rebellion with the arrival of the Germans in Iraq. They believed that a revision of the political status quo would then be possible, leading either to the creation of an autonomous Kurdish area in northern Iraq or to the reorganization of Iraq's political configurations altogether.

Although basic, these differences were temporarily blurred when danger threatened the community as a whole. An example of this was the united front the older and younger leaders formed when the withdrawal of 800 cadets from Baghdad's Military Academy to Sulai-maniya seemed imminent. Seeing the presence of the cadets (and their Palestinian followers) as an infringement on the community's *de facto* if not yet *de jure* rights over the Kurdish areas, the old and the young generations reacted in unison.

A delegation of notables who were particularly reluctant to engage in an unprovoked clash with Britain began to pressure Sulaimaniya's mutasarif, almost causing the former Commander of General Staff, Husein Fawzi, to resign. At the same time, the young officers of the Sixth and Eleventh Brigades, assembled by Rashid 'Ali on the outskirts of Baghdad, started planning an organized retreat of their Kurdish troops to Kirkuk. This radical step was meant to prevent a withdrawal of Rashid 'Ali's army to the northern districts in the event of his banishment from the capital by the British.[1] The crumbling of Rashid 'Ali's regime and his taking refuge in the town of Mosul, the second bastion of Arab nationalism, became a possibility after the collapse of the army's resistance against the British in the south.

The radicalism of the young Kurdish officers exceeded in certain aspects that of the irredentist aghas. A document drafted on 16 June 1941 by Sheikh Mahmud and Hajji 'Abbas, agha of the Pizhdar and representative of the irrendentists, is a good illustration. The document's first two clauses reiterated traditional claims, calling for the creation of a practically autonomous Kurdish territory in northern Iraq, administered by Kurdish officials, headed by a Kurdish muta-sarif, a Kurdish president of the judiciary, and a council composed of local notables in charge of budgets and credits. Clauses 3 and 4 reflected the changes that had occurred in the notables' position as a result of the strengthening of the state's institutions in general and their penetration into the Kurdish areas in particular. In effect, the third clause referred to the need to form a Kurdish military brigade modelled on the Levies, under the command of a Kurdish officer. This force would be responsible for the defence of Kurdish areas, a measure that implied the closing of these areas to government troops. The fourth clause focused on the need to establish an agricultural bank to provide more credit for the villagers. This measure was meant to stop the increasing impoverishment of the villagers resulting from the government's intervention in the marketing of agricultural produce. The fifth and sixth clauses reflected the aghas' distrust of the government, focusing on the need to have any agreement with Baghdad validated by the British Ambassador, still considered by the Kurds as the highest authority in the country and the person ultimately responsible for their political fate and security.[2]

This programme, referred to as 'The Six Points of 16 June', was officially adopted by a group of aghas assembled at Sulaimaniya under the auspices of Sheikh Qadir Qamchar Lesh in July 1941. The aghas reiterated that the programme was to be the basis for all future negotiations with the Iraqi authorities. However, the subsequent assembly of government troops in strategic points such as Qala Diza, Halabja and Panjwin and the proclamation of martial law in Sulaimaniya prevented the continuation of negotiations based on the Six Points programme.[3]

Rashid 'Ali's subsequent fall and the rise of Jamil al Midfa'i to the premiership did not bring radical changes in the relationship between the Kurds and the government. The disbanding of Sheikh Mahmud's followers allowed the re-emergence of moderate notables who still believed in a dialogue with the authorities if three main obstacles to a *modus vivendi* were removed. These were: (1) the government's policy restricting the expansion of secondary education to Kurdish areas; (2) the government's refusal to allow the establishment of a Kurdish cultural association in Baghdad; and (3) the government's refusal to forfeit its monopoly on the tobacco trade.[4] In other words, these were the same old claims regarding the preservation of the Kurdish culture and language and a demand to retain some liberty in the control of their main means of subsistence.

The government's monopoly on the tobacco trade – the main agricultural product in the northern provinces – had been made official in 1939. This measure was at first welcomed by aghas and villagers alike, as both sides felt exploited by city merchants. However, once implemented, the monopoly turned into a major point of dissension between the Kurds and the Iraqi authorities. The government's inability to take over some of the merchants' functions, such as providing loans to the cultivators and marketing their products, lowered the revenues of cultivator and landlord alike. These difficulties, coupled with problems caused by an inefficient and profit-seeking administration, severely damaged the economic structure in the Kurdish areas. The reiteration by the moderates of a point made earlier in Sheikh Mahmud's Six Points programme illustrated the real nature of the area's economic difficulties.

Moreover, the government's refusal to allow the establishment of a Kurdish cultural association in Baghdad – a right accorded to other minority groups – was seen by the moderates as blatant cultural discrimination, proving once more the weight of the cultural factor in the conflict between both sides.

The government's delay in establishing secondary education in the northern districts kept education on the agenda despite the partial solution reached on the language issue. Although Kurdish and Turkish were taught in the first four grades in primary schools in areas where those groups were in the majority, the general level of education remained the lowest in the country. The moderates asked that a committee be formed – headed by two Kurdish intellectuals – to draw up a new curriculum which would meet the requirements of modern education without relinquishing traditional values and culture.

Other demands made at this time by the moderates included the halting of the diversion of tax revenues from the provinces to the capital and the guarantee of a more sound investment of funds in the structure of the northern liwa's. Special mention was made of the need for an irrigation system to help drain the swamps of the Sharizur Valley, infested with malaria-carrying mosquitoes. The moderates pointed to the fact that state expenditure had been limited to works serving to consolidate the government's authority over the area (fortified serais and police posts) without improving living conditions for its inhabitants.[5]

The moderate aghas' platform demonstrated a willingness to negotiate with the authorities on what they considered a minimalist programme that was far less radical than the irredentists' views or the ideas of the younger leaders. However, Jamil al Midfa'i's response to their demands was as inflexible as Rashid 'Ali's reaction to Sheikh Mahmud's Six Points had been. Although showing some readiness to compromise on the tobacco issue, he bluntly refused to allow the establishment of a Kurdish cultural centre in Baghdad, a move reflecting more than anything else the real nature of the conflict between the Kurds and the Arabs. The very thought of forfeiting the state's monopoly on culture appeared to the Sunni authorities much more of a threat to the country's identity than losing total control over the economy in the northern districts.

This approach continued to shape the government's policy throughout the 1940s, preventing an agreement between the two sides. Education remained a disputed topic, as the government wrongly attributed the political activism of the uprising to the educational level of the younger generation, ignoring the fact that Kurdish youth were as active in Arbil (where a secondary school had been established years earlier) as in Sulaimaniya and Köe (where the struggle for secondary education was still on course).[6] In fact, disillusion and anger caused by the government's restrictive policy contributed to the failure of the national education scheme in the Kurdish areas.

Resentment towards the state in general and the government in particular grew during the early 1940s, reawakening Pan-Kurdish feelings. All sorts of publications, from pamphlets to magazines, pointed to a fundamental change in the Kurds' view of their situation. The cover of a magazine published in Badinan, a relatively quiet town, is a good illustration: it showed 'a maiden chained down on a map of Kurdistan – one hand made fast to Ankara, another to Teheran, and a foot to Baghdad'[7] – a protest against the division and submission of the Kurdish population to three masters.

Calls for the political unification of Kurdistan – 'the backbone of the Middle East' – became frequent.[8] The reawakening of Pan-Kurdish feelings – stifled during almost two decades of state-building – was also the result of the belief that times of war bring new opportunities. These beliefs were not totally unfounded. Although unofficial, swings in orientation had been registered on the British side, as mentioned. The belief that a revision in Britain's regional policy was necessary began to take root in British political circles during Rashid 'Ali's regime, when fears of German penetration were substantive. Variations on Britain's 'Kurdish policy' were then proposed, including redrawing the borders of Iran and Turkey.

> [A] situation might arise in which it [would] no longer [be] advisable for us to consider the feelings of either or both of the states in question and it would be well to start thinking of ways in which the future of the Kurds – particularly those in the proximity of: (a) the Caucasus approaches to Iraq; (b) the Turco–Syrian frontier – might be induced to help our plans and obstruct those of the enemy.[9]

This clause meant the creation of a Kurdish autonomous zone, turning it into a shield to protect Iraq from German or Russian invasion.

By an ironic turn of history, the creation of a Kurdish state seemed in the early 1940s a guarantee of Iraq's territorial integrity and the very condition for maintaining Britain's position in the area. These considerations were shelved once the immediate danger of an invasion from outside receded, and the traditional position of support for the Iraqi government was renewed. As soon as the war ended, the British covered the Iraqi army's advance into the northern provinces with the Royal Air Force, offering another illustration of Baghdad's difficulty in imposing its writ in the provinces. British ground troops also filled the role of local gendarmerie as clashes between the communities increased. Years after independence the Kurds and the Assyrians still preferred to rely on British troops rather than on Iraqi forces, considering the British as the *de facto* authority in the country. In fact, the arrival of British forces at a scene of contention brought the automatic retreat of Iraqi army units.[10]

However, Britain's main interest centred on the maintenance of order and Iraq's territorial integrity. As during the 1920s and the early 1930s, Britain's return to local politics in the 1940s was motivated by the need to reinstate the government's prestige in the northern provinces, where its authority had been shattered by the increasing pressure from the young Kurdish leaders for secession from Iraq. Given their inclinations towards and sympathies for Russia, the possibility of moves towards the incorporation of the Kurdish areas into the Soviet orbit at that time appeared greater.

The most outstanding figure among the young tribal leaders was Mulla Mustapha al Barazani, the younger brother of the famous Sheikh Ahmed al Barazani, who had led the uprising against the Iraqi forces in the early 1930s. In contrast to Sheikh Ahmed's retention of traditional authority, Mulla Mustapha emerged as a new type of leader, combining military and political functions that transcended the ones fulfilled by Kurdish leaders in the past. Although at this stage his role could not be characterized as that of a national leader, the composition of his permanent forces indicated new patterns of association inside the community itself.

Mulla Mustapha's forces consisted at the time of approximately 700 men, comprising Kurdish officers and soldiers who had deserted from the army and members of tribes, such as the Zibaris and Surahis, not traditionally linked to the Barazanis.[11] The protonational nature of Mulla Mustapha's position was reflected in the claims he put forward to General Muhammad Sa'id al Tikriti, the commander of the Iraqi forces in the north. Specific claims, such as the return of lands confiscated by the government and the liberation of Kurdish leaders detained in the south (among them Sheikh Ahmed himself), coupled with the traditional requests regarding the building of an economic, social and educational structure in the northern districts,[12] were once again on the agenda. The Mulla's assertiveness, expressed in his refusal to submit to the Tikriti general, contributed to an escalation of the situation and to a greater polarization of positions.

In January 1944, the Mulla's forces took control of twenty police posts in an area stretching from Rowanduz to 'Amadiya. From this position, new demands were made, demands that reflected a more developed sense of communal leadership than just combating the threats posed by nation-building measures. These new demands included the supply of grain to remote Kurdish villages and even more radical steps such as fiscal autonomy for the Kurdish districts.[13] On an ideological level, these demands represented a confrontation between two communities in search of political definition and of the very frame encompassing such a search. Some months later, this search led to Mulla Mustapha's march to Mahabad.

The independent Kurdish Republic of Mahabad – declared in 1946 and sponsored by the Soviets – was short-lived; it collapsed after one year. Its effects, however, were larger than reality. It provided the Kurds with a feeling that their minority status, created by the First World War misdeeds, had somehow been redeemed by the Second World War. A memorandum from a group of Kurdish notables to Nuri al Sa'id and Tawfiq al Wahbi, the Kurdish representative to the cabinet, reflects the first stirring of these feelings,[14] and it reiterates the Kurds' long-lasting desires for autonomy.

The Mahabad episode closed a period in the unresolved relationship between Iraq as a political entity and its Kurdish community. A new period opened more than twelve years later when General Qasem's *coup* of 1958 brought Mulla Mustapha back from his exile in the USSR.

7

The Southern Provinces in the 1940s

The waves of hope, protest and reappraisal that normally arise at the end of a war washed over Iraq's urban centres in the mid-1940s. Calls for a more liberal approach in politics and social affairs, including freer elections and a revision of the 1930 treaty, were heard in Baghdad.

The anti-British atmosphere in the Sunni urban centres contrasted with the situation in the provinces, where inhabitants turned again to the British as potential local mediators in their clashes with the central government. Britain's official comeback to Iraq in 1941 made it an influential factor in the struggle for control of the provinces' economic resources, the preservation of the cultural and religious patrimony of their inhabitants and the shaping of Iraq's intercommunal relationships in a wider context.

The population's divergent attitudes to the return of the British and the post-war situation in general were to be channelled into the reorganization of the electoral system, launched by the Regent in 1946. Although the amendment was intended to appease the urban sector, it was seen in the provinces as an opportunity to rectify past inequities. Officially, the amendment had two main objectives: to blur former geographical and administrative divisions between Baghdad and the provinces, and to break down the communitarian system in order to prevent easy penetration of traditional constituencies by Baghdad's politicians.

The first objective might have been obtained by dividing Iraq's territory into smaller districts. Article 5 of the 1946 Electoral Law set up new electoral circles on the basis of an arbitrary number of primary electors (from 15,000 to 70,000 adult males).[1] This clause permitted districts to be redrawn by adding to and subtracting from former electoral divisions. This measure reinforced the government's position in the provinces. The control exercised by government officials (in this case, the mudir of the nahiya) over the list of primary electors presented to him by the notables of each mahalla permitted the reshaping of electoral circles according to the government's interests. At the same time it made possible the government's direct interference in the determination of the number of deputies in each mahalla.

The government's control over the selection of secondary electors can be illustrated by the summoning to the capital of the mutasarifs of the fourteen liwa's, where they were given a list of the government's candidates[2] in an attempt to undermine the influence of local notables over their tribesmen and villagers. However, a deposit of 100 dinars (corresponding roughly to the relatively large sum of $400), to be credited to the municipalities in case the candidate failed to obtain 10 per cent of the votes, prevented independent candidates from presenting themselves.[3] As a result, the new electoral law that came into effect in June 1946 maintained the basic lines of a client–patron system in the rural areas, subordinating it *en bloc* to the government. Under these conditions, no political debate among the newly licensed political parties could be effective, nor could they appeal to the rural population in the provinces.

Two main parties operated in the Basra area at the time: (1) the National Democratic Party, a reminder of the Ahali group of the 1930s, whose programme included broad economic and social reform; and (2) the Istiqlal (Independence) Party, inspired by the anti-British parties of the late 1920s.[4] The Istiqlal Party appealed to the Sunni sector even though it was headed by Mahdi Kubba, a Shi'i politician, while the National Democratic Party found a response among the urban Shi'is, who were attracted to the ideas of sectarian egalitarianism implicit in the party's programme. These responses of the urban and more secular Shi'is to the prospects of democratization in the political system indicate a desire to participate in Iraq's political life,[5] whereas the relative indifference of the Shi'i rural population points to a lesser involvement in the country's politics in general.[6] The fellahin were still conditioned by feelings of sectarian and economic oppression which neutralized the supposed advantages of an alignment with any political party.[7] This was mainly due to the intertwining of sectarian and social causes that continued throughout the 1940s to determine the relationship between cultivator and landowner. Even the Naqib of Basra, the highest Sunni religious authority in the southern provinces, had acquired large tracts of cultivable land in Basra's outskirts, contributing indirectly to Sunni–Shi'i estrangement.[8]

The Shi'i fellahin lost all trust in the system. Whether they were cultivators on large plantations owned by Sunni landlords or dispossessed tribesmen in their own tribes' formal dira, the Shi'i fellahin witnessed the effects of their landlords' dependence on the system, a dependence that obliterated all hope of reforms.

The parliamentary elections in March 1947 resulted in a chamber composed of 178 deputies (68 Sunnis, 57 Shi'is, 6 Christians, 6 Jews and 1 Yazidi). However, neither this more balanced chamber nor the cabinet, composed of 3 Sunnis, 3 Shi'is, 2 Kurds, and 1 'other',[9] represented a truly equitable distribution of power between the different groups. This was mainly due to the principles on which the system was based. The most prominent Shi'i representatives at the time, Salih Jaber (the first Shi'i to become Prime Minister) and his fellow Shi'i Fadel al Jamali (in this cabinet fulfilling the function of Foreign Minister), were political figures shaped by the system and oriented towards it. They could hardly be defined as exclusive representatives of the Shi'is or as promoters of the community's needs, values and particular aims. Their belief in the possibility of a gradual integration of the Shi'is as individuals in Iraq's political life (once the prerequisites of education and modernization were fulfilled) undermined the weight of the community as a whole.

Another variant should be applied in the case of their Kurdish colleagues, Tawfiq al Wahbi and Jamal Baban, who were appointed as Minister of Education and Minister of Justice and Economics in the new cabinet. Although considered the representatives of the Kurdish community, Tawfiq al Wahbi and Jamal Baban came to be more indentified with the system. Long-time Baghdad dwellers, these politicians had already distanced themselves from the acute problems of their original constituencies. Their nomination was more the result of Nuri al Sa'id's attempt to convey the image of a new integrative regime than an indication of real national cohesion.

This illusory intercommunal harmony could not last long. Rumours spread in the Shi'i areas that the military was planning a *coup* to discharge Saleh Jabr from the premiership, adding to the tension brought about by the after-effects of a war economy.[10] The fall in revenues due to crop failures and the interruption of oil exports resulting from the paralysis of Haifa's refineries during the 1948 war in Palestine made the already difficult conditions in Iraq's countryside even worse. In fact, hardship was felt much more in the provinces than in the capital, where speculative profits resulting from war-time opportunities added to the merchants' wealth.

In the southern provinces, the suspension of already scarce investments in housing, irrigation, road-building, and other social and economic services worsened the plight of the inhabitants.[11] As a result, detribalized and impoverished fellahin moved to urban centres in search of better conditions. Concentrated mainly on the outskirts of the capital, the Shi'i fellahin remained socially marginalized, not even integrated into Baghdad's Shi'i community.

Increasing feelings of frustration and confusion caused by this rupture from the original community proved to be fertile ground for radical ideas. New political parties such as the Constitutional Union headed by Nuri al Sa'id; the Istiqlal Party, headed by Mahdi Kubba and Saddiq Shanshul; the Reform Party, headed by Sami Shawkat; the Popular Front, headed by Burhaniddin Basha'yan and Ja'far al Bader; and the National Democratic and Liberal parties, headed by Muhammad Hadid and Husein Jamil, competed in the political arena.[12]

These parties had influential newspapers: *Al Yaqza*, edited by Saddiq Shanshul; *Al Yawm*, edited by 'Abd al Fatah Ibrahim; *Liwa' al Istiqlal* a strong nationalist paper; *Al 'Alam al 'Arabi*, the Liberal Party's newspaper; *Sawt al Ahali*, edited by Kamel al Chadirchi; *Al Umma*, the mouthpiece of the Saleh Jabr group; and *Al Daftar*. Although papers such as *Al Yaqza* and *Liwa' al Istiqlal* had little appeal to the Shi'is as a whole, *Al Umma* and *Al Daftar* were read by the literate minority among the immigrant Shi'i fellahin. *Al Daftar* published articles on problems in agrarian areas, among them an ongoing discussion on the Lower Euphrates irrigation project at Dujaila. This project was especially important to the Shi'i immigrants, as its realization would mean a possible return to their native areas and the improvement of their living conditions there.[13]

The feelings of frustration made the uprooted fellahin even more easily influenced than their Baghdadi counterparts by the propaganda of two radical parties: Al Ittihad al Watani (National Union), headed by 'Abd al Fatah Ibrahim, and the Iraqi Communist Party, headed by Yusuf Salman Yusuf, widely known as Comrade Fahed.

However, the leanings of the uprooted Shi'i fellahin towards irredentist doctrines must be seen as stemming from social and sectarian causes artificially channelled into class-strife moulds, not as indications of new and suprasectarian allegiances. Although superficial, the scale of these new orientations brought a prompt reaction from Shi'i leaders, who considered them a threat to the community's cultural and religious patrimony.

A tribal conference was organized in November 1947 by Sheikh Muhan al Khairallah. This conference was officially designed as a mediating commission between the government and the tribal forces, commanded by the traditionally rebellious leaders Khawwam al 'Abbas, Sha'lan al Salman, 'Abd al Wahid al Hajj al Sikkar, Musa al 'Alwan, and others, whose names were directly linked to the uprisings of the 1920s and 1930s. Although a few Kurdish aghas, such as Mahmud, agha of the Zibari, and Sheikh Faidhala al Talabani, were invited to join the conference, enhancing its super-communal dimension, the conference's composition and its message remained essentially Shi'i.[14]

At the conference, tribal leaders, led by Sheikh Hasan al Suhail and 'Abd al-'Abbas Mizhir al Far'un from Diwaniya, attacked the new 'effendi' class. The effendis, 'those Iraqis living in the cities who have adopted a Western veneer and are susceptible to foreign ideologies', were seen as the direct cause of the fellahin's difficulties and the indirect cause of their further attraction to radical 'Western' ideologies.

Other associations such as parliamentary blocs were also formed, stressing the need to preserve the principles of the Muslim religion and the 'basic Arab traditions'.[15] These associations illustrated a genuine apprehension in the face of spreading radical trends. The tribal associations did not, however, transcend communal divisions, even if occasional associations emerged.

Alongside the organization in the tribal areas, other cultural and religious reactions took place in the religious centres of Najaf and Karbala'. Among them were such literary societies as the Rabita al Adabiyyun, which provided a framework for philosophers, writers and lecturers to gather and enliven the religious and cultural life of those centres with lively discussions.[16] The intellectual vigour of these societies illustrated the Shi'is' profound commitment to their traditions and to Arab culture and acted as a balance to the newly adopted allegiances of its more radical sectors. The depth of religious feeling was manifested by the large crowds participating in the procession following the death of Sayyid 'Abd al Hasan Musawi al Isfahani.

> Thousands of wailing mourners followed the casket, beating their bared breasts and giving vent to their spiritual agony in the most spectacular mass exhibition of sorrow seen in this city for many years ... The mourning processions at Nasiriya are said to have been most impressive, with tribesmen of the Ghazzi and Huseinat marching under their tribal standards.[17]

Mass demonstrations and associations of this kind proved that the norms of communal life remained basically unchanged.

The infiltration of Shi'i spiritual centres by the radical parties in the late 1940s has therefore to be understood in the context of the community's specific cultural and religious characteristics. Students in the Najaf and Karbala' seminaries were the group most attracted to the new ideas brought to the holy cities by Iranian pilgrims. But even they could hardly distinguish the interpretations of Ayatolla Kashani's preachings from the messages propounded by the followers of the Iranian Tudeh Party. The themes of both messages were similar, as they referred to the need to improve social and economic conditions in the rural areas. The parcellation of the land and its allocation to the farmers, together with a more equitable distribution of economic resources to the community as a whole,[18] were recurrent motifs in both messages.

The universal dimension of these messages appealed to the Shi'i students, who were just as sensitive to the welfare of their communities as were other youth to theirs. In this particular context, their sensibility was enlivened by a growing admiration for the Soviet Union, then seen as a possible counterweight to Britain, whose traditional support for the Sunnis was considered by Shi'i students as the root cause of the country's sectarian divisions.

In the late 1940s the Soviet Union stepped into the role filled by Germany ten years earlier, namely, an alternative to British influence, a focus of identification and a possible antidote to the social ills caused by the British–Sunni alliance. Ironically, some of the oldest Shi'i students infatuated with the Soviet Union had been attracted to Germany ten years earlier,[19] while their parents had believed in the benefits of an alliance with Britain.

These shifting convictions should be seen as tendencies of political minorities to seek assistance from great powers as a palliative against oppression at home.[20] Not only the Shi'i youth, but also Christian, Jewish, Armenian and Assyrian youth turned to the Soviets with the same hope that years earlier had induced the older generation to seek protection from Britain. The reason now was disenchantment with Britain. In fact, the Jews could hardly forget Britain's non-interference during the 1941 Farhud, the Assyrians resented Britain's low-key involvement in their earlier attempts to settle as a community in Iraq, while the Christians (mainly the Armenians) saw in the newly created Soviet republic of Yerevan a proof that the Soviet Union provided the 'goods' that Britain had failed to deliver.[21] That is to say, the leftist tendencies among Iraq's minority groups in the late 1940s should be seen as being pragmatically pro-USSR and not as stemming from deep communist convictions.[22]

The Shi'i youth's leanings towards the USSR fall, however, into a different category from the Kurds' alignment with the Soviets. Mulla Mustapha's exile in the USSR and the emergence of Mahabad, seen as a potential Soviet republic before its fall in 1947, provided the Kurdish Democratic Party with a different ideological starting point from that of the more radical Shi'i factions. The different realities in which both communities evolved contributed in large measure to this. The possible transfer of a Kurdish nucleus to territories beyond the Iraqi borders bestowed upon the Kurdish movement an additional trans-territorial dimension which was not felt in the case of the Shi'is. Effectively, the Shi'is' response to the radical leftist messages, characterized by an attraction to the egalitarian ideas contained in the Marxist message, was tinged by very local, Iraqi-focused characteristics.

The bulk of Iraq's population, however, remained untouched by communism. The unsettled tribes, Shi'i and Sunni alike, representing almost one half of Iraq's population, were immune to doctrines in general. By the same token the majority of the Shi'i fellahin in the rural areas, debilitated by malaria and malnutrition, could hardly be attracted to topics not directly linked to their daily survival.

This is why the growing polarization between Pan-Arabists and leftists was restricted to Iraq's urban sectors, whose population was more prone to shifting moods and political extremes.

The extent to which this polarization reflected clear-cut positions remains, however, an open question, one that must be analysed in the context of changing realities, volatile tendencies and clashing nationalisms.[23]

8

Shifting Loyalties, Accomplished
Identities? The 1950s

The 1950s epitomized all the tendencies and topics of debate that had
characterized Iraq's political life in the first decades of its existence.
The 1950s were also a decade of change and polarization in which two
opposite trends – communism and Pan-Arabism – gained in strength.
Their increased repercussions in the mainstream of political life
remain one of the most contradictory phenomena in Iraq's modern
history.

The Iraqi Communist Party (Hizb al Shuyu'i al Iraqi), formed in the
mid-1940s from an amalgamation of leftist groups and organizations,
presented in the early 1950s a rather broad platform that served as a
common denominator for many of these groups.[1] This broad platform
called for: (1) the abolition of the 1930 treaty, in force again after the
cancellation of the new British–Iraqi treaty signed in Portsmouth in
January 1948;[2] (2) the nationalization of the British bases of Habbaniya and Shu'ayba; (3) the rejection of the Middle East Defence
Organization (MEDO) and the Point IV Programme (as both
schemes permitted the perpetuation of British–American influence in
the Middle East); (4) the nationalization of oil and electricity concessions; (5) the removal of the country's trade from its dependence on
British currency; (6) the introduction of direct elections; and (7) the
promotion of a more sound distribution of funds to the different
sectors in the population.[3]

The Pan-Arabists, at the opposite end of the political spectrum,
focused on a possible fusion with other Arab countries by forming a
federation with Syria or Jordan. According to a secret scheme engineered in 1949 by Regent 'Abd al Ilah, Syria and Iraq were to be
united under the Hashemite crown as a first stage. Although Nuri al
Sa'id had previously dismissed the scheme, pointing to its economic

disadvantages, the idea re-emerged in the early 1950s when Fadel al Jamali was Prime Minister.[4]

The rationale behind the Syria–Iraq scheme was the one that inspired the idea of a Jordanian – Syrian – Iraqi federation: namely the reinforcement of Iraq's position in the Arab world as a first step in the creation of a united Pan-Arab state. This same rationale, when considered in the light of Iraq's interests in the internal arena, meant its definitive categorization as a Sunni Arab state. This approach encapsulated the idea of reviving the Futuwwa, the paramilitary organization of the 1930s. Its revival in the 1950s filled the same double purpose as in the 1930s: to attune youngsters to an assertive Iraqi nationalism and to meet the army's recruitment needs.[5]

The complex problem of Iraqi–Kuwaiti relations also re-emerged during a visit of King Feisal II to Kuwait in 1953 whose main objective was to undermine a possible Iran–Kuwait *rapprochement*.[6] All these topics fuelled the tendencies towards polarization in the capital.

However, these debates, when transplanted to the provinces, changed considerably in scope and in subject-matter. The leftists had to adjust their programme by omitting some of their platform's major points. Especially in agrarian areas, matters such as the promotion of a national industry, suffrage for women, the formation of labour unions and the termination of foreign concessions were omitted altogether.[7] In the southern provinces, the leftists' programme centred mainly on problems of land tenure and the need for complete reform of the agrarian structure.

As during the 1940s these issues overlapped with the messages disseminated by some of the Shi'i religious leaders, themselves influenced by the effects of the Tudeh Party ideology on the Shi'i clergy in Iran. This overlapping has to be understood in the context of the intertwined social, political and religious realities that had for generations characterized life in these areas. An illustration of these overlapping functions and messages is the dual role played by Sayyid 'Abdalla al Musawi.

Sheikh Musawi was a religious leader and a great landowner whose lands, extending from the Shatt al 'Arab to Qurna, north of Basra, were farmed by thousands of fellahin. Deeply concerned with the fellah's situation, Sheikh Musawi pressured the government to enforce the Miri Sirf Plan, by which large tracts of miri lands near Basra would be parcelled out to provide small farms for the fellahin. Although Sheikh Musawi's campaign can be seen as an attempt to find a solution that would not compromise his own lands, it should be analysed in the light of other landowners' apprehensions of its snowball effect on the whole agrarian structure of the southern provinces.

The complexity of the land tenure situation and the manifold aspects of the landowner – fellah relationship were often overlooked by the parties. By reducing the problem to its two-dimensional landowner–fellah aspect and by ignoring the fact that the relationship with the tribal sheikh, Sunni entrepreneur or Kurdish agha varied according to the landowner's other functions, the parties tried to capitalize on the fellah's or the villager's predicament.[8]

This was also true for the problem of crop shares. One of the most striking examples occurred in Shamiya, where the landlord Hajj Rayeh al 'Atiyya was involved in a dispute with his tenants of the Humaidat tribe over their share of the crops. The fellahin's initial share was as low as 30 per cent and was reduced to 22 per cent when seed and transport charges were deducted.[9] Although an order was issued by the government establishing a 50 per cent share for the fellah, the prospects of its materializing were slim, as the fellah was caught in a complex relationship with the landlord involving other social, economic and cultural aspects.

Although the leftist parties capitalized on the fellah's predicament, the wider context of the landlord – fellah connection was not duly appraised. The complexity of the situation and the duality of roles is illustrated by the involvement of religious leaders, landlords them-selves, in the daily problems of the fellah. Sheikh Musawi himself was reported to have fed thousands of his fellahin on the tenth of Mohar-ram in 1953 in order to prevent the political parties from taking greater advantage of the fellahin's hardship.[10]

The same concern was reflected in a petition drawn up by five religious leaders and presented to the King and the Regent during their visit to the southern provinces in February 1953. The petition demonstrated the growing concern of the Shi'i divines with the welfare of the fellahin and pointed to the impossibility of separating the social and religious aspects of the problem from the ideological and political ones. The petition raised such points as a reduction in food prices and taxes, particularly the abolition of the istihlak (the consumption tax instituted during the 1930s, which affected the lower classes in particular). The petition also called for the preservation of the cultural and religious rights of the Shi'is by keeping the waqf institution in its original form and by maintaining the holy cities' central role in the community's cultural and religious life.[11]

These last two topics deserve some explanation, as they encapsulate some of the basic points of conflict between the government and the Shi'i community at the time. A bill calling for the liquidation of hereditary awqaf was then being debated in parliament and was gaining the support of the deputies in spite of staunch opposition in the Senate. The bill had been drawn in order to provide a legal means for the government's interference in areas protected as hereditary awqaf. It drew some justification from the fact that awqaf beneficiaries frequently remained without resources to maintain their deteriorating properties, which as a result turned into slums.[12]

However, the interference of temporal authorities in the administration of a most sacred Islamic institution, the waqf, was seen in traditional circles as a dangerous precedent. Originally created as a means to protect the inheritors from the rulers and to prevent the fragmentation of real estate, the waqf was seen as a most basic institution in any Islamic society. Its supposed incompatibility with the needs of a modern economic system was therefore considered a political manoeuvre and not the reflection of real interests in the welfare of the community.

Promoted initially as a path to development and progress, the bill was attacked by Sunni and Shi'i religious authorities alike, who feared it would set a dangerous precedent for government interference in religious matters and would be used as a device for highly placed individuals to purchase awqaf properties at reduced prices.[13]

The second point in the petition needing explanation is the preservation of control over the education of Shi'i religious instructors. The intention to allow the state to supervise the formation of Shi'i mujtahids through the creation of a Shi'i religious seminary (modelled on the Egyptian Dar al 'Ulum) was seen by the 'ulama' as an attempt by Shi'i politicians to capitalize on the issue[14] rather than a means to redress the effects of an exclusive Sunni curriculum at the Kulliyat al Shari'a in Baghdad. The Shi'i 'ulama' wanted to restrict religious training to the religious seminaries at Najaf and Karbala' and to preserve the holy cities as the centre of all religious and cultural activities.

Preserving the prominence of Najaf and Karbala' became even more important at the time, given the secular tendencies of the new Shi'i generation. This was a generation of intellectuals, entrepreneurs, lawyers, doctors and other liberal professionals, who had acquired education by using the capital accumulated by the old generation of Shi'i landowners and merchants.[15] These young Shi'is tended to define the community's problems in political terms and to search for more congenial solutions. A greater participation in the country's political life was seen by them as the solution to be sought after, as they genuinely believed that political participation would solve the community's problems and bring full integration.

The Shi'i Umma Party, headed by Saleh Jabr, was seen as a first step in this direction. However, the Umma Party's participation in politics and its ability to bring change by constitutional means were widely contested. The 21 parliamentary seats the party gained in the June 1954 election hardly indicated a steady development towards greater Shi'i participation in political life. Although run according to the amendments introduced in December 1952 (direct elections in literate areas, meaning Sunni urban centres), the 1954 election not only preserved the government's ability to retain control over the elections in the rural areas,[16] but also enabled it to reverse the process whenever necessary. This happened some months later, in September 1954, when Nuri al Sa'id made his return to the premiership conditional on control of parliament.

Other Shi'i political associations, such as the one summoned by Fadel al Jamali in 1956 around the aforementioned question of Shi'i religious instructors,[17] also subscribed to the principle of integration through collaboration with the state. However, the temporary character of these associations, together with internal divisions among leading figures such as 'Abd el Hadi Chalabi (the Shi'i Vice President of the Senate), 'Abd al Karim al Uzri (the Shi'i deputy for Baghdad), and 'Abd al Ghanim Dalli (the Shi'i representative of the Muntafiq), proved the difficulty of shaping a more representative Shi'i leadership and of defining the problem of the Shi'is' integration in terms of modern and secular politics.[18]

The difficulty in finding the right formula to solve all aspects of the Shi'i–Sunni confrontation remained a constant in the decades to come. A major event that contributed to the impression that a unidimensional, class-oriented type of contention was at stake was the massive demonstration in December 1953 organized by the leftists at the installations of the British Petroleum Company at Basra. The demonstration, instigated by the National Democratic Party, reinforced the impression that the Shi'i workers forming the bulk of the company's labour force had chosen new forms of political expression, letting economic grievances outweigh religious and communal concerns.[19] However, this explanation emerges as partial when analysed in the context of decades of Shi'i discontent with modernization in general. The looting that followed the demonstrations proved that the former 'Amara tribesmen – now workers in the oil industry – used the same forms of protest in spite of the changes that had occurred in their political and social conditions.[20]

In fact, even more momentous changes were yet to come. They finally arrived in the form of a *coup* perpetrated in July 1958 by two army officers, Colonel 'Abd al Karim Qasem and Colonel 'Abd al Salam al Aref. I shall not delve into the developments in foreign policy leading up to the *coup*: the alignment of Iraq with Turkey and Pakistan in 1955, under the aegis of Britain; the Iraqi–Egyptian rivalry in the Pan-Arab arena; the nationalization of the Suez Canal; the formation of the Union of Arab Republics uniting Egypt and Syria on 1 February 1958; the subsequent Iraqi–Jordanian federation; and Lebanon's civil war. These events and their causes have already been explained by other writers.[21] I shall concentrate on the *coup*'s effect on Iraq's internal situation and its repercussions in the provinces.

The interim constitution, drawn up immediately after the *coup*, proclaimed Iraq as a republic and as part of the Arab nation.[22] It also declared Arabs and Kurds to be equal partners while recognizing the Kurds' national rights within the limits of the Iraqi state.[23] This was a most innovative step, as it implied a greater Kurdish imprint on the forging of Iraq's identity, which at the same time meant neutralizing Kurdish separatist tendencies.

Qasem's initial inward-looking policy was, theoretically at least, an attempt to forge an Iraqi society in which all the groups forming its population would find expression. His first months in power were, however, characterized by tensions between the regime's inward-looking orientation and an outwardly oriented Pan-Arab trend, embodied in Colonel 'Abd al Salam al 'Aref, Qasem's partner in the *coup*.

'Abd al Salam al 'Aref and his Pan-Arabist fellows saw in Qasem's approach a tendency to reify the confessional characteristics preserved during the monarchy. For them, the idea of a republic pointed to a total rupture of confessional boundaries and the fusion of all groups in a modern, revolutionary type of society modelled on Nasser's Egypt. A possible consequence of their Pan-Arab ideals, Iraq's joining the UAR, was, however, feared by many as an opening for Iraq's engulfment by Egypt.

Qasem's reluctance to opt for a Pan-Arab line was explained by an Iraqi official in the following terms: 'We have just rid ourselves of the Hijazis who ruled us for the last thirty-seven years. Now why for God's sake should we turn around and deliver ourselves to foreign domination [again]?'[24] With 'Aref's deposition and the temporary eclipse of the Pan-Arabists, the Iraqi Communist Party (ICP) and the National Democratic Party (NDP) set the tone and the directives of the new political debate.

It did not take long for the ICP to tinge its former pinkish platform with red and purple colours. Better prepared than the other leftist parties, the Communists organized rallies, parades and petitions. Their organizational skills were also reflected in the mushrooming of organizations associated with the party – the Teachers' Association, the Student Unions, the Unions for Writers and the Union of Cigarette Factory Workers are only a few examples. Among the most active groups were the League for the Defence of Women's Rights and the Peace Partisans. However, it is important to note that private and public figures saw their names listed without really belonging to these associations. The charged political atmosphere and the pressure exerted by the Communists prevented their standing up against this practice.[25]

The Communists' growing political assertiveness was also reflected in an open confrontation with the Pan-Arabists. The Ba'thists were characterized by them as 'Aflaqis', in reference to Michel Aflaq, the founder of the Syrian Ba'th Party. This categorization implied a rejection of the Ba'th ideology, as inspired by and directed towards Damascus. An open clash between the leftists and the Pan-Arabists in December 1958 and the demonstrations that followed the funeral of a student illustrate the Communists' massive presence in Baghdad's streets. Bookshops and news-stands were filled with Communist literature, and pictures of Mao Tse Tung, Lenin and Khrushchev hung everywhere.

Qasem's tilt to the left finally led to a collective resignation in February 1959 of the Pan-Arab members of the cabinet; Fuad Rikabi (from the Ba'th Party), Saddiq Shanshul and Muhammad Mahdi Kubba, both of the Istiqlal Party, resigned, paving the way for the leftists' control of the cabinet.

Qasem's immediate entourage – Colonel Wasfi Tahir and Colonel Fadel 'Abbas al Mahdawi (president of the famous people's tribunals) – appeared then as openly identified with the leftists. Moreover, the appointment of communists to top positions in the ministries of economics, education, agriculture and justice seemed to make official the country's new political direction.[26] The press contributed to this impression. 'Abd al Qader Isma'il, the Secretary General of the Communist Party, published editorials almost daily in the *Ittihad al Sha'b* (the Communist newspaper), and 'Abdallah Isma'il, a member of the Central Committee of the ICP, wrote articles in *Al Thawra*. The most widely read of all were the daily editorials of 'Aziz el Hajj in *Sawt al Ahrar*.[27] Other pro-Communist papers, *Al Ra'i al 'Amm*, *Al Bilad*, *Al Zaman*, and the NDP's *Al Ahali* added to the picture. These papers were read by the literate among the lower classes, by students, and by members of the Peace Partisans and other leftist organizations.[28] The nationalist papers *Al Hurriya, Al Yaqdza, Al Fajr al Jadid* and *Al Muwatin al 'Arab*[29] found their audience among the army officers, who remained essentially Pan-Arabist.

The growing polarization in Iraq's political arena and the instability thus created finally brought about an attempt by one of the poles to override the other. An anti-Qasem *coup*, presumably inspired by the Egyptian president Gamal 'Abd al Nasser, was perpetrated by Pan-Arab army officers. The Mosul *coup*, led by Colonel 'Abd al Wahhab Shawwaf, was presented as a reaction against the demonstrations organized by the Peace Partisans. During the demonstrations the Pan-Arabists followed the leftists by launching their own slogans against those of the demonstrators.[30] The Pan-Arabist forces relied also on elements which could be more easily characterized as anti-Qasem than pro-Naser. Among them were the Shammar tribesmen, whose paramount leader, Sheikh Ahmad 'Ajil al Yawar, was known for his antagonism to the leftist movement and who was ready actively to oppose the country's tilt to the left. The main leaders of the Dulaim and of the Muntafiq tribes were also expected to lead thousands of armed tribesmen to rebellion.

The initial confrontation in Mosul between the Pan-Arabists (led by Colonel al-Shawwaf's forces and the Arab tribesmen) and the pro-Qasem factions (including the leftists and the Kurds) deteriorated into bitter intercommunal and intertribal strife.

> Kurds and Yazidis stood against Arabs, Assyrians and Aramean Christians against Arab Muslems, the Arab tribe of Albu Mutaiwit against the Arab tribe of the Shammar, the Kurdish tribe of al-Gargariyyah against Arab Albu Mutaiwit; the peasants of Mosul country (Christian and Arameans) against their landlords (Moslem Arabs), the soldiers of the Fifth Brigade (Kurds) against their officers (Arabs).[31]

The above quotation could serve as an illustration that the multi-faceted conflict was communal in its essence, even if social and economic affiliations overlapped within it. Events after the *coup* further prove the acuity of the issues in focus. Colonel Shawwaf was killed, and the pro-Qasem factions tightened their position in Mosul and in the rest of the country by organizing the Committees for Defence of the Republic. A charter of the United National Front was issued on 28 June 1959, with the intention of safeguarding Qasem's regime.[32]

Some of the charter's points are worth mentioning, as they indicate the topics debated in the two camps at the time. In matters of foreign policy, the charter reiterated the necessity of rejecting the Baghdad Pact and disengaging from a defence alliance with the United States or Britain. In matters of internal politics, the charter indicated the government's intention to redress the situation in the provinces. Together with the need to reform the agrarian structure in general, special mention was made of the need to improve the fellah's predicament by providing loans and supplying seeds and fertilizers. This point was relevant mainly to the southern provinces, while the items focusing on the provision of financial and technical aid to tobacco growers were relevant to the northern districts.[33]

Another point in the charter indicated a tendency to subordinate Iraq's economy to the Eastern bloc. New regulations were established regarding the planting and trade of dates, with possible deals to be made with the socialist countries, ready to barter Iraqi dates for various goods.[34] This last point soon became a double-edged sword, for it implied a reduction in cultivation and in the export of crops, which affected the fellah personally and undermined the country's chances of becoming economically self-sufficient. A more immediate implication of the charter's regulations was the government's attempt to penetrate the agrarian sectors and bring about greater economic and political integration.[35]

However, the question of whether the leftists, with the ICP at their head, were capable of reaching the Shi'i fellahin and the Kurdish villagers remains controversial. Various attempts were made to address the question, and Batatu's was the most serious one. However, by focusing mainly on social and economic aspects and paying scant attention to the cultural and religious ones, these attempts failed to foresee long-term developments. The Shi'i fellahin and the Kurdish villagers, hardly fitting the category of a Western-type peasantry, did not respond to the norms of conduct imported from Western leftist theories. In many instances their reactions were fuelled by motifs other than cross-communal, class-oriented interests. The importance attributed to the leftist movement in the provinces therefore emerges as disproportionate, given the superficiality of its imprint and its short-term existence.

Seen in this light, the difficulty of imported ideologies in penetrating the deeper layers of cultural cognizance and reshaping identities in Middle Eastern societies is more easily understood.

As this study has tried to demonstrate, codes of belief and behaviour were so ingrained in the collective awareness of different communities that many attempts to uproot them failed, mainly be-

cause linguistic codes and cultural contexts were not taken into account. Leftist theories appealed mainly to certain factions of the urban population and to the Shi'i tribesmen who had been disconnected from their cultural matrix, elements whose feelings of stress and insecurity were caused by new kinds of economic hardship and by the weakening and even rupture of their communal roots. Leftist ideologies could penetrate the uprooted Shi'i farmers concentrated in the slums encircling Baghdad or Basra but could hardly reach the core of the agrarian population, in spite of the poverty characterizing daily life in the provinces.[36] The fellah in the south and the Kurdish villager in the north, although attracted by the messages of reform and agricultural development spread by parties and factions, rarely internalized the supracommunal message they contained.[37] The motifs advocated by the parties fell short of bringing radical changes in perception when not drawn from the context of common practices and cultural religious legacies.

All in all, communism in Iraq in the 1950s has to be taken with a grain of salt or considered as 'a brand of its own'.[38] In spite of the leftists' ability to stir up a disillusioned mass of urban 'proletariat', leading it to protest, the volatile character of this same population prevented the doctrine from striking roots in the deeper tiers of collective consciousness. Skin-deep convictions would be better understood when analysed in the context of the changes bringing the various sectors to subscribe to Nasserism or communism or, subsequently, to Ba'thism.[39]

The population's search for the appropriate political expression was a painful one. This search was exploited by the parties, movements and leaders of the day.

Qasem's regime was 'not a happy one',[40] proving itself unable to channel old loyalties into modern patterns of political debate and action. Traditional cleavages continued to determine the main categories of affiliation, even when new terminologies were adopted and modern ideologies emulated.

These conclusions would be better understood when analysed in the light of various attempts to change the pattern of relationships in Kurdish areas. Although active in the urban centres of Sulaimaniya and Mosul, the leftist parties proved unable to make radical changes in the tight network of social and cultural connections linking the agha to his villagers. In the Kurdish rural areas, the disagreements between the villagers and their aghas or between the tribal leaders themselves (such as the personal rivalries between Hamid and Hasan Beg from the Jaf tribes and Baba Ali and Sheikh Latif from Sulaimaniya) were

145

ironed out whenever a real danger to the community's survival presented itself.

The penetration of the leftists into the Kurdish movement was possible only when an appeal was made to protonational themes concerning the preservation of culture, language and the legacies from which the Kurdish community drew its identity and vital energy.[41] An article entitled 'Arab Liberal Policy and the Question of Kurdish Nationalism', published in January 1959 in *Ittihad al Sha'b*, is a good illustration of how a partial understanding of the communal roots of the Kurdish movement and the consequent setting up of an alternative order of priorities failed the test of political reality. Attempts to induce the Kurds to 'put first things first',[42] such as postponing their cultural priorities to a stage when national goals had already been achieved, demonstrated an underestimation not only of timetables and agendas but also of the very motifs leading the Kurds to political alignments.

The same can be said of the text of a secret agreement made between the ICP and the United Democratic Party of Kurdistan (Parti Democrati ba Gurtui Kurdistan).[43] The attempt to gain the Kurds' support by calling for a Kurdish–Assyrian alliance revealed a deep misunderstanding of the basic dissension between the two communities. Rivalry and animosity, anchored in decades of conflict, erupted even in the very first sessions. No permanent formula establishing a Kurdish President and an Assyrian Prime Minister was acceptable to the Assyrians, and a discussion on the rights and priorities encapsulated in the theoretical notion of rotation proved as difficult as the very obtaining of the autonomy in which the principle of rotation was to be applied.[44]

It is, however, difficult (and certainly historically wrong) to draw definitive and deterministic conclusions. Intercommunal alliances were formed temporarily when the need to defend a common territory from outsiders arose. An incident in Kirkuk in February 1959 is a good example. A temporary alliance between Kirkuk's Turkmen and Kurds in order to prevent leftists from strengthening their influence in the town led to the setting on fire of a Communist bookshop in Tuz-Khurmato and to their joining forces in attacking the leftists assembled on the spot.[45] The character of these alliances was, however, ephemeral, as any incident reset the Kurdish–Turkmen conflict in its communal parameters. The July 1959 riots are a good example of the kind of animosity existing between Kurds (workers in Kirkuk's oil industry) and Turkmen (merchants and artisans). During the riots there were reports of clashes between the two communities in which the Kurds (in spite of belonging to leftist organizations) kept together under ethnic-nationalist slogans and the 'Turkmen banded together under Turkmenian nationalist colours'.[46] The point to be made at this juncture is not the 'parallelism between racial and economic division',[47] but the redefinition of the nature of the conflict as communal, even if expressed through a modernized typology of contention.

Qasem himself understood the force of religious and communal legacies in the redefinition of political allegiances. He personally attended the inauguration ceremony of a new Assyrian church and praised 'freedom of worship', illustrating an understanding of the multiple dimensions of Iraq's divisions.[48] Qasem's personal intervention to appease the Shi'i 'ulama', hurt by leftist attacks on 'alim Muhsin al Hakim during the procession to the Haidar shrine in February 1959,[49] suggestion a revision of the assumption that the 'ulama' had at that point 'lost much of its prestige'.[50] Qasem's move was due not only to the repercussions on the regional level but also to the foreseeable national implications that would be caused by the 'ulama's alignment with or rejection of the regime. The role of the 'ulama' in stirring up opposition to the Ba'th regime years later indicates their prevalent role in shaping the community's political position.

Qasem's initial intention to open the way for a greater integration of the different communities did not, however, lead to the setting of new parameters for a supra-communal society, in which the predominance of the Sunnis could be shattered or challenged. Nor could Qasem go along with the attempts at cultural and administrative autonomy embodied in the Kurds' own search for the right expression of their collective identity. Qasem's further embroilment in a war with the Kurds[51] helped dissipate former illusions concerning the regime's search for new formulas of national cohesiveness.

In spite of the emergence in 1958 of new political, social and economic paradigms, Iraq's fundamental problems remained unsolved. Old alliances, loyalties and identities re-emerged in search of new definitions.

Conclusion

While accepting the premise that political behaviour rarely stems from a single cause, I have tried to rearrange priorities and to articulate the determinants that reshaped the self – and the collective images of Iraq's inhabitants during the period under discussion. For this purpose I had to plunge back in time and analyse the way in which different alliances, loyalties and identities contributed to the shaping of Iraq during its formative years. The extent to which these identities have been redefined in the process, however, deserves further attention.

Some difficulties presented themselves from the very beginning and others emerged as the work proceeded. The first difficulty was to find an appropriate theoretical model that could serve as a basis for a more elaborated theoretical analysis. However, no theoretical model seemed to render the subtleties and complexities of a reality in which overlapping identities – ethnic, religious and cultural – interacted.

Many stumbling blocks stemmed from the difficulties in determining the constituents of collective identities. 'Ethnic identities' normally suggest that the ethnic constituents override all others, whereas 'religious identities' suggest that the ethnic constituents are subordinate to the religious ones. 'Cultural identities' are even more difficult to define given the number and richness of the elements involved. Here again, it is worth noting – as an introduction to new or continuing debates – that one-dimensional definitions which reduce culture to language and its derivatives are unsatisfactory from the very outset. Culture implies religion, and religion, in some cases, corresponds to or creates ethnic bonds.

The difficulties increase with the realization that identities frequently overlap, inducing the observer to shift from one type of definition to another. This tendency is even more conspicuous when one tries to portray socio-economic realities during Ottoman times. This overlapping was duly reflected in the system of millets, the religious communities, which functioned as closed social units with an internal system of collective memories and symbols.

148

The role of religion was particularly conspicuous in the study of Muslim communities. Its mitigating effect (due to the solidarity among the members of the Umma Islamiyya) sometimes blurred the borders separating the different Muslim communities, creating the need to formulate new categories of analysis.

In Iraq's case, however, the mitigating effects of Islam appear to be less present than is generally believed. I soon realized that I was not only trying to describe the evolution of the three main Muslim communities (the Sunnis, the Shi'is and the Kurds) in the framework of a modern state, but was also engaged *ipso facto* in an attempt to understand the cultural and political implications of Islam in its local manifestations and their interaction. It did not take very long, as the evidence accumulated, to realize that I was in fact trying to evaluate the role of Islams as variants, reflecting specific local traditions.

This reference to Islam as a cultural system led to the need to rethink culture in a Geertzian context, namely to consider religion (or religions) as shapers of reality and – at the same time – as being shaped by it. I ventured therefore to refer to Islam as a basis for a political, cultural and social system. This was a system with 'powerful, pervasive and long lasting models'[1] and effects. The reference to Islam as a determinant of a cultural system (or systems) led to the perception of three cultural identities articulated during moments of opposition to the state and to other communities. Their articulation was shaped by factors internal to the community, and at the same time by the very source of this opposition.

This conclusion seemed to fit the complex reality of a Shi'i–Sunni conflict developed in the early stages of Iraq's formation, better than any other existing explanation. It also corresponded to other – more general – definitions of the Sunni–Shi'i conflict by which the theological and political differences between both groups were merely reduced to the primordial schism over the Caliphate, or were seen as a contest for the 'fruits of office'.

This conclusion was even more fascinating considering the fact that the Sunni–Shi'i contest in Iraq centred on Arab Shi'is, speaking Arabic and taking pride in their contribution to the Arab culture and heritage. In this case, Shi'i Islam, as a basis for a whole social structure, was no less influential than linguistic factors in shaping the parameters of cultural life.

It was also enlightening to realize that even among Sunnis (as in the case of the Arabs and the Kurds in Iraq), local variants of Islam shape different cultural systems, in this case, even competing with two primal factors such as language and ethnic origin.

The analysis of cultural units and their constituents emerged in all its complexity when a new factor was introduced into the equation: the state. Its emergence as a new frame of reference, which was supposed to alter the typology of relations among the different communities, posed new questions. Among them, the questions What state? Whose state?[2] set a useful paradigm for the re-evaluation of the basic relations between the state and Iraq's population. 'Whose state *is* it?' remains the very motif of Iraq's inner conflict.

Although the motifs helping to define Iraq's national identity seem to have contributed to the shattering of the identities of all the elements participating in the process, the conflict continues to centre on the revision of the elements forging these identities and on the way in which these elements can be used in the forging of supracommunal–national allegiances.

The difficulty in such a complex situation of delineating the parameters of the identities in question led me to conclude that in Iraq's case national identity cannot *yet* be seen as an overall frame of allegiance overriding all other ties.

It is, however, important to point out that my attempt was not – as might appear at first glance – an exercise in offering a reified interpretation of Iraq's history, but rather an attempt to underscore the effects of the various interacting identities and point to the need to redefine fluctuating categories of analysis. As mentioned earlier, I chose narrative as a way of showing the differences between the more persistent and the less persistent types of associations and as a means of reformulating impressions according to which economic interests forcefully bring about a reassessment of solidarities.

As I tried to demonstrate, the accumulation of wealth in the hands of the agha and the sheikh, on one hand, and the impoverishment of Kurdish villagers and the Shi'i fellahin on the other fall into the category of recurrent factors that led to temporary alliances and periodic crossings of communal borders. By the same token, the 'cultural package' (myths, collective memories, symbols, values) reappeared as the constant factor redefining the social and political functions of the community's leaders and the parameters of the community's resistance to external pressures.

Although modernization and economic development had in past decades contributed to a greater interaction between the different communities, they fell short of affecting the core of communal identities. The tendency to transact economic exchanges with partners of the same ethnic group, noted in the 1920s (when Mosul's Turkmen merchants tilted towards Turkey and the Arabs towards

Damascus and Aleppo), made room in the following decades for variations dictated by the intervention of an external factor – the state. But again, the question 'Whose state is (was) it?' conditioned relations between the provinces and Baghdad. Accordingly, in the 1930s and 1940s, each area's dominant group attempted to prevent the economic subordination of their provinces to the capital. This tendency prevailed as the years went by, especially in the northern districts. Some of its manifestations are even present nowadays. An example is Kirkuk's symbolic value to both the Kurds and the Arabs, as revealed in the aftermath of the Gulf War. The control over Kirkuk's oil, representing economic self-sufficiency and meaning political autonomy for the population in the area, acquires a new dimension when analysed in the context of past relations between the Kurds, the Turkmen and the Sunni authorities.

All this makes us realize that inter-communal alliances created on the basis of only economic interests rarely passed the test of time if their other aspects were not redefined in the process. The accumulation of wealth in the hands of the sheikh and the agha in the 1920s and 1930s did not radically change the rules in Iraq's political game in the following decades. Although richer, both the sheikh and the agha were, in fact, used by a system that ensured Baghdad's control through its political and administrative apparatus. This state of affairs, although altering the relationships in the communities, did not sever them altogether. The links between the agha and his villagers, or the sheikh and his tribesmen, continued, in spite of economic polarization, to be fuelled by social, cultural and religious legacies.

The 1950s brought radical changes that can be considered as changes more of form than of content. The advent of the leftist movement as a force to be reckoned with seemed at first to attempt to blur communal boundaries by establishing itself as a supracommunal current. However, a more careful examination of the movement's programme reveals elements of discontent and protest rather than an operational platform anchored in solid ideological precepts.[3] And in fact even discontent and protest were often fuelled by communal solidarities. The impact on Basra's Shi'i population of the Shi'i Arab members of the Iranian Tudeh Party (refugees from Khuzistan) seems to have been as deep as the effect of Baghdad-based leftist parties.[4]

The euphoria of the 1950s arose from the belief that social and economic deadlocks could be resolved if and when the right political solutions were applied and the right political forces mobilized. The overestimation of the role of the middle classes (again, defined according to categories of economic input and education) and the underestimation of the ethnic, cultural and religious links and barriers promoting or preventing the political interaction of the different sectors forming these middle classes contributed to the hastiness of the conclusions.[5] Similarly, the assumption that the 1958 revolution had disturbed the 'delicate balance between the various ethnic and sectarian communities of Iraq' by upsetting the power structure and the old class configuration seems precipitous.[6] As I have tried to demonstrate, this 'delicate balance' was promptly re-established after a short period alternating between hope and disillusion. It did not take long for communalist interests to re-emerge 'designed under modern ideological labels'.[7]

Although the urban sectors of both the Shi'i and the Kurdish communities found in adherence to communism an outlet for their conflicts with the state, the agrarian sectors of both communities did not cope with this conflict in a purely ideological way. The complex reality of the agrarian areas of the southern provinces, where religious leaders happened to be landowners and where a growing presence of Baghdadian entrepreneurs and politicians added a sectarian dimension to the 'peasant vs. landlord'[8] dichotomy, was the reason for this difficulty. By the same token, the mixed role of the agha as the agricultural entrepreneur in the less penetrable Kurdish areas and as a tribal, religious and sometimes protonational leader – as in the case of Mulla Mustapha al Barazani – required different parameters of analysis than the oversimplified landowner–tenant one. The villagers who followed the migrating Kurdish aghas to Iran after the expropriation of their lands in 1959[9] are proof of this.

All this leads to the conclusion that the sheikhs' and aghas' multi-faceted role included the protection of their communities against the state. Batatu's contention that 'life has been pumped in the sheikh-agha structure by an outside force (the British)'[10] holds true for the 1920s but must be reassessed when examining the 1930s and 1940s. The sheikhs' and aghas' strata, reduced to the parameters of 'economic burdens', appear to acquire 'a life of their own' as friction with the state evolved. The Iraqi leftist movement of the 1950s and early 1960s, when explained in communal terms, emerges as an amplified version of the 'Iraq first' approach adopted in 1936 by Bakr Sidqi and Hikmat Sulaiman and appears more as an attempt to prevent Iraq from being Baghdad-centred and Sunni Arab than as a movement stirred simply by the need to implement social and economic reforms.

Given all the above, the question whether communal and national identities can co-exist in modern Iraq remains unanswered. According to Batatu, nationalism and old loyalties co-existed in the pre-Ba'th period when nationalism, 'while corroding them, absorbed some of their psychological elements'.[11] But can Batatu's version of 'overlapping identities' (implying preservation of communal legacies in national moulds) be applied to the realities of Iraq in the 1990s?

In a country lacking one of the basic ingredients of the 'classic' national identity package – a single code of rights and duties applicable to all sectors of the population[12] – the very reference to these terms must be handled with the greatest care.

This book centred on the historical and cultural elements that influenced the shaping of the three or four different versions of the same story – the story of the formation of Iraq. In describing this search with directions, I would say that this was an attempt to present a historical case, not just from the 'top down' or from the 'bottom up', but from the sides to the centre.

To address these questions, it was necessary to show how Iraq's official nationalism developed and how it clashed with traditional social, economic and political patterns of interaction among the communities as they had developed after their collision with modernity. Reassessing the concept of nation-building and/or nationalism by reinserting it into its historical context led to some important conclusions. The first was that Iraq's official nationalism was not, in its beginnings, a reaction against the British. On the contrary, during the first stage, Iraqi nationalism was directly linked to and dependent upon the idea of nation as imported from Britain. Only in its second stage, when the state's institutions had already been established, was this official nationalism coloured by a resentment that grew in intensity until it appeared in its full spectrum in the second half of the 1930s.

And if one understands how resentment – 'a reaction of an imported nationalism to its source of importation'[13] – remains a constant as long as the nationalism in question does not possess sufficient elements to define itself otherwise, one can see how resentment against Britain and its imprint in the area still remains a constant in Iraq's official nationalism, long after the British era in Iraq has ended.

These three stages in the process of defining the essence of Iraqi nationalism – the transplantation to Mesopotamia of a foreign concept of nation, a redefinition of the same concept in terms of resentment against the matrix, and the further resentment, this time originating inside the country, against the the state – are essential in understanding Iraq's politics.

If the next question centres on the inability of the new official concepts to fulfil the national aspirations of all the groups involved in the process, the answer should point to the fact that the dominant idea of nation did not correspond to these groups' cultural and religious values.

Among other questions that emerged as the work proceeded was one centring on Iraq's territorial continuity as an outcome of British interests in the area to no less a degree than the interests of the Sunni political leadership. This is the reason why Britain played such an active role in helping Baghdad extend its writ to the provinces; this is also the reason why the tacit agreements between the British and the Sunni leaders – although providing the network of support without which no Sunni political hegemony would be possible – could not provide the legitimacy for a Sunni minority to rule over a Shi'i majority.

This legitimacy was drawn from the official recognition of Pan-Arabism as the country's national doctrine. The reference to this framework gave the Sunnis a theoretical platform from which their rule over the Shi'is and the Kurds was more easily undertaken.

This complex web of allegiances, agreements, tacit understandings and open resentments led to two interim conclusions: (1) that in Iraq's case, the classic example of ethnic conflicts fuelled by the colonial power as a means of preserving its presence in the country does not hold true; (2) that Britain continued to serve as a model of emulation and a source of resentment, even when the country was apparently immersed in different currents and different influences.

Emulation and resentment of the matrix – a classic theme in nascent nationalisms[14] – is a double thread tightly interwoven in the texture of Iraq's nationalism.

However, if we examine our story in the light of Gellner's definition of nation – 'an artifact of men's (common) convictions, loyalties, and beliefs'[15] – Iraq's path towards national crystallization is still a long one. This is so not only because the geographic, ethnic and religious chasms cannot be easily bridged by modernization and economic integration, but also because the idea behind the process itself does not correspond to the sets of loyalties, beliefs and cultural ties of the various groups forming its population. In other words, if nations are formed by a natural fusion of culture and polity,[16] and if the existence of a uniform culture is a prime condition in the formation of a nation, Iraq's experiment was doomed to failure from the outset. The idea of artificially promoting a culture that does not respond to widely accepted values cannot take root, and the attempt to circumvent or erase these values only brings reaction, rekindles resentment and further reinforces the imprint of these values on men. That is why the attempt to bring homogeneity through a monolithic education system did not elicit the expected response. That is also why 'Mesopotamian culture,' as promoted by Saddam Hussein's regime,[17] which underrates the specific cultural and religious traditions of different ethnic/religious communities, cannot provide a foundation for shaping a common identity. The attempt to emulate the idea of nation, by referring to 'fore-existing', historically inherited notions of culture, failed, as these notions of culture were not inherited, or fore-existent, or capable of replacing the existing sets of cultural references and social ties that kept the main communities in Iraq from forming a society, a nation or a nation-state.

Under these circumstances, can Iraq be considered a territorial state that is formed by more than one ethnic group?

By comparing what actually happened in Iraq with the process of state-formation as outlined in one of the widely accepted models,[18] we can perhaps get a partial answer. According to this model, a territorial state is formed when three overlapping processes occur: (1) economic integration, and implementation of a supervised communication system linking the centres of production and supply: this process implies a territory-wide employment system, having a potentially mobile workforce; (2) modernization of bureaucratic methods of control; and (3) standardization of culture, which implies the introduction of an administrative language by mass education to produce a standardized mode of communication.[19]

As I tried to demonstrate, none of these processes was successfully implemented during the formative years and it is rather doubtful whether these processes took place after the revolution. On the contrary, the patterns established during the first decades seem to influence the political, economic and social aspects of Iraq's internal politics nowadays as well.

Perhaps the right epilogue to this discussion is a conversation held in the spring of 1990 with Dr Fadel al Jamali, whose activities as the man responsible for education and culture in Iraq in the 1930s have been thoroughly depicted in this book. During this conversation, Dr Jamali resumed our debate by pointing out: 'You academicians try to find answers to questions that do not even bother the population in question. Believe me, the people in Iraq simply live on the face of the Earth, as other peoples in the world, without asking themselves if there is or there isn't a well-defined Iraqi identity.'[20]

Would Dr Jamali reconsider his words two years later?

Afterword

This project started years ago as an attempt to understand (and possibly explain) Iraq's oscillation between integration and dismemberment, and to make sense of history not by revising Iraq's formative years from today's perspective, but by reinserting facts into their own time-frame.

Although less fashionable and perhaps less appealing, this 'orthodox' approach connects the motifs rediscovered during the 1990–91 Gulf crisis more effectively than the comparative methods in fashion today. In addition, a study of Iraq *per se* and a review of its problems offer an even better key to understand Saddam Hussein's politics. Without providing a definitive answer to the question whether his moves were inspired by an attempt to redeem history or by personal ambitions, I have tried to reinsert some of the *ad hoc* explanations offered before and after the war within parameters of political cultures and collective identities. I tried to explain, among other things, why Saddam Hussein focused not on, say, the oil fields of Alaska or Saudi Arabia but on Kuwait, the 'branch severed from the tree', to quote Tariq Aziz, Iraq's Foreign Minister in the weeks preceding the war.

Looking for a confirmation of these assumptions, I approached leading scholars in the field, two of whom are historians of Iraqi origin. While agreeing with the outline of my analysis, both suggested a revision of the book's title. '*Identity* is perfect,' one said, 'because it really describes what we are all struggling for, but why *national*? It sounds like "Qawmiyism" [Pan-Arabism], or one-dimensional "Watanism" [Nationalism].'

After giving the matter some thought, I decided not to drop *national* from my title, because I am still inclined to believe that, even if temporarily deferred, nationalism in all its varieties and dimensions continues to be debated. Although Iraq's constant search for more suitable definitions of its identities – national and other – underwent some changes, its theoretical ingredients persist in Saddam Hussein's distorted interpretation of it. These ingredients, such as common myths, collective memories and cultural and linguistic standards, were exploited by his regime or artificially re-created. Although Saddam Hussein used the 'Mesopotamian' myth of common territory and common ancestry by referring to a period in history when the divisions tearing modern Iraq apart did not exist, it in fact served to divert attention from a return to the most primary types of kinship relations.

Another attempt, that of rewriting Iraq's history, was less aggressive but not less effective. A series of regime-inspired books were published, some of which are worth noting, as they cover the period explored here: *Nuri al Sa'id wa Dawrahu fi al Siyasa al 'Iraqiyya 1932–1945* ('Nuri al Sa'id and his role in Iraqi politics'),[1] *'Abd al Muhsin al Sa'dun wa Dawrahu fi al Ta'rikh al 'Iraq al Siyasi al Mu'asir* ('Abd al Muhsin al Sa'dun and his role in the contemporary political history of Iraq'),[2] *Harakat Rashid 'Ali al Kailani, 1941* ('Rashid 'Ali al Gailani's movement, 1941'),[3] *Ja'far al 'Askari wa Dawrahu al Siyasi wa al 'Askari fi Ta'rikh al 'Iraq hata 'am 1936* ('Ja'far al 'Askari and his political and military role in Iraq's history until 1936'),[4] *Mawlud Mukhlis Pachachi wa Dawrahu fi al Thawra al 'Arabiyya al Kubra wa fi al Ta'rikh al 'Iraq al Mu'asir* ('Mawlud Mukhlis Pachachi and his role in the Arab rebellion and in Iraq's contemporary history'),[5] *Muhammad al Sheikh 'Ali* ('Memoirs of Ali Muhammad al Sheikh 'Ali, Defence Minister in Rashid 'Ali's cabinet of 1941'),[6] *Awraq Awwami* (Personal papers, 1900, 1958),[7] *Faysal II, 'Ai'latuhu, Hayatuhu, Mu'allafatuhu* ('Feisal II, his family, his life, and his books'),[8] and *Al Malik Faysal al Awwal wa al Ingliz wa al Istiqlal* ('King Feisal I, the British and Iraq's independence').[9]

These titles indicate an attempt to skip over the Ba'th period and to connect Saddam Hussein's regime with the foundations of national life – as delineated during Iraq's formative years.

However, the attempt to create an artificial identification with the regime backfired. Reduced to Saddam Hussein's narrow circle[10] and sustained by a tight network of intelligence services, the regime could hardly present itself as the embodiment of Iraqdom. Periodic attempts were made to break this cycle by appealing to concepts inculcated over generations by national education. Once more, the myth of territorial integrity – embodied in Iraq's historic rights over Kuwait – was revived. In addition to the economic and strategic advantages to be gained from an annexation,[11] the invasion of Kuwait was meant to inspire adherence to the regime and at a later stage to launch the country into a campaign to lead the Arab world.

Ironically, this move contributed to Iraq's estrangement from its Arab counterparts and internally led to its near-disintegration. Moreover, the disparate attitude noted in the army – the Shi'i soldiers' lack of incentive contrasting with the motivation of the Sunni Republican Guards – points to divergent perceptions of national goals.

The conscripted army, conceived by the Sunni leadership of the 1920s and early 1930s as a symbol of national independence, cannot yet be seen as the nation's melting pot. Communal divisions in the army, in politics and in the administration re-emerge every time a political breakdown occurs.

The solution at this new crossroad lies in the ability of Iraq's population to rise above differences and ideological ebbs and flows and to find a way of collaborating politically. The Sunnis will be asked to forgo their monopoly of nationalism and power; the Shi'is will be asked to combine secularism and modernity with the precepts of their cultural and religious legacies; and the Kurds will be asked to relinquish separatism altogether.

The feasibility of this solution has yet to be proved. In any case, overlapping identities are more consistent with Iraq's characteristics than any attempt to overcome communal barriers by emulating other types of affiliations. This is especially true in a society where the components of class consciousness are still difficult to define.

The attempt to conclude this book on a hopeful note leads me to register the parliamentary elections that took place in the Kurdish autonomous area in the spring of 1992. Supervised by a Supreme Electoral Commission formed by representatives of major political parties,[12] these elections could mean a new direction for Iraq's northern provinces if the old patron–client pattern underpinning the political parties is dismantled.

Another point worth making is a still nascent tendency to overcome intercommunal feuds and differences. A declaration issued in April 1992 by the Kurdistan National Assembly (the *de facto* authority of Iraq's northern districts) granted the Assyrians and other Christian groups the right to nominate their own representatives to the Assembly. This measure gains in importance if analysed in the light of the relationship between the Assyrians and the Kurds during the last decades, in which the Assyrians' attempt to settle in northern Iraq implied their political and economic subordination to the Kurds.

However, the real proof of national integration will come when Iraq's National Congress (an outgrowth of the embryonic conference held in Beirut in February 1991) reaches the mainstream population within Iraq's borders. A charter issued after a conference in Vienna in

June 1992 will then constitute a turning point leading from unsolved continuities to the most promising of changes.

Center for Middle Eastern Studies
Harvard University
August 1992

Notes

PREFACE

1. E. Kedourie, 'Ethnicity, Majority and Minority in the Middle East', p. 26, in Milton Esman and Itamar Rabinovitch (eds), *Ethnicity, Pluralism and the State in the Middle East* (Ithaca, N Y: Cornell University Press, 1988), pp. 25–31.

INTRODUCTION

1. F. W. Axelgard, *A New Iraq? The Gulf War and Implications for U.S. Policy* (Washington, D C: CSIS, 1988).
2. Anthony D. Smith, *National Identity*, (Harmondsworth: Penguin, 1991), p. 14.
3. Ibid., p. 28.
4. Ibid., p. 14.
5. Ibid., p. 17.
6. Axelgard, pp. 20–5 and 27–9.
7. Clifford Geertz, *The Interpretation of Cultures* (New York, 1993, first published 1973), pp. 4–5.
8. Ibid., p. 17.
9. Michael C. Hudson, *Arab Politics: The Search for Legitimacy* (New Haven, CT: Yale University Press, 1977), p. 233.
10. Hanna Batatu, *The Old Social Classes and the Revolutionary Movements of Iraq: A Study of Iraq's Old Landed and Commercial Classes and of its Communists, Baathist and Free Officers* (Princeton, N J: Princeton University Press, 1978).
11. Ibid., pp. 6–8.
12. Ibid.
13. Esman and Rabinovich (eds), *Ethnicity, Pluralism and the State*; Anthony Hyman, 'Elusive Kurdistan: The Struggle for Recognition', *Conflict Studies* 214 (London, 1986); Ofra Bengio, *Mered Ha Kurdim be Iraq* ('The Revolt of the Kurds in Iraq'), ed. Hakibutz Hameuhad (Tel Aviv, 1989).
14. Anthony D. Smith, *The Ethnic Origin of Nations* (Oxford: Oxford University Press, 1983), p. 3.
15. Ibid., p. 17.
16. Ibid., p. 70.
17. Hanna Batatu, 'Shi'i Organizations in Iraq, al Da'wah al Islamiyah and al Mujahidin', in Nikkie Keddie (ed.), *Shi'ism and Social Protest* (New Haven, CT: Yale University Press, 1986); and Amatzia Baram, 'The Radical Shiite Opposition Movements in Iraq', in Emmanuel Sivan and Menachem Friedman (eds), *Religious Radicalism and Politics in the Middle East* (New York, NY: State University of New York Press, 1990).
18. Baram, op. cit.
19. Ibid.

20. Ibid.
21. Batatu, *The Old Social Classes*, p. 6.

CHAPTER 1

1. According to an estimate of the time, approximately 78, 800 Christians, 87,500 Jews, 26,650 Yazidis and Sabeans, 15,650 Bahais, 7,000 Armenians and 500,000 Kurds constituted the minority groups. The settled rural population was approximately 895,000 and the tribal rural population was approximately 1,351, 000; U.S. files 890 g42/18, *Report of the Educational Enquiry Commission* by Paul Monroe [Baghdad: Government Press, 1932]; and FO 371/14524 – E5895, Confidential, Brooke Popham, Acting High Commissioner, to Lord Passfield, Secretary of State for Colonies, 26 Sept. 1930. It is difficult to evaluate from these figures the real proportion of Sunnis and Shi'is. The Sunnis formed the bulk of the urban population in Baghdad and the town of Mosul, while the Shi'is, concentrated in the southern provinces, seem to have amounted to 60 per cent of the population at the time.
2. FO 371/14515 E125/125/93, Treaty Alliance between Britain and Iraq, 10 Oct. 1922.
3. Ibid.
4. Ibid.
5. CO 730/120/1, 40299, pt. 2, Conversation with Feisal at Aix-les-Bains, Report by Sir J. Shuckburgh, 12 Sept. 1927.
6. FO 371/20010, Annual Report, 1935.
7. Ibid.
8. CO 730/128/D.O./5h/14, G. Ellington, Air Headquarters Command, to H. Dobbs, High Commissioner of Baghdad, 5 Nov. 1928.
9. Ibid.
10. CO 730/120/40299, pt. 2, Conversation, Sir S. Wilson, Sir H. Trenchard, 28 June 1927. Conscription (National Defence Law) was finally introduced in 1934. See Ch. 3, pp. 70–1.
11. CAB 16/87, 'The Fuller Employment of Air Power Imperial Defence', Memorandum by the Chief of the Air Staff Secret, Nov. 1929; CO 730/125/40626, High Commissioner to Secretary of State for Colonies, Telegram no. 612, 20 Dec. 1927; CO 730/128/1 D.O. 5h 14, Ellington to Dobbs, 5 Nov. 1928; CAB/16/87, Memorandum by the Chief of Air Staff, Nov. 1929. According to the document, the expenditure dropped from £20,701,000 in 1921–22 to £2,107,000 in 1927–28.
12. CO 730/128, ibid.; and CO 730/123/40465, Ellington to Ormsby-Gore, 4 Oct. 1927.
13. CO 730/120/1, pt. 2, Trenchard to Sir S. Wilson, 28 June 1927.
14. CO 730/128/1, no. 58047, Minute by J. H. Hall, Colonial Office, 15 Nov. 1928; and P. Sluglett, *Britain in Iraq, 1914–1932* (Oxford: Ithaca Press, 1976), p. 49.
15. Rebellions after the end of the war started with Sheikh Mahmud's activities in May 1919. See Ch. 2.
16. See Ch. 2.
17. CO 813/14, Treaty of Alliance between Britain and Iraq and Annexures, 1926.
18. CO 730/120/40299, pt. 2, Secretary of State for Colonies to the Acting High Commissioner, Baghdad, Telegram no. 258, 21 July 1927; CO 730/120/40299, pt. 2, Report, by Shuckburgh, of a conversation with Feisal at Aix-les-Bains, 5–7 Sept. 1927.
19. CO 730/134/58400, pt. 1, High Commissioner to Secretary of State, 16 October 1928; and CO 730/119/40252, Secretary of State for Colonies, Amery, to Secretary of Air Ministry, July 1927.
20. Ibid.; and CO 730/119/40252, Draft Military Agreement.
21. CO 730/134/58400, ibid.
22. FO 371/13759 E 5492/6/93, Note by Butler, 29 Oct. 1929, and Brooke Popham, Acting High Commissioner, to Passfield, Secretary of State for Colonies, 23 Sept. 1929.
23. CAB 16/87, Memorandum by the Chief of Imperial Staff Committee of Imperial Defence, D.I.AP.2, Secret, June 1930.

24. CAB 16/87, Secret C.P. 332(29), Memorandum by the Secretary of State for Air, Nov. 1929, Appendix 1. 'Air Control in Iraq 1922–1929', p. 32; CAB 16/87, Appendix 5. Committee of Imperial Defence, Memorandum by the Secretary of State for Air, D.I.AP4, July 1930.
25. Ibid.
26. CO 730/128/1, no. 158047, Minute, J. H. Hall, 15 Nov. 1928; CO 730/128/1, Nuri al Sa'id to H. Dobbs, Personal, Unnumbered, 27 Oct. 1928; Minute, J. H. Hall, 15 Nov. 1928; and Nuri al Sa'id to H. Dobbs, 27 Oct. 1928.
27. Ibid.
28. CO 730/150/68593, Dobbs to Shuckburgh, 28 Dec. 1929.
29. Ibid.
30. FO 371/13760, Intelligence Report no. 8, 12 April 1929.
31. FO 371/16922 E2931/2831/93, Annual Report, 1932.
32. CO 730/128/1, Nuri al Sa'id to Dobbs, Personal, 27 Oct. 1928.
33. FO 371/16052 E6843/5666/93 C.P., no. 1157, Humphrys to Simon, Secret, 15 Dec. 1932.
34. Ibid.
35. CO 730/162/7, Note by Dobbs, 8 May 1931.

CHAPTER 2

1. LP&S/12/2873 PZ7041/1933–E6229/7/93, F. Humphrys to J. Simon, 12 Oct. 1933.
2. Ibid. In the following years, the British also recruited Kurds and even Arabs into the Levies' forces. However, the majority continued to be Assyrians.
3. Ibid.
4. The composition of the commission, its work and conclusions, as well as the question of the Mosul vilayet, will be dealt with later; I shall concentrate here only on the implications of its conclusions regarding the Assyrian question. See also Elie Kedourie, 'The Kingdom of Iraq: A Retrospect', in the Chatham House Version and Other Middle Eastern Studies (New York, 1970), pp. 236–82.
5. R. S. Stafford, The Tragedy of the Assyrians (London, 1935).
6. CO 730/172/16358, Intelligence Summary no. 16, 10 Aug. 1932.
7. FO 371/15317 E5097/75/93, Observations by H. E. Holland (Secretary of the Iraqi Minorities Rescue Committee in London), 16 June 1931.
8. Ibid.
9. Ibid.
10. Ibid., p. 117; and CO 730/178/1, no. 96602, pt. 4, Flood to J. Pedler, from the Colonial Office, no. 96602/32, 5 Sept. 1932. Enclosure, Observations on Petition by the Patriarch and Leaders of Assyrians in Iraq to the High Commissioner, with copy to the League of Nations.
11. Ibid.
12. Ibid.
13. LP&S/12/2873, PZ 7041/1933, E6229/7/93, F. Humphrys to J. Simon, 12 Oct. 1933.
14. Ibid.
15. Ibid.; and FO 371/14524 E5895, R. Brooke Popham, Acting High Commissioner, to Lord Passfield, Secretary of State for Colonies, 26 September 1930.
16. FO 371/14524 E5895, ibid.; LP&S/12/2873, ibid.
17. Ibid.
18. Gertrude Bell, Review of the Civil Administration of Mesopotamia (London, 1920. Cmd 1067), pp. 51–5; FO 371/15316 – E3087/751/93, Position of the Non-Moslem Minorities in Iraq, Memorandum sent to the League of Nations, 3 Sept. 1930.
19. Ibid.
20. Ibid.
21. LP&S/12/2873, PZ 7041/1933, E6229/7/93, ibid.

22. Ibid.
23. Ibid.
24. FO 371/14524 E5375/4891/93; *The Spectator*, 9 Aug. 1930; *The Times*, 1 Aug. 1930; FO 371/14524 – E6119, Petition to the League of Nations by H. Rassam, 23 Sept. 1930.
25. Ibid.
26. Ibid. In a letter of 20 July 1930 to Sir Elie Kadoorie K.B.E., 6 Princes Gate, London SW7, a Jew from Mosul wrote: 'The condition of the Jewish community in Mosul Vilayet is deplorable [and] in no way better than that of other communities.' The writer of the letter, a certain Nahim, asked for help to be given in London to Captain Rassam, the unofficial intermediary between the Assyrians and the League.
27. LP&S/12/2873, ibid.
28. Ibid.
29. Ibid., and Stafford, *Tragedy*, p. 102.
30. Stafford, *Tragedy*, p. 103; S. Longrigg, *Iraq 1900 to 1950: A Political, Social and Economic History* (London, 1953), pp. 229–31; and M. Khadduri, *Independent Iraq (1932–1958): A Study in Iraqi Politics* (London, 1960), pp. 38–40.
31. FO 624/24/469 E3577/3245/93, no. 397, O. Forbes to J. Simon, 22 June 1933; and FO 624/24/469 E4617/3245/93, J. G. Ward to J. Simon, 3 Aug. 1933.
32. Stafford, *Tragedy*, pp. 141–58.
33. FO 624/16901 E6076, Memorandum by G. Rendel, F.O., on the Assyrian question, 11 Oct. 1933. And FO 624/16901 E7962, Memorandum on the Assyrian question by U.K. representative to the League, 26 Dec. 1933; CO 730/172/96358 E69091/75/93, League of Nations Memorandum, Guarantees for the Minorities, 8 Dec. 1931; CO 730/162/7, no. 80858, pt. 1; E2728/75/93, Draft declaration to be made by representatives of Iraq on application for admission to League of Nations, May 1931.
34. CO 730/178/1, no. 96602, pt. 4, Minute by J. E. W. Flood, 15 Aug. 1932
35. CO 730/172/5 E6091/75/93, Rendel to Flood, 1 Feb. 1932.
36. CO 730/162/7, Minute, Hall, 4 June 1931.
37. CO 371/15317 E5097/77/93, Observation HMG on Petition to League of Nations by Captain Rassam and by Iraq Minorities Rescue Committee of London, Oct. 1931; FO 371/14524 E5375, ibid.; and FO 371/14524–E6119, ibid.
38. CO 730/162/7, 88058, pt. 1, 'Taxation under Turkish Government and Now', Enclosure to Assyrian petitions to the League, May 1931.
39. Ibid.
40. FO 371/15317 E3241, Enclosure letter, H. Rassam to League of Nations, 12 May 1931.
41. CO 730/178/1, pt. 4, 96602/32, J. E. W. Flood to H. J. Pedler, Colonial Office, 5 Sept. 1932.
42. CO 730/162/7, no. 88058, pt. 1, E2728/75/93, Declaration of the Iraqi Government to the League of Nations, May 1931.
43. Ibid.; and Rashid 'Ali's letter to Feisal, 26 June 1933, no. 2247, p. 159. 'Abd al Razzak al Hasani, *Ta'rikh al Wizarat al 'Iraqiyya*, Vol. 3 (Sidon, 1939), pp. 175, 176. Feisal's cable of 28 July 1933 to Rashid 'Ali. Edmonds Papers, Draft of letters of 27 July 1933, and Letter of 26 June 1933, no. 2447, to Cornwallis. 'Abd al Mariyati, *A Diplomatic History of Modern Iraq* (New York, 1961), pp. 68, 69; and Khaldun Sati' al Husri, 'The Assyrian Affair of 1933', *IJMES*, 1974, 5:161–76, 344–60.
44. LP&S/10/781 P 5546/18/B 303, Note by the Political Department of the India Office, 14 Dec. 1918. The census of 1947 refers to a Kurdish population of 900,000. Cecil J. Edmonds, *Kurds, Turks and Arabs* (New York, NY: Oxford University Press, 1957), p. 13.
45. LP&S 10/782, no. 10202, Z 3523 59/100, Baghdad, 23 March 1920. Memorandum by Gertrude L. Bell. LP&S/10/781 P 5546/18/B 303, Note by the Political Department of India Office, 14 Dec. 1918.
46. Edmonds, *Kurds, Turks and Arabs*, p. 7.
47. LP&S/10/781 P 5546/18/B 303, ibid.
48. LP&S 10/752, p. 8765; Bell, *Review*.
49. Bell, *Review*, pp. 60, 61.

50. Ibid.
51. Ibid.
52. Ibid.
53. Ibid.
54. Ibid.
55. Ibid.
56. Ibid. Edmonds, *Kurds, Turks and Arabs*, pp. 9, 57, 58. The most important ones were the principality of Bahdinan in the northern qadas of Mosul (Zakho, Dohuk, 'Aqra, 'Amadiya and Zebar), the principality of Soran (corresponding to Arbil), and the principality of Baban (corresponding to Sulaimaniya and Kirkuk).
57. Bell, *Review*, pp. 60, 61.
58. LP&S 10/782, Secret 2170, Feb. 1920. Interdepartmental Conference on Middle Eastern Affairs.
59. Edmonds, *Kurds, Turks and Arabs*, p. 116.
60. Ibid.
61. Ibid.
62. Edmonds Papers, box 3, file 2 – NK S/23/12. Memorandum by Edmonds of 11 May 1929, 'The Kurdish Question'.
63. FO 371/14521 E 2558/2558/93, High Commissioner Humphrys to Lord Passfield, Secretary of State for Colonies, 23 April 1930. Enclosure, Note by K. Cornwallis, adviser to the Ministry of Interior, 'Pledges Given to the Kurds'.
64. Edmonds Papers, box 3, file 2, Edmonds to Hooper, adviser to the Ministry of Justice, 16 March 1929; Edmonds, *Turks, Kurds and Arabs*, p. 118; and Special Report on Progress of Iraq, Colonial no. 58.
65. Edmonds, *Turks, Kurds and Arabs*, pp. 124, 301, 302.
66. Edmonds Papers, box 3, file 2. Edmonds to Hooper, 16 March 1929; and FO 371/14521 E2558/2558/93, Humphrys to Passfield, 23 April 1930. Enclosure, Note by K. Cornwallis, 'Pledges Given to the Kurds'.
67. Ibid.
68. Edmonds, *Turks, Kurds and Arabs*, pp. 314, 315; Edmonds, 'A Kurdish Newspaper – Rozh-i-Kurdistan', *Journal of the Central Asian Society* (1925), Edmonds Papers.
69. *Special Report of Administration*, Colonial Papers no. 58 (1925), p. 20.
70. Bell, *Review*.
71. Edmonds, *Turks, Kurds and Arabs*, p. 224.
72. Ibid., p. 146.
73. A. D. Smith, *National Identity*. See William A. Graham, 'Traditionalism in Islam – An Essay in Interpretation', *Journal of Interdisciplinary History*, XXIII: 3, Winter 1993, pp. 495–522.
74. The term *tariqa* implies the way to God or the path to Sufism. See A. R. Nicholson, *Islamic Mysticism* (Cambridge University Press, 1980).
75. Ibid., pp. 61, 62, 63.
76. Batatu, *The Old Social Classes*, p. 43.
77. Edmonds, *Turks, Kurds and Arabs*, p. 319.
78. Bell, *Review*.
79. Edmonds, *Turks, Kurds and Arabs*, pp. 209–71. Among them, the British allowed the Talabanis to administer the oil wells in the vicinity of the Gil nahiya. The Naftchizada (as their name indicates) were also owners of oil wells.
80. Edmonds, *Turks, Kurds and Arabs*, pp. 8, 264–5, 416.
81. Edmonds Papers, box 1, secret no. K 361, Edmonds, Political Officer in Kirkuk, to Cornwallis, adviser to the Ministry of Interior, June 1923; and Edmonds Papers, box 3, file 2, Edmonds to Hooper, adviser to the Ministry of Justice, 16 March 1929.
82. Edmonds, *Turks, Kurds and Arabs*, pp. 302, 303.
83. Ibid., pp. 266, 302–4.
84. Edmonds Papers, box 1, secret no. K 361, Edmonds, Political Officer in Kirkuk, to Cornwallis, adviser to the Ministry of Interior, 2 July 1923 and 22 Oct. 1923.
85. Edmonds Papers, box 3, file 2, Edmonds to Hooper, 16 March 1929.

86. FO 371/14521 E2558/2558/93, Humphrys to Passfield, 23 April 1930. Note from Cornwallis, 'Pledges Given to the Kurds'. Edmonds, *Turks, Kurds and Arabs*, pp. 344, 345.
87. Ibid.
88. Edmonds Papers, box 1, Report from Edmonds to Bourdillon, Secretary of the High Commissioner, unnumbered, Kirkuk, 26 Oct. 1922.
89. Ibid.
90. Ibid.
91. Ibid.
92. FO 371/70B33, Intelligence Report, 8 Jan. 1925; Edmonds Papers, box 7, Edmonds to Cornwallis, June 1923; and Confidential Report no. 7, Sept. 1923.
93. Electoral Law of May 1922, CO 813/1, published in Iraqi government *Gazette*, 24 Nov. 1924.
94. Ibid. The Electoral Law is based on a system of primary and secondary electors. The secondary electors, each representing 250 primary electors, were to elect a deputy. However, the secondary electors and the deputies themselves were, in practice, appointed by the government.
95. Bell, *Review*.
96. Edmonds Papers, box 3, file 2, Edmonds to Hooper, adviser to the Ministry of Justice, 16 March 1929.
97. Edmonds, *Turks, Kurds and Arabs*, p. 10.
98. FO 371/10113 E6144/5711/65, Colonial Office to Foreign Office, 18 July 1924: FO 371/10113 E6144/5711/65, Minute, D. G. Osborne, 17 July 1924; and CO 730/33 CO6570, Memorandum by Colonel Meinertzhagen, Feb. 1922.
99. Edmonds Papers, box 1, D 579 9K. Diary no. 3 of the liaison officer, 22 Feb. – 3 March 1925.
100. Ibid.
101. Ibid.
102. Ibid.
103. Edmonds, *Turks, Kurds and Arabs*, p. 398; Marion Kent, *Oil and Empire, British Policy and Mesopotamian Oil 1900–1920* (London: Macmillan, 1986), pp. 5, 13, 39, 98, 99, 118, 156. The discovery of oil in commercial quantities happened only in the late 1920s, and only then did it become a factor shaping politics. CO 730/123/10, no. 40465, Memorandum by H. Dobbs, 18 Oct. 1927.
104. CO 730/173/1, pt. 1, no. 96378, C. P. E369/9/93, 21 Jan. 1932, Appendix 2.
105. Ibid.; Edmonds Papers, box 1, Diary no. 33.
106. CO 730/1162/7 E2728/75/93 G–12427, G. Murray, Chairman of Executive Committee of League of Nations, to Henderson, Under Secretary of State for Colonies, 21 May 1931; U.S. National Archives 890 goo/130. From Sloan, Baghdad, to Secretary of State, Washington, DC, 12 Aug. 1930.
107. FO 371/14521 E4976/1923/93, Sir G. Clerk to Mr A. Henderson, CP no. 330, Constantinople, 4 Sept. 1930; and FO371/14521 – E5504/1932/93, Memorandum of Conversation between Nuri al Sa'id and Ismet Inönü, no. 3031, 20 Sept. 1930.
108. Air 23/417 – S.S.O., Arbil to Air Staff Intelligence at Hinaidi, ref. no. I/A/40, 31 July 1930, Constitution of Yanai-Sarkastan-i-Kurdan (Kurdish Progress Society); and Air 23/417, Enclosure in the Report from S.S.O. Mosul, Secret I/M/33, to Air Staff, Hinaidi, 6 Aug. 1930.
109. *Special Report on Progress of Iraq*, Colonial Papers no. 58.
110. Ibid.
111. Air 23/417, secret S.S.O. Sulaimaniya to Air Staff, AHQ Enclosure to report no. I/S/I, 13 Aug. 1930.
112. Ibid.
113. Edmonds Papers, box 3, file 2, extract from *Baghdad Times*, 9 Aug. 1930; Air 23/244, Summary of Intelligence no. 33, 18 Aug. 1930; and 890 goo/130, Sloan to Secretary of State, 12 Aug. 1930.
114. Air 23/412, Kurdish Petitions to the High Commissioner, 26 Aug. 1930.

115. Edmonds Papers, box 3, file 2, Memorandum on Kurdish policy, 11 Nov. 1930.
116. Edmonds, *Turks, Kurds and Arabs*, pp. 204, 205.
117. Air 23/415, Secret I/Bd/70, from S.S.O. Baghdad to Air Staff, 7 Nov. 1929; and Air 23/
     412, Enclosure to dispatch from S.S.O. Arbil, 10 July 1930, to Hinaidi. Ref. no. I/A/
     40.
118. CO 730/161/1, Humphrys to Kenneth Williams of *The Near East and India* Magazine,
     26 March 1931.
119. Local Language Law no. 74, 1931. CO 730/157/78315, High Commissioner to Secre-
     tary of State for Colonies. Dispatch Secret A, 19 Dec. 1930; FO 371/15372 E4302/31/
     93.
120. Local Language Law no. 74, 1931.
121. CO 730/161/1, Nuri al Sa'id to F. Humphrys, 16 Feb. 1931; Air 23/419. Secret note,
     imprinted, unnumbered, and unsigned, p. 25B, 9 Nov. 1931, attached to Secret
     Dispatch of 18 Dec. 1931, RI/S/25, from S.S.O. Sulaimaniya to Air Staff.
122. Secret note, 9 Nov. 1931, ibid.
123. Ibid.
124. Ibid.
125. Edmonds Papers, box 3, file 2, Memorandum by C. J. Edmonds, *The Kurdish
     Question*, NKS/23/12, 11 May 1929.
126. FO 371/15312 E3052, J. Pedler to Dixon, Observations on Tawfiq Beg Petition, 10
     June 1931.
127. FO 371/15312 E3455/31/93, Nuri al Sa'id to Major Young, no. 2251, 30 May 1931.
128. FO 371/18945 E2296/278/93, Enclosure no. 1, C. P. A. Clark Kerr to J. Simon, 8
     March 1935; and FO 371/18949 – E1198, RAF, *Monthly Intelligence Summary*, Jan.
     1935.
129. Air 23/413, Enclosure to Report no. 1/1/72, from S. S. O. Sulaimaniya to AHQ, 4 Jan.
     1928.
130. Annual Report 1935; FO 371/20010 and FO 371/18945 E3432/278/93, C.P. no. 281, A.
     Clark Kerr to J. Simon, 22 May 1935; and FO 371/18945 E2296/278/93, C. P. no. 174,
     A. Clark Kerr to J. Simon, 8 April 1935.

CHAPTER 3

1. D. Warriner, 'Land Tenure Problems in the Fertile Crescent in the 19th and 20th
   Century', in Charles Issawi (ed.), *The Economic History of the Middle East* (London,
   1966), pp. 71–2.
2. Albertine Jwaideh, *Midhat Pasha and the Land System of Lower Iraq*, St Antony's
   Papers no. 16, A. H. Hourani (ed.) (London, 1963), p. 195.
3. Ibid.; Warriner, loc. cit.
4. Jwaideh, op. cit.; Warriner, op. cit.
5. Sluglett, *Britain in Iraq*, p. 231; Warriner, op. cit.
6. Ibid.
7. Bell, *Review*.
8. Ibid.
9. Ibid.
10. Ibid.
11. Ibid.
12. Ibid.
13. Iraq was considered by the Ottomans as a conquered province whose land was defined
    as the property of the conqueror; therefore the lands of Iraq were mostly *miri* (state
    property). However, land was divided into several other categories:
    (1) *Mulk*, land owned as freehold and usufruct.
    (2) *Miri*, or *aradi amiriyya*, state-owned lands with usufruct enjoyed by the in-
    dividual. This category was divided into three sub-categories: (a) *miri sirf*, land over
    which the state had retained ownership; (b) *tapu miri*, an estate on which the govern-

ment had, by a deed known as *tapu sanads*, granted the cultivator rights of occupancy and usufruct (*tasarruf*) after ten years of use, while the *riqba* (supervision) remained in the hands of the state; and (c) *miri lazma*, regulated by rules similar to those of the miri tapu. The main difference was the government's right to prevent the transfer of the land to the cultivators (returning land to the state) if the parcel had not been properly cultivated.

(3) *Waqf* land, reserved for pious purposes; the usufruct was transferred to the community and used for pious purposes while remaining in possession of the previous owner. Waqf land could not be sold or parcelled. This type of title was used in order to evade inheritance laws and to keep the estate intact. There were subdivisions in this type of tenure: (a) *waqf-madbuta*, waqf lands that were administered by the Awqaf Department in Istanbul; (b) *waqf mulhaqa*, administered by the mutawalis or the guardians of the property for the special benefit of the community; (c) *waqf-dhurriyya*, held as a trust for the benefit of the direct descendants of the dedicator; (d) *waqf ma'aruf*, dedicated to educational purposes; (e) *waqf-ifta'*, administered by the *mufti* for charitable bequests.

(4) *'Uqr*, a tenure peculiar to Baghdad, consisting of rights to a fixed proportion of the produce (1/20 to 1/30). Of obscure origin, this kind of tenure was regulated by a commission convened by Midhat Pasha in 1872. Not really entering in the category of waqf, the 'uqr related to absentee landlords who were not permitted to interfere in the land's management.

(5) *Mawat*, unreclaimed and unused land.

(6) *Matruka* land, reserved for public purposes; in general, gardens and other public places.

Sources: A. Jwaideh, 'The Sanniyya Lands of Sultan Abdul Hamid in Iraq', in *Arabic and Islamic Studies in honor of Sir H. Gibb* (Leiden, 1965), pp. 327–39; Jwaideh, *Midhat Pasha*, p. 125; and Bell, *Review*.

14. S. Haider, 'Land Problems in Iraq', in Issawi (ed.), *Economic History of the Middle East*, pp. 164–7.
15. Ibid.
16. Sir E. Dowson, *An Inquiry into Land Tenure and Related Questions* (Letchworth: Garden City Press, 1932), p. 26.
17. Land Code 1858, pt. 2, Chs 8 and 9, quoted in Haider, op. cit., p. 166.
18. Ibid.
19. Jwaideh, 'Sanniyya Lands', pp. 327–90.
20. Bell, *Review*.
21. Ibid.
22. Ibid.
23. Ibid.
24. Warriner, op. cit.; Sluglett, *Britain in Iraq*, p. 231. See note 13 above.
25. Haider, op. cit., pp. 163–6. The sirkals in practice organized such common tasks as the cleaning of canals, sowing, harvesting, providing money and seeds for the fellah. At the same time they collected taxes, which were increased by the inclusion of their share.
26. FO 371/16049 E3588, Dowson to the High Commissioner, 15 Jan. 1932.
27. Ibid.
28. Jwaideh, 'Midhat Pasha', pp. 134, 135.
29. FO 371/16049 E3588, Dowson to Humphrys, 15 Jan. 1932. Dowson, *Inquiry into Land Tenure*, p. 74. 'Where small holders paying their land revenue were found to exist, they should be recognized.' The same applied to large holders, 'provided relations with cultivators and tenants were healthy'. In addition, in areas where tribal tenure survived and was 'favoured by the tribe as a whole,' this usage should be recognized. FO 371/16049, ibid.
30. Ibid. Dowson argued that the administrative division of Iraqi territory (into 14 liwas, 47 qadas and 139 nahiyas) would easily allow the application of his policy.
31. Ibid.
32. CO 730/130, Dobbs to Amery, Secretary of State for Colonies, Secret, 4 Dec. 1928.
33. Dowson, *Inquiry into Land Tenure*; and CO 813/5, *Iraq Government Gazette*, no. 23, 5

June 1932, pp. 422–3.

34. 890 goo 313, from Baghdad to Washington, Dispatch of 26 May 1928; 'Special Report on Progress of Iraq'. 1920–31, p. 198; and *Iraq Government Gazette*, no. 52, 28 Dec. 1938.

35. FO 371/17858 E191/191/93, Enclosure in Dispatch no. 807, 428/7/33, Humphrys to J. Simon, 22 Dec. 1933, Note by Webster, Inspector General of Agriculture, 'Law Governing the Rights and Duties of Cultivators', June 1933, published in the *Iraq Government Gazette*, no. 31, 30 July 1933; and FO 371/17858 – E191.

36. AIR 23/104, Appendix to the Monthly Report on Muntafiq liwa', Sept. 1926, received from the High Commissioner under HQ/1223 in 31 Oct. 1926.

37. Ibid.

38. Ibid.

39. Ibid.

40. Ibid.

41. Ibid.

42. *Iraq Government Gazette*, no. 31, 30 July 1933; and FO 371/17858 E191/191/93. Note by Webster, Inspector General of Agriculture, on Law Governing the Rights and Duties of Cultivators, no. 28, June 1933. Enclosure in Baghdad dispatch no. 807, 22 Dec. 1933.

43. FO 371/17858. Note by Webster, ibid.; Gabriel Baer, 'Agrarian Problems in Iraq', *Middle Eastern Affairs*, Vol. 3, no. 12 (Dec. 1952), p. 382.

44. AIR 23/560, Very Secret. From the office of the Administrative Inspector at Diwaniya to the adviser of the Ministry of Interior, referring to C/2089, 12 Oct. 1923; and AIR 23/104, S.S.O. Basra to AHQ NCD/1/251, 22 May 1926.

45. FO 371/12264 E3782/121/65, Intelligence Report, 28 Aug. 1927.

46. Ibid.

47. Among the Baghdadi politicians who greatly increased their personal fortunes and acquired large estates of agricultural land, by taking advantage of the land tenure system, were Yasin al Hashimi and Rashid 'Ali al Gailani. A 1934 report tells how dispossessed Shi'i tribesmen rushed into Yasin's gardens demanding the return of their land. 890 goo 303 no. 410 Confidential 29 Nov. 1934, from the U.S. Embassy in Baghdad to the Secretary of State, Washington, and FO 624/24/489, Note on Rashid 'Ali by Hikmat Sulaiman, July 1941.

48. By 'sectarian' I mean factional, as I am referring to the two main factions in Islam – the Sunna and the Shi'a.

49. FO 371/12264 E3782/121/65. Intelligence Report, 28 Aug. 1927; AIR 23/105, Secret from AHQ to AOC, 6 Oct. 1927; AIR 23/121, Administrative Inspector Kut and 'Amara to the adviser of the Ministry of Interior, Confidential, no. C.93, 18 Oct. 1927; AIR 23/105, Appendix to Report I/Bd/39 S.S.O. Baghdad to Air Staff, 16 Feb. 1927, 'The History of the Sa'dun'; AIR 23/105, S.S.O. Baghdad to Air Staff Intelligence I/Bd/ 39, Appendix A, 16 Feb. 1927; and AIR 23/105, no. I/N/25, Nasiriya to Intelligence Branch in the Air Staff, 9 March 1927.

50. AIR 23/121, Translation of letter no. 888 from the qaimaqam of Hai qada to the mutasarif of Kut liwa', 13 March 1928; AIR 23/105, Appendix to report I/Bd/39 from S.S.O. Baghdad to Air Staff, 16 Feb. 1927; AIR 23/105, Extract from S.S.O. Mosul IM/ 03/A of 30 June 1927; FO 371/12264 E3782/121/65, Intelligence Report, 28 Aug. 1927; AIR 23/121, Secret no. I/N/4 S.S.O. Nasiriya to Air Staff Intelligence, 7 Aug. 1927; AIR 23/121, Secret I/5/9 I/N/4, From S.S.O. Nasiriya to Air Staff AHQ, 8 Aug. 1927; and AIR 23/432 – J/26, S.S.O. Hai, Capt. Jeffreys to AHQ Baghdad, 8 Aug. 1927.

51. AIR 23/105 – no. C/3247. C. J. Edmonds, acting adviser to the Ministry of Interior, to the High Commissioner, 19 Sept. 1927; AIR 23/105, Secret from the Air Head Quarters to AOC, 6 Oct. 1927; FO 371/12264 E3298/121/65, Intelligence Report, 7 July 1927; FO 371/12264 E3782/121/65, Intelligence Report, 28 Aug. 1927; AIR 23/121, Memorandum no. 2048, Situation on the Shatt al Gharraf, 17 March 1928; and AIR 23/121 – I/N/ 4, from Nasiriya to AHQ, 7 Aug. 1927.

52. Batatu, *The Old Social Classes*, p. 47; Marion Farouk-Sluglett and Peter Sluglett, 'Some Reflections on the Sunni Shi'i Question in Iraq', *British Society for Middle East Studies Bulletin*, Vol. 4.5 (1977–78).

53. Bell, *Review*,
54. Ibid.
55. Ibid.
56. Moojan Momen, *An Introduction to Shi'i Islam. The History and Doctrines of Twelver Shi'ism* (New Haven, CT: Yale University Press, 1985), p. 50.
57. Sluglett, *Britain in Iraq*, pp. 41, 43; Kedourie, 'The Kingdom of Iraq', p. 262; and Longrigg, *Iraq 1900 to 1950*, pp. 16–124.
58. W. J. O. Nadhmi, 'The Political, Social and Intellectual Roots of the Iraqi Independence Movement of 1920', unpublished Ph.D. dissertation, Durham University, 1974.
59. FO 371/E3203 E5764/7, Air Liaison Officer J. P. Domville to Air Intelligence Staff, 17 June 1939; Kedourie, 'The Kingdom of Iraq', pp. 190, 191.
60. Air 23/385, S.S.O. Baghdad to Air Staff. Ref: Bd/28, 27 Nov. 1931.
61. Air 23/589, Abstract of Intelligence no. 20, 20 May 1933.
62. Ibid.
63. Sluglett, *Britain in Iraq*, pp. 82, 83.
64. CO 703/40/37008, Intelligence Report, 5 July 1923.
65. CO 703/123/44065, Note on Political Situation, 27 Sept. 1927.
66. Ibid.
67. Ibid.
68. Ibid.
69. Air 23/432, Weekly Report from S.S.O. Basra to Air Headquarters, 10 Sept. 1927; Air 23/432, Extract from S.S.O. Basra Report no. I/896, 31 Dec. 1927.
70. Air 23/432, S.S.O. Baghdad to Air Staff. AHQ. Secret I/Bd/II, 19 Dec. 1927.
71. Air 23/432, Weekly Report S.S.O. Basra, 10 Sept. 1927; Air 23/106, Confidential no. 3312, from Secretariat of the Council of Ministers in Baghdad, 'Abd al Muhsin Sa'dun to Dobbs, 11 Dec. 1928, and Dobbs's answer to 'Abd al Muhsin Sa'dun, no. P.O. 425, Baghdad, 22 Nov. 1928, ibid.; Air 23/432, S.S.O. Baghdad Report no. I/Bd 35, 12 Dec. 1927; 23/432, S.S.O. Baghdad to Air Staff, AHQ Secret I/BD/II, 19 Dec. 1927; Air 23/432, S.S.O. Baghdad Report no. I/Bd 35, 12 Dec. 1927; Air 23/432, S.S.O. Baghdad to Air Staff, AHQ Secret I/BdII, 19 Dec. 1927; CO 730/125, Note by C. A. Hooper, 28 Dec. 1927; FO 371/18945 E2295, Enclosure in Baghdad's dispatch of 28 March 1935; and Bell, *Review*.
72. Air 23/106, Intelligence Report, 26 Nov. 1927; Air 23/432, Extract from S.S.O. Basra, Report no. I/1896, 31 Dec. 1927: Air 23/105 pt. 3, no. I/N/25; and S.S.O. Nasiriya to Air Headquarters, Secret, 11 Oct. 1927 and 17 Oct. 1927. Yasin al Hashimi was reported to have offered in 1927 a reward of Rs 100,000, together with promises of a Shi'i semi-autonomous administration, if conscription measures could be implemented in Shi'i areas.
73. Abstract of Intelligence Report, 18 April 1925, quoted in Sluglett, *Britain in Iraq*, p. 311; CO 730/124/40488, Secret B, Acting High Commissioner Bourdillon to S/S Colonies, 15 July 1927; and Air 23–/105, pt. 3, no. I/N/25, S.S.O Nasiriya to AHQ Secret, 11 Oct. 1927.
74. Air 23/453, From S.S.O. Hilla to Air Staff, Baghdad, 2 July 1923; Edmonds Papers, box 1, Secret C/1097, from the adviser to the Minister of Interior K. Cornwallis to C. J. Edmonds, then political officer in Kirkuk, 14 June 1923.
75. Air 23/105, no. I/N/25, S.S.O. Nasiriya to Air Staff, 17 Oct. 1927; FO 371/12264 E3298/121/65, Intelligence Report, 7 July 1927; Air 23/432 – I/Bd/II, S.S.O. Basra to AHQ, 19 Dec. 1927; ibid., Report I/892, S. S. O. Basra to AHQ, 24 Dec. 1927; FO 371/12264 E3298/121/65, Intelligence Report, 7 July 1927; and ibid., E121/121/65, Intelligence Report, 22 Dec. 1926; Air 23/432, Weekly Report, S. S. O. Basra, 10 Sept. 1927; and Enclosure, minute by the Chief Staff Officer, 6 May 1927; Air 23/432 – Secret I/Bd/35, S. S. O. Baghdad to Air Staff, 19 Dec. 1927; Air 23/432, S. S. O. Baghdad to AHQ Ref. I/Bd/35, 21 Nov. 1927; and Air 23/432. S. S. O. Baghdad Report I/Bd/135, 23 Dec. 1927.
76. Air 23/431, S. S. O. Diwaniya, Report for the period 15 May 1930 to 26 May 1930; Air

23/432, S. S. O. Basra to AHQ I/799, 17 July 1927; FO 371/17858 E191/191/93, Enclosure to Baghdad Dispatch, 22 Dec. 1933, 'Law Governing the Rights and Duties of Cultivators', June 1933; Air 23/43, S. S. O. Diwaniya, Report for period 15 May 1930 to 26 May 1930; Air 23/383, Secret no. 900, from the Administrative Inspector in Diwaniya to the adviser at the Ministry of Interior, 16 Nov. 1930; Air 23/432 – I/Bd/39, S. S. O. Baghdad to A.H.Q, 21 July 1930; Air 23/806, Secret Report no. 110 – I/Bd/28, from Air Liaison Officer in Baghdad to Air Staff, Hinaidi, 25 March 1934; CO 730/123/10 – 40465, Note on the Political Situation, by Edmonds, 27 Sept. 1927; ibid., Ellington to Ormsby-Gore, no. D.O. 26/2, 4 Oct. 1927; and ibid., Minute, Hall, 11 Oct. 1927.

77. FO 624/24/469 E6677/3245/93, Extract from Intelligence Summary, Sept. 1933; and Air 23/105 – I/Bd/39, Enclosure appendix A, from S. S. O. Baghdad to Air Staff, 16 Feb. 1927.

78. FO 371/18949 E898, Review of Events 1934; and FO 371/16924 E5521/5250/93 no. 595, Confidential, Humphrys to Simon, 14 Sept. 1933. The best description of Ghazi can be found in Maurice Peterson's *Both Sides of the Curtain* (London, 1950), p. 138. 'Ghazi was weak and unstable as water and his intemperate habits combined with his choice of companions from among the wildest of the young army officers and his own servants at the palace, made him impossible to control, difficult to influence and dangerous to all, especially to himself.'

79. 890 goo 297, ibid.; 890 goo 300, no. 410, Confidential, Knanbeshue to Dept. of State, Washington, 29 Nov. 1934; and FO 371/18949 E898, Review of Events.

80. 890 goo 325, Strictly Confidential, Knanbeshue to Dept. of State, Washington, 21 March 1935; and FO 371/18952 E1198, Monthly Intelligence Summary, 1935.

81. FO 371 E623/278/93, Humphrys to Simon, 17 Jan. 1935; 890 goo 310, Knanbeshue to Dept. of State, 6 Feb. 1935; Capt. A. D. McDonald, 'The Political Development of Iraq Leading Up to Rising in Spring 1935', *Royal Central Asian Society Journal* (1936), p. 30.

82. FO 371/18945 E434/278/93, C. P. Humphrys to Simon, 10 Jan. 1935; 890 goo 316, Knanbeshue to Dept. of State, 16 March, 1935; FO 371/18945 E2096/278/93, C. P. no. 159, A. Clark Kerr to J. Simon, 21 March 1935; and 890 goo 325, Knanbeshue to Sec. of State, 21 March 1935.

83. 'Abd al Razzak al Hasani, *Ta'rikh al Wizarat al 'Iraqiyya*, Vol. 4 (Sidon, 1940), pp. 46–8. Taha al Hashimi's letter, 26 June 1939; and FO 371/18953 E716/1583/93, Telegram, Humphrys to FO, 13 March 1935. Reports about 'soldiers reduced to tears by the appeal of Shi'i women not to shed their brothers' blood' were current in those days.

84. 890 goo 316, Knanbeshue to Dept. of State, 16 March 1935.

85. 890 goo 325, Strictly Confidential, 21 March 1935, Knanbeshue to Dept. of State; 890 goo 330, Confidential, Knanbeshue to Dept. of State, 2 July 1935; and 890 goo 327, Enclosure to Telegram from Knanbeshue to Dept. of State, 20 May 1935.

86. Khadduri, *Independent Iraq*, p. 60.

87. FO 371/18945 E2096/278/93, O. P. A. Clark Kerr to J. Simon, 21 March 1935.

88. FO 371/18945 E2455/278/93, C. P. no. 178, A. Clark Kerr to J. Simon, 2 April 1935; and 890 goo 329, Knanbeshue to Murray, 13 May 1935.

89. FO 371/18945 E2295/278/93, Enclosure Dispatch no. 171, A. Clark Kerr to J. Simon, 28 March 1935. Kerr wrote in his report of June 1935: '[G]reat chieftains . . . had to submit to the insolence of officials drawn from the effendi classes of the towns whom they despised both as venal and affected townees and as a product of shameless nepotism' (FO 371/18945 C.P. E3731/278/93, no. 300, A. Clark Kerr to J. Simon, 17 June 1935). FO 371/16923 E6677, Extract of the Intelligence Summary, 1933. Among numerous other examples of inconsiderate treatment on the part of the authorities, special mention was made of the arrest of 'Abd al Jawad Kelidar, the brother of Sayyid 'Abbas al Kelidar, titular holder of the keys of the shrine at Najaf, for the publication of an opposition article in *Al Ahrar*. CO 730/132, the Iraqi Constitution; CO 730/125, Note, C. A. Hooper, 28 Dec. 1927; FO 371/18945 E2295, Enclosure in Baghdad Dispatch of 28 March 1935. This manifesto can be compared with the 'Proclamation of the Executive Committee of the Shi'a in Iraq', quoted in Kedourie, 'The Kingdom of Iraq',

pp. 283–5: the chief claims there were for government offices to be distributed proportionally, revenues of awqafs to be directed to Muslim institutions, and usurped land to be returned to former owners. The manifesto in the mid-1930s followed the main lines of the earlier one. The addition points reflected the same problems, which had if anything worsened after independence.

90. CO 730/125, Note by C. A. Hooper, 28 Dec. 1927, and Review on the Progress of Iraq 1920–1931; Edmonds Papers, box 3, file 1, DS7952, Recent Events at Rumaitha, 1 June 1936.

91. FO 371/18945 E2295/278/93, Enclosure, Baghdad Dispatch no. 171, 28 March 1935. Also quoted in al Hasani, *Ta'rikh al Wizarat al 'Iraqiyya*, Vol. 41, pp. 76 and 64.

92. FO 371/18945 E2563/278/93, A. Clark Kerr to J. Simon, C.P. 200, 11 April 1935.

93. McDonald, 'Political Development in Iraq', pp. 38, 39; Edmonds, DS7952 BIII F.I., 1 June 1936.

94. Edmonds, ibid.

95. Ibid.; Air 23/105 S.10155, from AHQ to the High Commissioner, 18 Oct. 1927; and 890 goo 362, Knanbeshue to Murray, 5 March 1936.

96. 890 goo 362, ibid.; FO 371/20015, ibid.; FO 371/20015 E1575/1575/93, C.P. no. 127, A. Clark Kerr to Eden, 5 March 1936; FO 371/20015 E2530/1575/93; *The Times*, 5 May 1936; and FO 371/20015 E3062/1575/93, A. Clark Kerr to Eden, 22 May 1936. In this atmosphere, the agreement signed by Iraq and Saudi Arabia was considered by the Shi'is as a threat, because memories of the Wahabis' looting in Karbala' and Najaf at the beginning of the nineteenth century were still fresh.

97. FO 371/20010, Annual Report 1935.

CHAPTER 4

1. George Antonius, *The Arab Awakening* (Beirut, 1936).

2. Batutu, *The Old Social Classes*, pp. 153–318.

3. CO 730/120/1, Note, Dobbs, no. 40299, pt. II, 2 Aug. 1923.

4. CO 730/123/40465, Note on the political situation by C. J. Edmonds, 27 Sept. 1927.

5. CO 730/123/40465, Bourdillion to Dobbs, 15 Aug. 1927.

6. CO 730/120/1 Pt. 2. E. L. Ellington to Sir H. M. Trenchard, 15 June 1927.

7. CO 730/130/13, Report of conversation with Feisal, by Dobbs, 3 April 1928; CO 730/123/404/65, Dobbs to Shuckburgh, 31 Aug. 1927.

8. CO 730/139/680/5, Pt. II. Teleg. High Commission to Sec. of State, 22 June 1929.

9. 890 goo/130, Sloan to Sec. of State, 12 Aug. 1930; 890 goo/133 Sloan to Sec. of State. Despatch No. 132, 14 Oct. 1930.

10. FO 371/15324 E3799/3715/93, Message from C.W.C. East India to Admiralty, 21 July 1931.

11. The TCCDR had been created by the British at first to safeguard tribal customs. Purely tribal cases were not to be subject to decisions of ordinary courts but should come before a tribal majlis, or court, with the sentence confirmed by the mutasarif. *Report on Administration*, p. 35. Article 40 of the TCCDR allowed the authorities to transfer disruptive elements from tribal areas. This regulation was also employed in urban areas, serving as a political instrument in the hands of the authorities. FO 371/15324 E4619, H. Young, Acting High Commissioner, to Passfield, Secretary of State for Colonies, 14 Aug. 1931.

12. 890 goo/Faysal/36, Dispatch by Sloan, 22 July 1932.

13. To quote just two of them, Taha al Hashimi, *Mudhakkirat Taha al Hashimi, 1919–1943* (Beirut, 1967), pp. 140–8; and Tawfiq al Suwaidi, *Mudhakkirati* (Baghdad, 1969).

14. Anthony D. Smith, *The Ethnic Origin of Nations*.

15. Sylvia G. Haim, *Arab Nationalism: An Anthology* (Berkeley, 1962).

16. Tawfiq al Suwaidi, op. cit., pp. 263, 274, 275; Taha al Hashimi, op. cit., pp. 158, 159.

17. FO 371/20803, Annual Report 1936.

18. Ibid.
19. FO 371/20014 E7145/419/95, A. Clark Kerr to Eden, 10 Nov. 1936.
20. FO 371/20014 E71747/419/93, Sir A. Clark Kerr to Eden, 16 Nov. 1936.
21. Taha al Hashimi, op. cit., p. 139.
22. Annual Report 1936, ibid.
23. FO 371/29794 E659, Enclosure in Baghdad dispatch no. 25 of 13 Jan. 1937. Quarterly Report on Royal Iraqi Air Force.
24. Annual Report 1936.
25. Ibid.; al Hasani, *Ta'rikh al Wizarat al 'Iraqiyya*, p. 189.
26. Al Hasani, ibid.
27. Annual Report 1936; FO 371/20013 E6783/1419/93 Teg. no. 265 from the Embassy at Baghdad to the F.O., 29 Oct. 1936.
28. Ibid.
29. 890 goo 395 – Dispatch from Baghdad to Washington, 24 Dec. 1936; and FO 371/20014 E7181, Summerscale, of the Commercial Secretariat at Baghdad, to Lacy Bagallay, London, 2 Nov. 1936.
30. Edmonds's papers, DS. 70.92; DS. 79.52; box 3, File 2, Narrative of Events, 1 June 1936.
31. In fact, Hikmat Sulaiman's first act after the *coup* was to send a message to the British Ambassador assuring him of the new government's intention to maintain friendly relations with Britain. Annual Report 1936.
32. Edmonds, ibid.
33. Ibid.
34. Ibid.
35. FO 371/20014 E7145/1419/93, A. Clark Kerr to Eden, 16 Nov. 1936; FO 371/20013 E6860/1419/93, minute of J. G. Ward, 3 Nov. 1936; and E6819/1419/93, minute of J. G. Ward, 2 November. 1936. Ibid., and E6784/1419/93, A. Clark Kerr to F.O., 29 Oct. 1936.
36. FO 371/20013 E6784/1419/93, Minute, Rendel, 30 Oct. 1936.
37. FO 371/20013 E6784/1419/93, Minute, J. G. Ward, 29 Oct. 1936; FO 371/20013 E6797/1419/93, Minute, J. G. Ward, 30 Oct. 1936.
38. FO 371/20013 E6818/1419/93, Minute, J. G. Ward, 26 Nov. 1936.
39. Ibid., E6825/1418/93, G.O.C. Egypt to the War Office, Dispatch no. 1750, 29 Oct. 1936.
40. FO 371/20015 E7917/1419/93, Rendel to A. Clark Kerr, 30 Dec. 1936; and FO 371/20803 – Annual Report 1936.
41. Ibid. and FO 371/20014 E7474/1419/93 – CP, A. Clark Kerr to Eden, 15 Nov. 1936, and E7479/1419/93, A. Clark Kerr to Eden, 1 Dec. 1936, ibid. According to Hasani, op. cit., p. 199, more than two officers were involved in Ja'far's murder, among them Jamal Jamil, Muhammad Jawad and a Christian officer named Lazar Brudarmus.
42. FO 371/20015 E7627, Notes on Bakr Sidqi, Enclosure in dispatch from A. Clark Kerr to Rendel, 26 Nov. 1936.
43. FO 371/20013 E6814/1419/93, Telegram A. Clark Kerr to F.O., 30 Oct. 1936, and FO 371/20015 E7625/1419/93, Minute of J. G. Ward, 11 Dec. 1936.
44. Annual Report 1936.
45. FO 371/20014 E7624/1419/93, A. Clark Kerr to Rendel, 21 Nov. 1936; and 890 goo/303, No. 410, Confidential, Baghdad to Secretary of State in Washington, 29 Nov. 1934.
46. FO/624/24/489, A note on the origin and career of Rashid 'Ali, extract from Hikmat Sulaiman's book *During the Hashimi Administration*, July 1941.
47. FO 371/20801 E368, No. 10, 28 Jan. 1937, A. Clark Kerr to Eden, 5 Jan. 1937.
48. FO 371/12264 E3660/121/65, Intelligence Report – 2 Aug. 1927; FO 371/10098, Intelligence Report, 27 Nov. 1924.
49. FO 624/24/489, ibid.; and Longrigg, *Iraq 1900 to 1950*, p. 152.
50. Ibid.; FO 371/10098 E111069 and E11709, Intelligence Reports of Dec. 1924.
51. Annual Report 1936; FO 371/20014 E7624/1419/93, A. Clark Kerr to Rendel, 21 Nov. 1936; and CO813/3, the Awqaf Administration Law No. 27, 1929.

52. FO 624/24/489, ibid., and FO 371/20014 E7624/1419/93, ibid.; FO 371/23217 E4745/4745/93, Report on the Leading Personalities in Iraq.
53. FO 371/13760, Report no. 9, 26 April 1929; and 890 goo/132 – Dispatch from Baghdad no. 129, 24 Oct. 1930.
54. FO 371/20013 E5650/1419/93, Confidential, Bateman to Eden. The stipulations that Britain would participate for twenty years in the board of directors and that Iraq would have to pay £650,000 to Britain aroused great criticism. FO 371/20010 – Annual Report 1935.
55. Annual Report 1936.
56. Ibid. and FO 371/20013 E6906, A. Clark Kerr to F.O., 31 Oct. 1936. FO 371/20014 E7147/1419/93, A. Clark Kerr to Eden, C.P. No. 548, 16 Nov. 1936.
57. FO 371/20014 E7351/1419/93, Minute, Scott Fox, 28 Dec. 1936. For a more detailed account of the Ahali group, see Batatu, *The Old Social Classes*, pp. 300–6.
58. FO 371/20014 E7351/1419/93, Minute, Scott Fox, 28 Dec. 1936; and C.P. No. 565, A. Clark Kerr to Eden, 25 Nov. 1936.
59. Ibid.; FO 371/20795 E660/14 a, Clark Kerr to Eden, 13 Jan. 1937.
60. FO 371/21853, Personalities, ibid.
61. FO 371/20795 E3929/14/93, no. 258 401/5/37, A. Clark Kerr to Eden, 28 June 1937.
62. 890 goo 407 – Report, 12 May 1937, from Baghdad to Sec. of State in Washington; and FO 371/21856, Annual Report 1937. One of the enterprises receiving special government attention was the Abu Ghuraib project near Baghdad, FO 371/20014 E7351/1419/93 C. P. 565, A. Clark Kerr to Eden, 25 Nov. 1936; and 890 goo 407, ibid., and FO 371/20795 E3699/1419/93, A. Clark Kerr to Eden, no. 237, 15 June 1937.
63. FO 371/20795, ibid.
64. Ibid.
65. Ibid.; FO 371/21856 E794/794/93, Annual Report 1937.
66. Khadduri, *Independent Iraq*, p. 117.
67. FO 371/20795 E1967, No. 100/27/37, A. Clark Kerr to Eden, 31 March 1937.
68. FO 371/20715 E1235/14/93, A. Clark Kerr to Eden, 14 Feb. 1937.
69. 890 goo, General Conditions 108, 890 goo B/9; *The Baghdad Times*, 3 Aug. 1937; al Hasani, op. cit., p. 288; and FO 371/20795 E3478/14/93; *The Times*, 25 June 1937.
70. FO 371/20795 E4112/14/93, No. 274–100/49/37, A. Clark Kerr to Eden, 3 July 1937.
71. FO 371/20015 E7627/1419/93, Notes on Character of Bakr Sidqi, Nov. 1936.
72. FO 371/20013 E172/172/93, Records of Leading Personalities, Jan. 1936; FO 371/17864 E653/653/93, Records of Leading Personalities, Jan. 1934; FO 371/20015 E7627/1419/93, Notes on Bakr Sidqi; Annual Report 1937; and FO 371/20015 E7795/1419/93, Rendel to A. Clark Kerr, Secret, 31 Dec. 1936.
73. FO 371/20015 E7795/1419/93, A. Clark Kerr to Rendel, 19 Jan. 1937.
74. Annual Reports 1936 and 1937.
75. Taha al Hashimi, op. cit., pp. 185–6.
76. Ibid., pp. 155–6.
77. FO 371/20014 E7437, A. Clark Kerr to Rendel, 17 Nov. 1936.
78. FO 371/20015 E7790/1419/93, Interview Bakr Sidqi to Sawt al Sha'b, 29 Nov. 1936.
79. FO 371/20795 E61/14/93, A. Clark Kerr to Rendel, 18 Dec. 1936.
80. Taha al Hashimi, op. cit.; FO 371/20795 E1235, A. Clark Kerr to Eden, 14 Feb. 1934.
81. FO 371/20013 E6922/1419/93, Minute, J. G. Ward, 5 Nov. 1936.
82. FO 371/20013 E6784/1419/93, Minute by G. Rendel, 30 Oct. 1936.
83. FO 371/20014 E7062/1419/93; *The Times*, 4 Nov. 1936. Hikmat Sulaiman was the brother of Shawkat Pasha, one of the leaders of the CUP and the son of Kethuzada Sulaiman Beg, the Ottoman Vali of Basra.
84. FO 371/27095 E4688/14/93, Minute by J. G. Ward, 12 Aug. 1937.
85. FO 371/20015 E7917/1419/93, Rendel to A. Clark Kerr, 30 Dec. 1936.
86. FO 371/20014 E7147/1419/93, Minute by J. G. Ward, 18 Nov. 1936, and A. Clark Kerr to Eden, No. 548, 16 Nov. 1936.
87. FO 371/27095 E4112, No. 274 100/49/37, A. Clark Kerr to Eden, 3 July 1937; FO 371/27095 E1235, A. Clark Kerr to Eden, 14 Feb. 1937.

88. FO 371/20013 E6814/1419/93, A. Clark Kerr to F.O., 30 Oct. 1936.
89. Annual Report 1936 and FO 371/20795 E1235, A. Clark Kerr to Eden, 14 Feb. 1937.
90. Annual Reports 1936 and 1937.
91. FO 371/20013 E6922/1419/93, Minute by J. G. Ward, 5 Nov. 1936.
92. FO 371/20795 E4455/14/93, A. Clark Kerr to L. Oliphant, 24 July 1937.
93. FO 371/20029 E7217, A. Clark Kerr to Rendel, 7 Nov. 1936.
94. Annual Report 1937.
95. Ibid.
96. Ibid. and FO 371/20795 E5071/14193, No. 3420, Scott to Eden, 18 August 1937.
97. Ibid.
98. Ibid.; also quoted in E. Kedourie, 'The Kingdom of Iraq'.
99. FO 371/20795 E4730/14/93, Minute by J. G. Ward, 14 Aug. 1937.
100. Longrigg, *Iraq 1900 to 1950*, p. 255.
101. Khadduri, *Independent Iraq*, pp. 122, 123.
102. Longrigg, pp. 255, 256.
103. Khadduri, p. 123; Annual Report 1937.
104. FO 371/20795 E5071/14/93, No. 342 – O. Scott to Eden, 18 Aug. 1937; FO 371/20795 E4815; *The Times*, 18 Aug. 1937.
105. U.S. files 890 goo B9 890, goo General Conditions 108 Comment of Press, Aug. 1937.
106. U.S. files 428, Dispatch No. 862 from Baghdad to Secretary of State Washington, 2 Sept. 1937.
107. FO 371/21856, Annual Report 1937.
108. U.S. files 890 goo 461, Knanbeshue to Sec. of State, 29 Dec. 1938.
109. FO 371/21846 E455, A. Clark to Rendel, 4 Jan. 1938.
110. See Reeva Simon, *Iraq Between the Two World Wars: The Creation and Implementation of a Nationalist Ideology* (New York, NY: Columbia University Press, 1986), pp. 10–26.
111. Muhammad Tarbush, *The Role of the Military in Politics. A Case Study of Iraq*, pp. 73, 87; and Khadduri, *Independent Iraq*, pp. 69, 70.
112. FO 371/17850 C.P. 797 E10/10/93, F. Humphrys to J. Simon, 1 Jan. 1934.
113. FO 371/17850 C.P. No. 19 E658/10/93, F. Humphrys to J. Simon, 10 Jan. 1934.
114. FO 371/18949 E7418/464/93, Intelligence Summary, Nov. 1935; FO 371/21846 E2011, Edmonds to Holt, 16 March 1938.
115. Ibid., and AIR 23/590, Intelligence Summary, 16 Nov. 1935.
116. FO 371/21856, Annual Report 1937; FO 371/23213 E2181/655/93, Monthly Intelligence Summary, Feb. 1939.
117. Ibid.; CO 730/162/7, Intelligence Report No. 4, 18 Feb. 1931.
118. Ibid.; 890 goo 351, Henry Field to Wallace Murray at the Dept. of State, 5 Nov. 1935; 890 goo 355, Knanbeshue to Washington, confidential, no. 558, 27 Nov. 1935; AIR 23/439, Views of Ja'far al 'Askari regarding the formation of an army for the Iraqi state, 12 Nov. 1920; Longrigg, *Iraq 1900 to 1950*, p. 246.
119. FO 371/20013 E6797/1419/93, Minute by J. G. Ward, 30 Oct. 1936.
120. AIR 23/120 Bd/I/56 from the Wing Commander S.O.I. of the Air Staff Intelligence in Hinaidi to the A.O.C. Baghdad, 31 July 1929; AIR 23/120 I/Bd/56, S.S.O. Baghdad to Air staff at Hinaidi, 17 July 1930.
121. Bassam Tibi, *Arab Nationalism: A Critical Enquiry*, quoted in Simon, *Iraq Between the Two World Wars*, p. 26.
122. Simon, loc. cit.
123. op. cit., pp. 14–43.
124. Ibid.
125. FO 371/21859 E6083/1982/93, R. A. Leeper, F.O., to K. R. Johnstone, the British Council, 10 Nov. 1938.
126. FO 624/24/448/3/41, Nazi Propaganda; Simon, pp. 36–9.
127. FO 371/23203 E5164/1, From Air Liaison Officer J. P. Domville to Air Staff Intelligence, 17 June 1939.
128. Ibid.; FO 371/20013 E6940/1419/93, Minutes by J. G. Ward, 6 and 10 Nov. 1936.

129. Ibid.; FO 371/20006 E5853/375/93, Bateman to F.O., 14 Sept. 1936; F. Grobba, *Männer und Mächte im Orient* (Berlin, 1967), p. 167; and H. H. Kopietz, 'The Use of German and British Archives in the Study of the Middle East: The Iraqi Coup d'Etat of 1936', in A. Kelidar (ed.), *The Integration of Modern Iraq* (London: Croom Helm, 1979).

130. FO 371/20013 E6940/1419/93, Minutes by J. G. Ward, 6 and 10 Nov. 1936.

131. Ibid.; Kopietz, op. cit.

132. FO 371/23203 E5164/1, Air Liaison Officer J. P. Domville in Basra to Air Staff at Habbaniya, 17 June 1939. Although Taha al Hashimi, in his memoirs, *Mudhakkirat Taha al Hashimi 1919–1943* (Beirut, 1967), denies his links with German arms dealers, the great amount of the evidence in British files proves the contrary.

133. FO 371/23203 E5164/77/93, Air Liaison Officer J. P. Domville in Basra to Air Staff at Habbaniya, 17 June 1939.

134. Ibid.

135. FO 624/24/448/3/41, Nazi Propaganda; Peterson, *Both Sides of the Curtain*, pp. 144–5; FO 371/23203 E5164/1, ibid.

136. FO 371/23203 E5164/1, ibid.; FO 371/23214, Annual Report 1938.

137. Ibid.; Grobba, *Männer und Mächte*, pp. 171, 172.

138. Edmonds Papers, box 3, file 2, Edmonds to Cornwallis, 25 June 1941, PS no. 104; FO 371/27078 E42311/1/93, Cornwallis to Eden no. 185, 11 July 1941.

139. FO 371/23213 E3647, Monthly Intelligence Report, May 1939; FO 371/23200 E2476/72/93, Telegram to F.O. from Houston Boswall, 4 April 1939; FO 406/77 E2817/77/93, Houston Boswall to Halifax, 11 April 1939.

140. FO 371/23213 E3647, Monthly Intelligence Report, May 1939, no. 119.

141. FO 371/23200, Telegram, H. Boswall to F.O., no. 119, 6 April 1939; FO 371/23202 E7693/72/93, Telegram, B. Newton to F.O., 23 Nov. 1939; Note by Crosthwaite, 24 Nov. 1939, ibid.

142. FO 371/23213 E7339, Monthly Intelligence Report, Sept. 1939.

143. Ibid.

144. FO 371/23218 E6406/6263/93, B. Newton to F.O., 9 Sept. 1939; FO 371/23213, ibid.; Daniel Silverfarb, *Britain's Informal Empire in the Middle East: A Case Study of Iraq, 1929–1941* (New York: Oxford University Press, 1986), p. 108.

145. FO 371/23213, ibid.

146. FO 406/78 E918/448/93, no. 65, B. Newton to Halifax, 18 Feb. 1940.

147. FO 406/78 E711/448/93, C.P. no. 46, B. Newton to Halifax, 17 Feb. 1940; FO 371/24551, ibid.; FO 406/78 E779/4481/93, B. Newton to Halifax, 21 Feb. 1940; and FO 406/78 E918/448/93, no. 65, B. Newton to Halifax, 18 Feb. 1940.

148. *Phebe Marr, The Modern History of Iraq* (Boulder, CO: Westview, 1985), pp. 81, 82.

149. FO 371/24551, Secret Report no. 30 on the Iraqi Army and the RAF, Feb. 1940; FO 406/78 E2228/G, C. P. no. 342, B. Newton to Halifax, 8 July 1940.

150. Ibid.

151. FO 371/24558 E1724, Enclosure, Baghdad Dispatch, no. 144, 3 April 1940.

152. FO 406/78 A E2228/G, C.P. no. 342, B. Newton to Halifax, 8 July 1940; FO 371/24558, ibid.

153. FO 371/24558 E2228/G, Telegram no. 285, B. Newton to F.O., 5 July 1940.

154. FO 371/21859 E7805/1982/82, Report by Consul McKereth in Damascus to Halifax, no. 60, 2 Dec. 1938; FO 371/23203 E5164, Domville to AHQ, 17 June 1939; FO 371/24558 E2105, Telegram, B. Newton to F.O., 22 June 1940; E2228, B. Newton to F.O., 3 July 1940; Telegram no. 285. Conversation between Mustapha al 'Umari and Edmonds.

155. FO 371/24558 E2228, Telegram no. 258, B. Newton to F.O., 3 July 1940; Telegram no. 342; B. Newton to F.O., 8 July 1940.

156. FO 371/24558 E1375/448/93, Minute, Crosthwaite, 28 March 1940.

157. FO 624/23 214/1/41, Holt to Forester, 20 Jan. 1941; Simon, *Iraq Between the Two World Wars*, pp. 136–40.

158. FO 371/24552 E2703/471/93, Talbot, F.O., to Gorell Barnes, Cabinet Office, 5 Oct.

1940; FO 371/24558 E2228, Telegram no. 285, B. Newton to F.O., 3 July 1940; ibid., Telegram no. 342, B. Newton to F.O., 8 July 1940.
159. FO 371/24554 E2703/47/93, Minute, C. Price, 30 Sept. 1940.
160. FO 371/24558 E2228, Telegram nos. 285 and 342.
161. FO 371/24558 E1724, Enclosure, Baghdad Dispatch, no. 144, 3 April 1940; Simon, *Iraq Between the Two World Wars*, pp. 141, 142.
162. FO 371/27079 E4732/1/93, Foreign Office, Minute, 13 Aug. 1941.
163. FO 371/24558, Extract, War Cabinet Conclusions, 1 July 1940; FO 371/24558 E2105/ G, Secret Memorandum of War Cabinet WP (40) 205, 14 June 1940; FO 371/24558 E2228/G, Telegram no. 342; FO 371/24558 E2228/G, Extract meeting COS (40), War Office, 27 June 1940; FO 371/24558 E2105/G, Secret Memorandum, ibid.; FO 371/ 27076 E3286/1/93, A. Clark Kerr to Eden, 24 June 1941.
164. Ibid.
165. FO 371/24558 E2905/448/93, Minute, Crosthwaite, 12 Nov. 1940; FO 371/24558 E2339/448/93, Telegram no. 530, F.O. to B. Newton, 20 Oct. 1940; FO 371/24558 E2905, F.O. to B. Newton, 14 Nov. 1940.
166. Edmonds Papers, box 2, file 3, Political Situation, DS 79, 53, Edmonds to B. Newton, 1 April 1941.
167. Ibid.; FO 371/27076 E3286/1/93, C.P. 143, Cornwallis to Eden, 28 April 1941 and 24 June 1941.
168. FO 371/27062 E1276/1/93 and E1277/E1291/1/93, K. Cornwallis to F.O., 4 and 5 April 1941.
169. Silverfarb, *Informal Empire*, pp. 118–41; FO 571/24558, Newton to F.O., 18 June 1940; E2105/E2228/448/93, 3 July 1940.
170. Silverfarb, p. 126.
171. FO 371/27077 E3426/1/93, no. 1485/843/41, Cornwallis to Eden, 6 June 1941.
172. Ibid.
173. Ibid.
174. India Office, R/1S/S/168 D.O. no. 192–22, From the Publicity Officer at Bahrein to Major A. C. Galloway, Political Agent in Kuwait, 6 May 1941; FO 371/16095 E175, Treaty of Alliance between Britain and Iraq, 1930.
175. FO 371/21851 E5707, Extract Note by the Eastern Department at the Foreign Office, Oct. 1938; FO 371/21858 E2176/298/93, Baxter to the Secretary of the Air Ministry, 24 May 1938; FO 371/27067 E1790, Cornwallis to F.O., 25 April 1941; FO 371/27067 E1837, Iraqi Legation in London to F.O., 29 April 1941.
176. FO 371/27067 E1815/1/93, Cornwallis to F.O., 30 April 1941, and F.O. to Cornwallis, 30 April 1941; FO 371/27077 E3426/1/93, no. 148, Cornwallis to Eden, 6 June 1941; FO 371/27069 E2261/1/93, Telegram, F.O. to Ankara, no. 1121, 17 May 1941; FO 371/ 27069 E2261/1/93, Telegram, F.O. to Ankara, no. 1121, 17 May 1941; FO 371/27073 E2724/1/93, Telegram no. 388, F.O. to Baghdad, 31 May 1971.
177. Haim Cohen, 'The Anti-Jewish Farhud in Baghdad', *MES*, Vol. 3, no. 1 (Oct. 1966); Elie Kedourie, 'The Sack of Basra and the Farhud in Baghdad', *Arabic Political Memoirs* (London, 1974), pp. 297, 298.
178. FO 371/27069 E2112/1/93, Minute, Seymour, 13 May 1941; FO 371/27074 E2923, no. 528, from Baghdad to F.O., 7 June 1941; FO 371/27075 E2952, Telegram no. 535, 9 June 1941.
179. FO 371/27077 E3426/1/93, no. 148, Cornwallis to Eden, 6 June 1941; Edmonds Papers, box 2, file 2, Edmonds to Cornwallis, unnumbered, 12 July 1941.
180. Smith, *National Identity*.
181. Tawfiq al Suwaidi, *Mudhakkirati*, and Taha al Hashimi, *Mudhakkirat Taha al Hashimi*.
182. Silverfarb, *Informal Empire*, pp. 65–73.
183. Ibid. The redress of damage caused by the smuggling of goods and arms into Iraqi territory, the low taxation of the Emir's date gardens in Iraq, and the establishment of an Iraqi port city on the Bay of Kuwait, as well as control of the Bubiyan and Warba islands, were at the basis of Iraq's arguments at the time.

184. Sati' al Husri, *Dirasat 'an Muqaddimat Ibn Haldun* ('Studies on the Muqaddima of Ibn Haldun'), 2nd edn (Cairo, 1961), p. 21.
185. Tawfiq al Suwaidi, op. cit., pp. 209, 210, 219.
186. Sati' al Husri, *Abhath Mukhtara fi al Qawmiyya al 'Arabiyya* (Cairo, 1963), pp. 33–81.
187. Sati' al Husri, *Ma hiya al Qawmiyya? Abhath wa Dirasat 'ala Daw al Ahdath wa al Nazariyyat* ('What is Nationalism? Empirical and Theoretical Studies and Researches'), 3rd edn (Beirut, 1963), p. 259.
188. Edmonds Papers, box 3, file 2, Edmonds to Cornwallis, PS no. 104, 25 June 1941.

CHAPTER 5

1. Batatu, *The Old Social Classes*, p. 954.
2. Air 23/432.
3. 'Azzam al Hadid, 'Le Développement de l'Éducation Nationale en Iraq', *Revue des Études Islamiques*, 932–6, pp. 237–67.
4. William L. Cleveland, *The Making of an Arab Nationalist: Ottomanism and Arabism in the Life and Thought of Sati' al Husri* (Princeton, NJ: Princeton University Press, 1971); Sylvia Haim, *Arab Nationalism: An Anthology* (Los Angeles, CA: University of California Press, 1962).
5. Sati' al Husri, *Mudhakkirati fi al 'Iraq* (Beirut, 1967), vol. II, p. 340 and pp. 463–76.
6. Cleveland, p. 182.
7. Reeva Simon, 'The Teaching of History', *Middle Eastern Studies* (1986), pp. 37–51, 82–5; and Phebe Marr, 'The Development of a Nationalist Ideology in Iraq 1920–1941', *Muslim World* (1985), p. 92.
8. Al Husri, Reply to Yasin al Hashimi, 5 May 1935, *Mudhakkirati*, II, pp. 298–9.
9. Ibid., I, p. 80. Also quoted in Marr, 'Nationalist Ideology', p. 93.
10. Al Husri, *Mudhakkirati*, I, pp. 105–11.
11. Ibid., I, pp. 116, 358.
12. Ibid., I, p. 116.
13. Ibid., I, pp. 117–127 and 311.
14. Ibid., I, pp. 117–27, 171–4 and 166. According to al Husri, Muslim students were in the majority in 'Amara, Kirkuk and Nasiriya, whereas the majority of non-Muslim students were concentrated in the Mosul area.
15. Ibid., I, pp. 126–7.
16. Ibid., I, p. 174.
17. Ibid., II, p. 7.
18. Ibid., II, p. 54.
19. Ibid., II, p. 68.
20. Ibid., I, p. 457.
21. Marr, 'Nationalist Ideology', pp. 88–93.
22. Simon, *Iraq Between the Two World Wars*, p. 79.
23. Al Husri, *Mudhakkirati*, I, p. 340.
24. Simon, pp. 83–96.
25. Ibid., pp. 86–9; al Husri, II, pp. 325 and 344.
26. 890 g. 42/18; *Report of the Educational Inquiry Commission* (Baghdad Government Press, 1932).
27. Ibid., pp. 121–4.
28. Ibid., pp. 25–8, 121–4.
29. Ibid., p. 122.
30. Ibid., pp. 122 and 93.
31. Ibid.
32. Ibid.
33. Ibid., p. 93.
34. Simon, *Iraq Between the Two World Wars*, pp. 89–92.
35. Ibid.

TABLE 1

Liwa'	Population[1]	Tables[2] Rs	Spent on Schools Rs
Mosul	320,000	6,480,000	669,436
Arbil	106,000	1,530,000	91,636
Sulaimaniya	94,000	1,720,000	68,992
Kirkuk	160,000	1,009,000	118,165
Diyala	240,000	2,480,000	130,933
Baghdad	388,000	1,350,000	1,223,765
Dulaim	147,000	1,006,000	87,241
Karbala'	90,000	1,420,000	77,449
Hilla	103,000	2,320,000	86,866
Kut	170,000	330,000	80,550
Diwaniya	238,000	3,950,000	89,974
Muntafiq	340,000	1,970,000	136,890
Amara	238,000	60,000	136,596
Basra	190,000	1,620,000	315,394
Total	2,824,000	27,245,000	3,313,887

[1] Based upon the estimates of the liwas' authorities. No complete census has yet been taken.
[2] Land revenue only, collected from each liwa' but not necessarily within the liwa'. The payments are of 1929 and for summer crops, winter crops, dates, other fruits and tobacco.

TABLE 2: GOVERNMENT INTERMEDIATE SCHOOLS, 1931–32[1]

Liwa'	Boys		Girls	
	Schools	Pupils	Schools	Pupils
Baghdad	3	968	1	163
Kut	1	26	–	–
Diyala	1	33	–	–
Hilla	1	83	–	–
Karbala'	2	121	–	–
Ramadi	1	36	–	–
Kirkuk	1	99	–	–
Total Baghdad area	10	1,366	1	163
Basra	–	–	1	30
Amara	1	40	–	–
Muntafiq	1	56	–	–
Diwaniya	1	12	–	–
Total Basra area	3	108	1	30
Mosul	1	460	1	93
Total Mosul area	1	460	1	93
Sulaimaniya	1	51	–	–
Arbil	1	58	–	–
Total Kurdish area	2	109	–	–
Grand total	16	2,043	3	286

[1] Figures from the Ministry of Education, February 1932.

TABLE 3: GOVERNMENT SECONDARY SCHOOLS, 1931[1]

Liwa'	Boys		Girls	
	Schools	Pupils	Schools	Pupils
Baghdad	1	245	–	–
Basra	1	184	–	–
Mosul	1	51	–	–
Total	3	480	–	–

[1] Figures from the Ministry of Education, February 1932.

36. Ibid.
37. Ibid.
38. Informal Conversation with Dr Fadel al Jamali held at Harvard University, Cambridge, MA, Spring 1990.
39. Simon, p. 94.
40. *Report of the Educational Inquiry Commission*, pp. 99 and 100. Table 1 shows the estimated population of each liwa', the land revenue collected from each liwa', and the sums spent on schools in each liwa' in 1929. Tables 2 and 3 show the totals for Government schools in 1932.
41. *Report of the Educational Inquiry Commission*, p. 94.
42. FO 371/14521 E3249 12558/93, June 1930.
43. Ibid.
44. Al Husri, *Mudhakkirati*, II, pp. 165–8.
45. Ibid., II, p. 172.
46. Ibid., II, pp. 183–245.
47. Ibid., II, pp. 202–3.
48. Ibid., II, p. 206.
49. Ibid., II, p. 232.
50. Ibid., II, p. 271.
51. Ibid., II, p. 211.
52. Simon, *Iraq Between the Two World Wars*, pp. 91–107; and Kedourie, 'The Kingdom of Iraq', p. 273.
53. FO 371/23218 E6666, Enclosure in Baghdad Dispatch, no. 454, Draft, New Public Education Law, 16 Aug. 1939.
54. Ibid.
55. Ibid.
56. 890g 42/35, no. 1347, Baghdad to Washington, 5 Aug. 1939.
57. 890g 42/37; *Istiqlal*, May 1939.
58. 890g 408/1, P. Knanbeshue to Washington, 7 June 1939.
59. Ibid.; *Al Bilad*, 30 March 1939; Haim, *Arab Nationalism*, pp. 97–9.
60. Al Husri, *Mudhakkirati*, I, p. 160.
61. Sami Shawkat, in Haim, op. cit.
62. Fadel al Jamali, in Haim, p. 68.
63. Ibid.
64. Al Husri, *Mudhakkirati*, II, p. 375.

CHAPTER 6

1. Edmonds Papers, Secret Note, *The Kurds in May 1941*, 27 July 1941; Letter, Edmonds to Cornwallis, Very Secret, 26 June 1941.
2. Edmonds Papers, Note from Edmonds to Cornwallis, PS no. 104, 25 June 1941.
3. Edmonds Papers, Note by Edmonds, 13 July 1941.
4. Edmonds Papers, Note no. 339, Very Secret, Edmonds to Cornwallis, 26 June 1941.

5. Edmonds Papers, Note no. 339, 24 June 1941.
6. Edmonds Papers, Secret, DS no. 789, Memo: 'Nationalist Manshars in Sulaimaniya', 15 July 1943.
7. Ibid.
8. Ibid.
9. Edmonds Papers, Note on the Kurdish Question, 24 June 1941.
10. 890 goo/7 1744, Confidential, no. 362, 17 July 1944, Loy W. Henderson to Secretary of State; and 890 goo/679, Strictly Confidential, 'Deterioration of the Situation in Northern Kurdistan', 1 Jan. 1944, Loy W. Henderson to Secretary of State.
11. Ibid.; 890 goo/669, no. 490, Strictly Confidential, 13 Oct. 1943, Daniel Gaudin, Jr, to Secretary of State; 890 goo/674, Strictly Confidential, no. 517, 13 Nov. 1943, Daniel Gaudin, Jr, to Secretary of State and 890 goo/679, Strictly Confidential, no. 41, 'The Deterioration of the Situation in Northern Kurdistan', 1 Jan. 1944, Loy W. Henderson to Secretary of State.
12. 890 goo/674, Strictly Confidential, From Daniel Gaudin, Jr.
13. 890 goo/674, no. 517, Strictly Confidential, Daniel Gaudin, Jr, to Secretary of State; and 890 goo/3–2245, no. 674, William Moreland to Secretary of State, 22 March 1945.
14. 890 goo/3–2245, no. 674, 22 March 1945, William Moreland to Secretary of State; see annex.

CHAPTER 7

1. 890 goo/7–1646 in 1325, James S. Moose, Jr, to Secretary of State, Washington, DC, the Electoral Law, no. 11, of 1946, *Al Waqa'i' al 'Iraqiyya* (official Gazette no. 237), 8 June 1946.
2. 890 goo/4–347, Airgram to Secretary of State, 3 April 1947; 890 goo/7/1646, no. 1325, James S. Moose, Jr, to Secretary of State, 14 Aug. 1946.
3. Ibid.
4. Marr, *Modern History of Iraq*.
5. 890 goo/3/1947, Report on the Election for Parliament in Basra, by William Burdett, Jr, Basra, 19 March 1947.
6. Ibid.
7. Ibid.
8. Ibid.
9. 890 goo/3–3147, ibid., Airgram from Baghdad, 31 March 1947.
10. 890 goo/12–947, Confidential, 22 Dec. 1947.
11. *The Times*, 14 May 1948, in 890 goo/12–246, 2 Dec. 1946, James S. Moose, Jr, to Secretary of State.
12. 890 goo/12–1749, Airgram from Baghdad, 26 Dec. 1949.
13. 890 g 91/7–1946; 890 goo/12–1749, Airgram, ibid.
14. 890 goo/10/2747, Airgram, 27 Oct. 1947.
15. 890 goo/3–845, Walter W. Birge, Jr, to Secretary of State, 8 March 1945.
16. 890 goo/7/1544, no. 361, Confidential, 18 July 1944, Visit to Holy Cities of Najaf and Karbala'.
17. 890 goo/12–246, 2 Dec. 1946, James S. Moose, Jr, to Secretary of State.
18. 890 goo/6–2145, ibid.; 787.001 1/2850, Airgram, 28 Jan. 1950.
19. 787.001 1/2850, Airgram, 28 Jan. 1950.
20. 890 goo/6–2145, ibid.
21. 787.001/1–2850, ibid.
22. Ibid.
23. 787.001/1259, Report of Dr Ernest F. Penrose, 12 Jan. 1959.

CHAPTER 8

1. 890 goo/6/2145, no. 783, William Moreland, Jr, to Secretary of State, 21 June 1945. Among these groups are: Al Qa'ida (the Pedestal); Wahdat al Nidal (Unity of Struggle); Al Sharara (The Sparkle); Rabitat al Shuyu'i al 'Iraqiyyun (League of Iraqi Communists); Hizb al Taharrur al Watani (National Liberation Party).
2. Marr, *Modern History of Iraq*, pp. 101–6.
3. 787.001/2–1153, Air Pouch, 11 Feb. 1953, by Philip Ireland to Department of State.
4. Marr, *Modern History of Iraq*, pp. 108–9, 113–14.
5. Ibid.
6. 787.11/4–1053, Airgram, 10 April 1953.
7. 787.001/7–753, Dispatch from Baghdad, 7 July 1953.
8. 787.2/8–453, Dispatch no. 102, 4 Aug. 1953; 887.413/9–1553, 25 Sept. 1953, James Cortado to Department of State.
9. 787.00/3–3054, Dispatch no. 686, 30 March 1954.
10. 887.413/9–2553, ibid.
11. 787.11/3–1053, Air Pouch, 10 March 1953; 787.11/3–1053, Dispatch no. 632, 18 March 1953.
12. 787.344/3–354, Airgram, 3 March 1954.
13. Ibid.
14. 887–413/7–156, Dispatch no. 1, by Herman Frederik Eilts, 1 July 1956.
15. 787.00/3–2559, Dispatch no. 75, 25 March 1959; and Marr, *Modern History of Iraq*, p. 107.
16. 787.34/12–3152, Dispatch no. 437, 31 Dec. 1952; 787.00/7–1454, 14 July 1954; 787.00/9–1654, Dispatch no. 25, From Basra, 16 Sept. 1954.
17. 887.413/7–156, Dispatch no. 1, by Herman Frederick Eilts, 1 July 1956.
18. Whether these politicians represented their constituencies remains an open question. When Fadel al Jamali (elected as the representative of Diwaniya) was asked whether he had received a public ovation when he went there during the campaign, he responded: 'I cannot say I was given a great ovation by the public but I was well received by the army.' Also 787.00/1–2753, Air Pouch, 27 Jan. 1953.
19. 787.00/1–654, Dispatch no. 75, 6 Jan. 1954.
20. Ibid.
21. Marr, *History of Modern Iraq*, pp. 116–25; Uriel Dann, *Iraq Under Qassem: A Political History* (Jerusalem and New York, 1969), pp. 10–12, 25–6.
22. 787.03/7–295 8, Dispatch no. 45, 29 July 1958.
23. Ibid.
24. 787.001/11–1358, Dispatch no. 127, 18 Nov. 1958.
25. 787.00/1–659, Dispatch no. 370, 6 Jan. 1959; 787.00/9–1059, Dispatch no. 218, 10 Sept. 1959; 787.00/1–955, Dispatch no. 393, 9 Jan. 1959.
26. 787.00/1–559, Dispatch no. 372, 5 Jan. 1959.
27. 787.00/3–1659, Dispatch no. 691, 16 March 1959.
28. 787.61/7–159, Dispatch no. 1, 1 July 1959.
29. Ibid.
30. 787.00/3–1659, Dispatch no. 576, 16 March 1959.
31. Batatu, *The Old Social Classes*, p. 866; 787.00/3–1959, Dispatch no. 126, 19 March 1959; 787.00/3–2059, Dispatch no. 851, 20 March 1959.
32. 787.00/9–1059, Dispatch no. 218, 10 Sept. 1959, Enclosure no. 2.
33. Ibid. Enclosure no. 2.
34. Ibid.
35. 787.00/9–1059, Dispatch no. 218, 10 Sept. 1959.
36. Ibid.; 787.005/–1359, Dispatch no. 755, 13 May 1959.
37. Ibid.; 787.00/5–2559, Dispatch no. 797, 25 May 1959; 787.00/1–1259, Dispatch no. 403, 12 Jan. 1959.
38. 787.005/5–2559, ibid.
39. 787.005/5–1359, ibid.

40. 787.001/5–1259, ibid.
41. 787.00/2–659, Dispatch no. 465, 6 Feb. 1959; 787.00/1–654, Dispatch no. 75, 6 Jan. 1954; 787.00/8–454, Dispatch no. 51, 4 Aug. 1954; 787.00/12–2054, Dispatch no. 278, by W. L. Eagleton, Jr, 12 Dec. 1954; 787.001/1–259, Dispatch no. 39, 2 Jan. 1959; 787.005/2159, Dispatch no. 794, 21 May 1959.
42. 787.00/2–659, Dispatch no. 465, 2 Feb. 1959.
   787.00/1–2159, Dispatch no. 424, 21 Jan. 1959.
44. 787.00/2–459, Dispatch no. 459, 4 Feb. 1959; 887.413/4–3059, 30 April 1959.
45. 789.00/2–1759, Dispatch no. 59, 17 Feb. 1959.
46. Batatu, *The Old Social Classes*, pp. 912, 913.
47. Ibid.
48. 887.413/4–3059, 30 April 1959.
49. 787.002/959, Telegram no. 3298, Feb. 1959; 787.002/1759, Dispatch no. 509, 17 Feb. 1959.
50. Batatu, p. 954.
51. Marr, *Modern History of Iraq*, pp. 176–9.

CONCLUSION

1. Bassam Tibi, *Islam and the Cultural Accommodation of Social Change* (Boulder, CO: Westview, 1990), p. 9.
2. Roger Owen, 'Class and Class Politics in Iraq Before 1958: The Colonial and Post Colonial State', in Robert A. Fernea and William Roger Louis (eds), *The Iraqi Revolution of 1958: The Old Social Classes Revisited* (London: Tauris, 1991), p. 168.
3. 787.00/5–1359, Dispatch no. 755, 13 May 1959; 787.00/1–659, Dispatch no. 370, 6 Jan. 1959; 787.00/1–1259, Dispatch no. 403, 12 Jan. 1959; 787.00/1–559, Dispatch no. 372, 5 Jan. 1958.
4. 787.11/3–1053, Dispatch no. 632, 10 March 1953; 887.413/9–2553, Dispatch no. 32, 25 Sept. 1953.
5. Batatu, *The Old Social Classes*, p. 807.
6. Ibid.
7. Sami Zubaida, 'Community, Class and Minorities in Iraqi Politics', in Fernea and Louis, op. cit p. 202.
8. FO 371/44041 E1903/37/93, 14 March 1944, the regent's proposal to stop the distribution of land to influential individuals.
9. 787.00/1–259, Dispatch no. 39, 2 Jan. 1959; 787.001/11–2458, Dispatch no. 32, 24 Nov. 1958; and 787.00/10–2758, Dispatch no. 25, 27 Oct. 1958.
10. Batatu, *The Old Social Classes*, p. 98.
11. Ibid., p. 22.
12. Smith, *National Identity*.
13. Liah Greenfeld, *Nationalism, Five Roads to Modernity* (Cambridge, MA: Harvard University Press, 1991), p. 78.
14. Ibid.
15. Ernest Gellner, *Nations and Nationalism* (Oxford: Blackwell, 1983), p. 7.
16. Ibid., p. 13.
17. Amatzia Baram, *Culture, History and Ideology in the Formation of Ba'thist Iraq, 1968–89* (Oxford: St Antony's, Macmillan, 1991).
18. Smith, *The Ethnic Origin of Nations*, pp. 131–41.
19. Ibid.
20. Informal conversation at the Harvard Faculty Club, Cambridge, MA, Spring 1990.

AFTERWORD

1. By Sa'd Ru'uf Shair Muhammad (Baghdad: Maktab al Yaqza al 'Arabiyya 1988).
2. By Lutfi Ja'far Faraj 'Abd Allah (Baghdad: Maktab al Yaqza al 'Arabiyya, 1988).
3. By 'Uthman Kamal Haralu (Sidon: Maktab al 'Asriyya, 1987).
4. By 'Ala' Jasim Muhammad (Baghdad: Maktab al Yaqza al 'Arabiyya, 1987).
5. By Dr Muhammad Husein al Ziyadi (Baghdad: Faculty of Letters, Baghdad University, 1979).
6. By Dr Muhammad Husein al Ziyadi (Baghdad: Dar al Wasit, 1985).
7. By Talib Mushtaq (Beirut: Dar al Tali'a, 1968; reprinted in Baghdad, 1989).
8. By Ahmad Fawzi (Baghdad: Dar al Hurriyya, 1988).
9. By Kazim Ni'ma (Beirut: Dar al 'Arabiyya fi al Mawsuat, 1988).
10. Marion Farouk-Sluglett and Peter Sluglett, 'Iraq Since 1986: The Strengthening of Saddam', *Middle East Report* (Nov.–Dec. 1990), pp. 19, 24.
11. Ibid.
12. *Sawt al Ittihad al Demoqrati al Iraqi fi America*, 22 May 1992.

Glossary

Agha (pl. *Aghawat*): Kurdish tribal leader. Originally a title of military distinction among the Turks.

Ahl al Haqq (lit., People of Truth, of God): heretical sect found among Persians, Turkmen and Kurds in Iraq and Iran. Their doctrine focuses on Seven Divine manifestations (among them 'Ali, the Prophet's cousin and son-in-law). Their doctrine, like those of the Yazidis and the 'Alawis, is considered a variation of Sevener Shi'ism.

Al Ahd (lit., covenant): the secret Arab Nationalist Society, formed before the First World War by Arab officers serving in the Ottoman army.

Amir prince.

Assyrians: Christian community whose members were known for their belligerent qualities. The Assyrians fled the Turks at the end of the First World War and settled in northern Iraq. Many of them were recruited to the Levies in 1921, continuing a tradition of collaboration with the British which dated from pre-war times. See also *Nestorians* and *Levies*.

Awqaf (pl. of *waqf* – lit., standing, hence the sense of perpetuity of a Moslem endowment): money or property given in perpetuity to the Islamic authorities for pious purposes or for public good. Over time the waqf became an institution used to avoid property being expropriated by the state.

Ba'th (lit., resurrection or renaissance): Arab Socialist Ba'th Party.

Bid'a (lit., innovation): a practice or belief not revealed in the Qur'an nor established through tradition.

Caliph: successor to the Prophet Muhammad. Caliphs were the political and military leaders of the Umma (the Muslim community) after the death of the Prophet (in 632).

Darwish: a member of the Qadiriyya, the most popular mystic order in Iraq and Turkey.

Dhimmis (or Ahl al Dhimma – lit., protected people): the members of

184

monotheistic religions (Jews, Christians and Sabeans) who were granted cultural and religious autonomy and protected by the Islamic state. The dhimmis paid special taxes: the jiziyah (head tax) and the kharaj (exemption tax). Their special status has been abolished since the establishment of modern states.

Dira: land belonging to a tribe by customary right.

Diwan: a council or cabinet.

Fallah (pl. *Fallahin*): peasant.

Fatwa: a formal legal opinion on religious matters issued by a mufti (among the Sunnis) and by the mujtahid (among the Shi'is).

al Futuwwa: originally a medieval brotherhood, inspired by the ritualistic practices and chivalry of the Crusades; in Iraq in the 1930s, a paramilitary youth organization set up by the government.

Haqq (lit., truth, right): used in the mystical language of the Sufi orders to mean Divine Reason.

Hiwa (lit., hope): Kurdish party formed in the early 1940s.

Hukumiyyun (lit., partisans of the government): in monarchic Iraq, the name for the Shi'i tribal chiefs collaborating with the government of the day.

Ibtida'iyya: primary school.

I'dadiyya: secondary school.

Iltizam: contract between the multazim and the state, appointing the former as the collector of taxes from the cultivators.

Imam: for Sunnis, a prayer leader; for Shi'is, one of the twelve descendants of 'Ali. For the Twelvers (the largest Shi'i sect in Iraq), the Imam is the intermediary between man and God.

Intifada (lit., uprising): a term normally used to describe the riots of 1952.

Istiqlal (lit, independence): a nationalist party active in Iraq during the 1940s and 1950s.

Kelidar: the titular holder of the keys to the shrine at Najaf.

Khums (or *Khums-al Miri* – lit., the fifth part): originally the portion of the spoils of war reserved for the leader/ruler of the community. In Shi'i areas, the share allotted to the mujtahid. In modern times, the quota from crops allocated to the state.

Koda: tax paid by Kurdish flock owners to the agha.

Lazma: a type of land tenure by which the right of occupancy and cultivation of miri (state) land was accorded to the title-holder, but its permanent transfer to the fellahin could be prevented in cases of improper use. The lazma differed from other types of miri land over which the fellahin could acquire a more permanent hold after ten years of labour.

185

Levies: troops of Assyrian soldiers (later including Arabs and Kurds), formed in 1921 and led by British officers. Their chief roles in monarchic Iraq were guarding British air bases and keeping order in the provinces.

Liwa': the largest unit of local administration in monarchic Iraq. The liwa' was governed by a mutasarif and was similar to the Turkish sanjaq.

Madrasa: religious secondary school, focusing on Islamic theology and jurisprudence; the current word for school.

Mahakim nizamiyya: civil courts introduced after 1869 in the Ottoman provinces.

Mahakim shar'iyya: religious courts dealing with personal matters.

Majlis (lit., a sitting or session): originally, a gathering of notables or a ruling council; in modern times, the parliament; among Sufis, a gathering dedicated to the reading of mystic texts, and to other forms of collective elation.

Majlis Idara: administrative council of a district.

Maktab: religious primary school in which reading, writing and the Qur'an were taught. The maktabs were usually part of the local mosque.

Malik: tribal leader among the Assyrians.

Mallak: landowner.

Mallakiyya: land tax normally paid by a cultivator to the mallak.

Matruka (lit., those left aside): land for general public use, such as communal pastures and places of worship.

Mawat (lit., dead lands): unoccupied grazing land not under any kind of title deed.

Millet: sect or spiritual community. Term used by the Ottomans to designate the different religious communities within the Empire. Millet members enjoyed cultural, administrative and religious privileges.

Miri: land owned by the state on which the cultivator benefited from its usufruct without being officially recognized as the owner. Miri lands were leased under various conditions (see Lazma).

Mudawwara (lit., converted): the lands formerly owned by the Sultan. With the advent of the Young Turks (1908) the Sanniyya lands were converted to state property.

Mudir (lit., director): administrator of a nahiya, a small unit in local administration.

Mufti: in Sunni Islam, a jurist with the authority to issue a fatwa.

Mujtahid (pl. *Mujtahidun*): religious Shi'i leader entitled to practise ijtihad (lit., the personal effort to find answers to questions not covered by the Qur'an or the Sunna). In modern times, a Shi'i mujtahid has the authority to reinterpret religious precepts according to changing needs. No reinterpretation of the Qur'an is allowed among the Sunnis.

Mulk: lands belonging to a private person and held in freehold.

Multazim: tax collectors linked to the state by a contract (Iltizam) and acting as intermediaries between the authorities and the fellahin.

Mu'min: Shi'i itinerant preachers.

Murshid: guide, instructor or spiritual leader; an instructor in an Islamic mystic order.

Musha'a: a type of collective land ownership under which the pieces of land were periodically redistributed.

Mutamarridun (lit., the rebels): in monarchic Iraq, the name for the Shi'i tribal leaders rebelling against the government of the day.

Mutassarif: governor of a *liwa'*, the largest administrative unit.

Mutawalli: the guardian or administrator of waqf property.

al Muthana: Arab leader famous for having conducted the first attacks against the Sassanian Empire in 635 in the name of Islam. In Iraq of the 1930s, the name of a nationalist organization active in Sunni quarters.

Nahiya: the smallest unit in local administration, governed by a mudir.

Naqib or *Naqib al Ashraf*: chief of the descendants of the Prophet (the Ashraf or Shurafa') in a Muslim town; a religious leader endowed with great prestige and occasionally consulted on current political affairs.

Naqshabandiyya: Islamic mystic order founded in the fourteenth century by Muhammad Baha-ad-Din-Naqshaband.

Nestorians: a branch of Christianity named after Nestorius, Patriarch of Constantinople in 428. Distinct from other Christian sects by their belief in the duality of Jesus. For them Jesus was not *one* person with two natures (one human and one Divine) but, in fact, two persons. The Nestorians are also known as Assyrians. Nestorians who later accepted the Vatican's authority are called Chaldeans.

Peshmerga (lit., those who face death): followers of the Kurdish leader Mulla Mustafa al Barazani.

Qada: an administrative unit, between a *nahiya* and a *liwa'*. The qada's head was the qaimaqam.

Qadi: a judge responsible for the religious courts, the mahakim shari'a. Sunni qadis are expected to make judgements only according to past precedents and traditions.

Qadiriyya: Islamic mystic order founded in the eleventh century by 'Abd al Qader al Kailani. One of his descendants, the Naqib al Ashraf of Baghdad, was appointed in 1920 as the head of Iraq's first Arab administration.

Qaimaqam: administrative governor of a qada.

Quraish: the tribe of Mecca. The Prophet belonged to the Banu Hashem clan of the Quraish.

Ramadan: the ninth and holy month of the Islamic calendar in which fasting during daytime is imperative.

Rushdiyya: intermediate school (in Ottoman times).

Sabeans: an ethnic group in northern Mesopotamia with roots in ancient Babylonian religions. Different Christian groups have been associated with the name, giving rise to the supposition that it was in fact a general term.

Sanjaq: see Liwa'.

Sanniyya: the Sultan's private lands, administered separately until 1908. With the advent of the Young Turks Sanniyya lands became the property of the state, under the name mudawwara.

Sarifa: a mud house or hut with a reed-mat roof.

Sassanians: the last pre-Islamic dynasty to govern Persia, overthrown in 651.

Shari'a: canonical Islamic law of the Qur'an and the Sunna. The Shari'a encompasses all sorts of regulations, from religious duties to questions of daily conduct and behaviour.

Sheikh (lit., the old man): among the Arabs, the head of a tribe or a village. It is also the title for a venerable man enjoying spiritual and political authority. Among the Kurds, the head of the Sufi order who can lead his followers to direct knowledge or truth.

Sherif (pl. *Shurafa'* or *Ashraf* – lit., noble): descendants of the Prophet through his daughter Fatima and his cousin 'Ali. Today, two ruling families are Sharifians, those of Morocco and Jordan.

Shi'a (lit., the Party or the Party of 'Ali): originally, those who supported the claim of 'Ali to the Caliphate after Muhammad's death, rejecting the nomination of Abu Bakr (one of the Prophet's closest companions) to the post. Today, one of the two major sects in Islam – a minority in the Islamic world, but having a small majority in Iraq, and a larger majority in Iran.

Shi'ism: the religious doctrine that developed after the split between the Sunnis and the Shi'is following the Prophet's death. The largest group among the Shi'is is the Twelvers (Ithna 'Ashiriya – to which the majority of the Iraqi Shi'is belong) who believe in the sanctity of Twelve Imams and in the return of the Twelfth Imam as the Mahdi.

Sirkal: the agent of a tribal sheikh. In southern Iraq a sirkal is responsible for the distribution of labour and irrigation water.

Sirkala: the sirkal's share of the crops.

Sufi (lit., the one wearing woollen (suf) clothes): the first followers of the Islamic mystic orders.

Sunna (lit., custom, usage): the precepts of daily conduct and religious duties established by the Prophet and his companions.

Sunnis (lit., those who follow the Sunna): the largest group of Muslims; known as the 'orthodox'. The Sunnis recognize the first four Caliphs, dismissing 'Ali's right to the Caliphate.

Tanzimat: the set of reforms launched in 1839 envisaging the legal and administrative reorganization of the Ottoman Empire.

Tapu: a title deed formalizing the private ownership of land. The name derives from the initials of the department issuing the deeds in 1868.

Taqiyya: dissimulation of one's real intentions and beliefs. The recourse to taqiyya is legally permitted whenever the community and its members face dangers of any kind. Taqiyya is common practice among the Shi'is.

Tariqa (lit., the way or the path to God): a general name for an Islamic mystic order and/or its local branches.

Tathlith: the state's share of the crops. Introduced in Iraq after independence and collected on the basis of an average of the three previous years.

Tithe: tax paid by a Kurdish cultivator to an agha.

'Ulama' (sing. *'Alim*): scholars, theologians and authorities in religious sciences. The body of learned authorities competent to decide on religious and, occasionally, on temporal matters.

Umayyad: the first dynasty in Islam (661 to 750), named after Ummaya of the Quraish tribe. The Umayad capital was Damascus.

'Uqr: a type of land tenure in the Baghdad area in which the cultivator's rights varied from one-twentieth to one-thirtieth of his produce.

Waqf: see Awqaf.

Wali: governor of a *wilaya*.

Wathba: uprising. More specifically the uprising against the Portsmouth Treaty of 1948.

Wilaya or *vilayet*: a large province and the main administrative unit in the Ottoman Empire. (Three former Ottoman wilayas – Mosul, Baghdad and Basra – were formed by the British after the First World War – into the territory known as Iraq.) A wilaya was administered by a wali and was divided into liwa's (which were administered by mutasarifs). Each liwa' was divided into qadas (administered by qaimaqams) and each qada was further divided into nahiyas (administered by mudirs).

Yazidis: an obscure sect found among the Kurds in northern Iraq, Syria, Turkey and Iran. Their centre is the tomb of Sheikh 'Adi ibn Musafir in the district of Mosul. Widely known as 'devil worshippers', the Yazidis have close ties with other sects such as the Ahl al Haqq.

Bibliography

UNPUBLISHED SOURCES

Public Record Office

Air Ministry
AIR 20   Unregistered papers of the Air Ministry
AIR 23   Papers of overseas commands
AIR 40   Papers of the Directorate of Intelligence

Cabinet Office
CAB 16   Subcommittees of the Committee of Imperial Defence
CAB 23   Conclusions of the Cabinet

Colonial Office
CO 730   Colonial Office papers on Iraq
CO 935   Colonial Office confidential print

Foreign Office
FO 371   General correspondence of the Foreign Office
FO 406   Foreign Office confidential print
FO 624   British Embassy in Baghdad

War Office
WO 201   Middle East forces

India Office Library and Records

L/P&S/12 Correspondence of the India Office's Political and Secret
          Department
L/P&S/18 Memoranda of the India Office's Political and Secret
          Department
R/15/1   Bushire political residency

R/15/5   Kuwait political agency

Middle East Center, St Antony's College, Oxford
C.J. Edmonds' papers

National Archives, Washington
Decimal Records relating to the internal affairs of Iraq File 890G
(1930–1949) and File 787 (1950–1959)

PUBLISHED SOURCES

Documents

Great Britain. Colonial Office. *Special Report by His Majesty's Government in the United Kingdom of Great Britain and Northern Ireland to the Council of the League of Nations on the Progress of Iraq during the period 1920–1931.* London, 1931.
——. Colonial Office. *Report by His Majesty's Government in the United Kingdom of Great Britain and Northern Ireland to the Council of the League of Nations on the Administration of Iraq for the period January to October, 1932.* London, 1933.
——. Admiralty War Staff, Intelligence Division. *A Handbook of Mesopotamia*, Vols. I and III. London, 1916–17.
——. Foreign Office, Historical Section. *Mesopotamia.* London, 1920.
——. India Office. *Review of the Civil Administration of Mesopotamia.* London, 1920.
——. *Report by His Britannic Majesty's Government to the Council of the League of Nations on the Administration of Iraq for: October 1920–March 1922* (London, 1922); *April 1922–March 1923* (1924); *April 1923–December 1924* (1925); *1925* (1926); *1926* (1927); *1927* (1928); *1928* (1929); *1929* (1930); *1930* (1931); *1931* (1932); and *January–October 1932* (1933).
——. *Report of the Financial Mission Appointed by the Secretary of State for the Colonies to Enquire into the Financial Position and Prospects of the Government of Iraq.* London, 1925.
——. *Special Report by His Majesty's Government in the United Kingdom to the Council of the League of Nations on the Progress of Iraq during the Period 1920–1931.* London, 1931.
United States. Department of State. *Documents on German Foreign Policy 1918–1945*, Series D (1937–1945), Vols. X – XIII: *The War Years.* Washington, 1957–64.

——. Department of State. *Foreign Relations of the United States: Diplomatic Papers 1940*, Vol. III, and *Diplomatic Papers 1941*, Vol. III. Washington, 1958–59.

Bell, Gertrude. *Review of the Civil Administration of Mesopotamia*. HMSO, London, 1920.

Hurewitz, J. C. (ed.). *The Middle East and North Africa in World Politics: A Documentary Record*, Vol. II: *British–French Supremacy 1914–1945*. New Haven, CT, 1979.

Books

Al Sa'id, Nuri. *Arab Independence and Unity*. Baghdad, 1942.

Amery, L. S. *My Political Life*, Vol. II: *War and Peace 1914–1929*. London, 1953.

Antonius, George. *The Arab Awakening: The Story of the Arab Nationalist Movement*. London, 1938.

Arfa, Hassan. *The Kurds: An Historical and Political Study*. London, 1966.

Atiyyah, Ghassan R. *Iraq: 1908–1921, A Socio-Political Study*. Beirut, 1973.

Baer, G. *Population and Society in the Arab East*, London, 1964.

Baram, Amatzia, *Culture, History, & Ideology in the Formation of Ba'thist Iraq 1968–1989*. Oxford, 1991.

Barker, A.J. *The Neglected War: Mesopotamia 1914–1918*. London, 1967.

Barth, Frederick. *Principles of Social Organization in Southern Kurdistan*. Oslo, 1953.

Batatu, Hanna. *The Old Social Classes and the Revolutionary Movement of Iraq: A Study of Iraq's Old Landed and Commercial Classes and of its Communists, Bathists, and Free Officers*. Princeton, NJ, 1978.

Beeri, Eliezer. *Army Officers in Arab Politics and Society*. New York, 1970.

Bell, Gertrude Lowthian. *Amurath to Amurath*. London, 1911.

Bell, Lady. *The Letters of Gertrude Bell*. 2 vols. New York, 1928.

Bentwich, Norman. *The Mandates System*. London, 1930.

Birdwood, Lord. *Nuri al-Said: A Study in Arab Leadership*. London, 1959.

Bond, Brian. *British Military Policy between the Two World Wars*. Oxford, 1980.

Bowman, Humphrey. *Middle East Window*. London, 1942.

Browne, Brigadier-General J. Gilbert. *The Iraq Levies 1915–1932*. London, 1932.

Bruinnessen von, M.M. *Aghas, Sheykhs and State*, Rijswijk, Utrecht, 1978.

Burgoyne, Elizabeth. *Gertrude Bell from her Personal Papers 1914–1926*. London, 1961.

Churchill, Winston S. *The Second World War*, Vol. III: *The Grand Alliance*. Boston, 1950.

Cleveland, William. *The Making of an Arab Nationalist: Ottomanism and Arabism in the Life and Thought of Sati' al Husri*. Princeton, 1971.

Cohen, Michael J. *Palestine: Retreat from the Mandate, The Making of British Policy, 1936–45*. New York, 1978.

Cohen, Stuart A. *British Policy in Mesopotamia 1903–1914*. London, 1976.

Connell, John. *Wavell: Scholar and Soldier, To June 1941*. London, 1964.

Dann, Uriel. *Iraq Under Qassem: A Political History, 1958–1963*. New York, 1969.

Davison, Roderic. *Reform in the Ottoman Empire 1856–1876*. Princeton, N J, 1963.

Dawn, E. *From Ottomanism to Arabism: Essays on the Origins of Arab Nationalism*. Urbana, 1973.

Dowson, Sir Ernest. *An Inquiry into Land Tenure and Related Questions*. Letchworth, 1931.

Edmonds, C. J. *Kurds, Turks and Arabs*. London, 1957.

Erskine, S. *King Faisal of Iraq*, London, 1935.

Fernea, Elizabeth, W. *Guests of the Sheik: An Ethnography of an Iraqi Village*. Garden City, 1969.

Fernea, Robert A. *Shaykh and Effendi: Changing Patterns of Authority among the El-Shabana of Southern Iraq*. Cambridge, 1970.

Fernea, Robert A. and Louis, William Roger (eds). *The Iraqi Revolution of 1958: The Old Social Classes Revisited*, London, 1991.

Ferrier, R. W. *The History of the British Petroleum Company*, Vol. I: *The Developing Years 1901–1932*. Cambridge, 1982.

Fichte, Johann Gottlieb. *Addresses to the German Nation*. New York, 1968.

Gallman, Waldemar J. *Iraq Under General Nuri*. Baltimore, 1964.

Gaunson, A.B. *The Anglo French Clash in Lebanon and Syria 1940–1945*, London, 1987.

De Gaury, Colonel Gerald. *Three Kings in Baghdad, 1921–1958*. London, 1961.

Geertz, Clifford. *The Interpretation of Cultures*. London, 1993 (2nd edn).

Gibb, H.A.R. and Bowen, H. *Islamic Society and the West*, Vol. I, Part I. London, 1950.

Glubb, Brigadier-General John B. *The Story of the Arab Legion*. London, 1948.

Glubb, Lieutenant-General Sir John B. *Britain and the Arabs: A Study of Fifty Years 1908 to 1958*. London, 1959.

Greenfeld, Liah. *Nationalism, Five Roads to Modernity*. Cambridge, MA. 1991.

Haim, Sylvia. *Arab Nationalism*. Berkeley, 1962.

Haldane, Lieutenant-General Sir Aylmer L. *The Insurrection in Mesopotamia, 1920*. Edinburgh, 1922.

Hamdi, Walid M.S. *Rashid Ali al-Gailani: The Nationalist Movement – Iraq 1939–1941*. London, 1987.

Hirszowicz, Lukasz. *The Third Reich and the Arab East*. London, 1966.

Hobsbawm, E.J. *Nations and Nationalism since 1780: Programme, Myth, Reality*. Cambridge, 1990.

Horne, Alistair. *A Savage War of Peace: Algeria 1954–1962*. London, 1977.

Hyde, H. Montgomery. *British Air Policy Between the Wars 1918–1939*. London, 1976.

International Bank for Reconstruction and Development. *The Economic Development of Iraq*. Baltimore, 1952.

Ireland, Philip W. *Iraq: A Study in Political Development*. London, 1937.

Issawi, Charles (ed.). *The Economic History of the Middle East 1800–1914*. Chicago, 1966.

Jackson, Stanley. *The Sassoons*. London, 1968.

Al Jamali, Muhammad Fadel. *The New Iraq: Its Problems of Bedouin Education*. New York, 1934.

Joseph, John. *The Nestorians and their Muslim Neighbors: A Study of Western Influence on their Relations*. Princeton, N J, 1961.

Keddie, Nikki. *Scholars, Saints and Sufis, Muslim Religious Institutions since 1500*. Los Angeles, 1978.

Kedourie, Elie. *England and the Middle East: The Destruction of the Ottoman Empire 1914–1921*. London, 1956.

——. *The Chatham House Version and Other Middle-Eastern Studies*. New York, 1970.

——. *Arabic Political Memoirs and Other Studies*. London, 1974.

——. *In the Anglo-Arab Labyrinth: The McMahon–Husayn Correspondence and its Interpretations 1914–1939*. Cambridge, 1976.

——. *Islam in the Modern World and Other Studies*. London, 1980.

Kelidar, Abbas (ed.). *The Integration of Modern Iraq*. London, 1979.

Kennedy, Paul. *The Realities Behind Diplomacy: Background Influences on British External Policy, 1865–1980*. London, 1981.

Kent, Marian. *Oil and Empire: British Policy and Mesopotamian Oil 1900–1920*, London, 1976.

Khadduri, Majid. *Arab Contemporaries: The Role of Personalities in Politics*. Baltimore, 1973.

——. *Political Trends in the Arab World: The Role of Ideas and Ideals in Politics*. Baltimore, 1970.

——. *Independent Iraq 1932–1958: A Study in Iraqi Politics*. London, 1960 (2nd edn).

——. *Republican Iraq: A Study in Iraqi Politics since the Revolution of 1958*. London, 1969.

Kimche, John. *The Second Arab Awakening: The Middle East 1914–1970*. New York, 1970.

Kleiman, Aaron S. *Foundations of British Policy in the Arab World: The Cairo Conference of 1921*. Baltimore, 1970.

Longrigg, Stephen H. *Four Centuries of Modern Iraq*. Oxford, 1925.

——. *Iraq 1900 to 1950: A Political, Social, and Economic History*. London; 1953.

——. *Syria and Lebanon under French Mandate*. London, 1958.

——. *Oil in the Middle East: Its Discovery and Development*. London, 1968 (3rd edn).

Luke, M. *Mosul and its Minorities*. London, 1925.

MacDonald, A. D. *Euphrates Exile*. London, 1936.

al-Mariyati, A. *A Diplomatic History of Modern Iraq*, New York, 1961.

Marlowe, John. *Late Victorian: The Life of Sir Arnold Talbot Wilson*. London, 1967.

Marr, Phebe. *The Modern History of Iraq*. Boulder, CO, 1985.

Meinertzhagen, R. *Middle East Diary (1917–1956)*. London, 1959.

Mejcher, Helmut. *Imperial Quest for Oil: Iraq 1910–1928*. London, 1976.

Monroe, Elizabeth. *Britain's Moment in the Middle East 1914–1956*. Baltimore, 1963.

Moojan, Momen. *An Introduction to Shii Islam. The History and Doctrines of Twelver Shi'ism*. New Haven, 1985.

Mottahedeh, Roy P. *Loyalty and Leadership in an Early Islamic Society*. Princeton, 1980.

Penrose, Edith and E. F. *Iraq: International Relations and National Development*. London, 1978.

Peterson, Maurice. *Both Sides of the Curtain: An Autobiography*. London, 1950.

Philby, H. St. John. *Arabian Jubilee*. London, 1954.

Porath, Y. *The Palestinian Arab National Movement 1929–1939: From Riots to Rebellion*. London, 1977.

——. *Bemivhan Hama'se Hapoliti*. Jerusalem, 1985.

Reisner, Edward H. *Nationalism and Education since 1789: A Social and Political History of Modern Education*. New York, 1929.

Sassoon, D. S. *A History of the Jews in Baghdad*. Lechworth, 1949.

Shwadran, Benjamin. *The Middle East, Oil and the Great Powers*. New York, 1973 (3rd edn).

Silverfarb, D. *Britain's Informal Empire in the Middle East, A Case Study of Iraq 1929–1941*. New York, 1986.

Simon, Reeva. *Iraq between the Two World Wars – The Creation and Implementation of a National Ideology*. New York, 1986.

Sluglett, Peter. *Britain in Iraq 1914–1932*. London, 1976.

Smith, Anthony D. *National Identity*, London, 1991.

——. *The Ethnic Origin of Nations*. Oxford and New York, 1983.

Soane, E. B. *To Mesopotamia and Kurdistan in Disguise*. London, 1912.

Sollors, Werner. *The Invention of Ethnicity*. Oxford and New York, 1991.

Stafford, Lieutenant-Colonel R. S. *The Tragedy of the Assyrians*. London, 1935.

Stark, Freya. *The Arab Island*. New York, 1945.

——. *Baghdad Sketches*. New York, 1938.

——. *Dust in the Lion's Paw*. London, 1961.

Stivers, William. *Supremacy and Oil: Iraq, Turkey, and the Anglo-American World Order, 1918–1930*. Ithaca, NY, 1982.

Taggar, Y. 'The Iraqi Reaction to the Partition Plan for Palestine, 1937' in Gabriel Ben-Dor (ed.), *The Palestinians and the Middle East: Studies in their History, Sociology, and Politics*. Haifa, 1976.

Tarbush, Mohammad A. *The Role of the Military in Politics: A Case Study of Iraq to 1941*. London, 1982.

Thesiger, W. *The Marsh Arabs*. London and New York, 1964.

Tibi, Bassam. *Islam and the Cultural Accommodation of Social Change*. Boulder, CO, 1991.

Toynbee, Arnold J. *Survey of International Affairs 1925*, Vol. I: *The Islamic World since the Peace Settlement*. London, 1927.

——. *Survey of International Affairs 1928*. London, 1929, 1931, 1935, 1937.

Warner, Geoffrey. *Iraq and Syria 1941*. London, 1974.

Warriner, Doreen, *Land and Poverty in Middle East*. London, 1948.

——. *Land Reform and Development*. London, 1957.

Wigram, Reverend W. A. *Our Smallest Ally: A Brief Account of the Assyrian Nation in the Great War.* London, 1920.

Wilson, A. T. *Loyalties, Mesopotamia 1914–1917.* London, 1936.

——. *A Clash of Loyalties Mesopotamia 1917–20.* London, 1937.

Woodward, Sir Llewellyn. *British Foreign Policy in the Second World War*, Vol. I. London, 1970.

Zeine, Zeine N. *The Emergence of Arab Nationalism.* New York, 1973.

Articles

Akrawi, Matta. 'The Arab World: Nationalism and Education', *The Yearbook of Education* (1949), pp. 422–39.

——. *Curriculum Construction in the Public Primary Schools of Iraq.* New York: Columbia Teachers College, 1943.

——. 'The New Educational System in Iraq', *The Open Court* (1935), 49:162–76.

Arjomand, Said Amir. 'The Ulama's Traditionalist Opposition to Parliamentarism: 1907–1909', *Middle Eastern Studies*, 17 (2) (April 1981).

Al-'Askeri, Ja'far. 'Five Years Progress in Iraq', *Journal of the Central Asian Society* (1927), 14:62–72.

Baer, G. 'Agrarian Problems in Iraq', *Middle Eastern Affairs*, 3 (12) (1952).

Baram, Amatzia. 'Saddam Hussein: A Political Profile', *Jerusalem Quarterly* (1980), 17:115–44.

Batatu, Hanna. 'Iraq's Underground Shii Movement – Characteristics, Causes and Prospects', *Middle East Journal*, 35 (4) (1987).

Cohen, Hayyim. 'The Anti-Jewish *Farhud* in Baghdad, 1941', *Middle Eastern Studies*, 3 (1966).

Cole, Juan R. I. 'Indian Money and the Shi'i Shrine Cities of Iraq 1786–1850', *Middle Eastern Studies*, 22 (4) (Oct. 1986).

——. 'Imami Jurisprudence and the Role of the Ulama' in Nikki Keddie (ed.) *Religion and Politics in Iran.* New Haven, 1983.

Connor, W. 'Self Determination, The New Phase', *World Politics*, 20 (1) (October 1967).

Dann, Uriel. 'The Kurdish Nationalist Movement in Iraq', *Jerusalem Quarterly*, 9 (1978), 131–44.

Davison, Roderic. 'Westernized Education in Ottoman Turkey', *Middle East Journal* (1961), 15:289–301.

Dawn, E. 'The Question of Nationalism in Syria and Lebanon' in W. Sands, *Tension in the Middle East.* Washington DC, 1956.

——. 'The Rise of Arabism in Syria', *Middle East Journal*, 6 (2) (1962).

Edmonds, C. J. 'Kurdish Nationalism', *Journal of Contemporary History*, 6 (1971).

——. 'A Bibliography of Southern Kurdish 1920–1936' *Royal Central Asia Society Journal* (1937).

——. 'The Kurds of Iraq', *Middle Eastern Studies* (1957).

Al-Gailani, Rashid 'Ali. 'Mudhakkirati' (Memoirs) in *Majallat Akhari Sa'a*. Cairo, 1957.

Haim, Sylvia G. 'Aspects of Jewish Life in Baghdad under the Monarchy', *Middle Eastern Studies*, 12 (1976).

——. 'Islam and the Theory of Arab Nationalism' in W. Laqueur (ed.), *The Middle East in Transition*. New York, 1958.

Hodgkin, E. C. 'Lionel Smith on Education in Iraq', *Middle Eastern Studies*, 19 (1983).

Husri, Khaldun S. 'The Assyrian Affair of 1933', *International Journal of Middle Eastern Studies*, 5 (1974).

——. 'King Faysal I and Arab Unity, 1930–33', *Journal of Contemporary History*, 10 (1975).

——. 'The Political Ideas of Yunis al-Sabawi,' in Marwan R. Buheiri, (ed.), *Intellectual Life in the Arab East, 1890–1939*. Beirut, 1981.

Al-Husri, Abu Khaldun Sati'. 'The Historical Factor in the Formation of Nationalism' in Kemal H. Karpat (ed.), *Political and Social Thought in the Contemporary Middle East*. New York, 1968.

Al-Jamali, M. Fadel. 'The Theological Colleges of Najaf', *The Muslim World* 50 (1) (1960), 15–22.

——. 'John Dewey, the Philosopher Educator', *Middle East Forum* (1969), 45: 75–89.

Jwaideh, A. 'Midhat Pasha and the land system of lower Iraq'. *St Antony's Papers*, No. 16, A. H. Hourani (ed.), London, 1963.

——. 'The Sanniyya Lands of Sultan Abdul Hamid in Iraq' in *Arabic and Islamic Studies in Honour of Sir H. Gibb*. Leiden, 1965.

Kedourie, Elie. 'Continuity and Change in Modern Iraqi History', *Asian Affairs* (1975), 62: 140–6.

——. 'Wavell and Iraq, April – May 1941', *Middle Eastern Studies*, 2 (1965–66).

Kelidar, Abbas, 'Iraq, the Search for Stability', *Conflict Studies*, 59 (July 1975).

Kenny, L. M. 'Sati' al-Husri's View on Arab Nationalism', *Middle East Journal* (1963), 17: 231–56.

Khadduri, Majid. 'The Coup d'Etat of 1936: A Study in Iraqi Politics', *Middle East Journal* (1948), 3: 270–92.

——. 'The Role of the Military in Middle Eastern Politics', *American Political Science Review* (1953), 47: 511–24.

——. 'General Nuri's Flirtations with the Axis Powers', *Middle East Journal*, 16 (1962).

Kopietz, H. H. 'The Use of German and British Archives in the Study of the Middle East: The Iraqi Coup d'Etat of 1936' in 'Abbas Kelidar (ed.), *The Integration of Modern Iraq*. London, 1971.

MacDonald, A. D. 'Political Developments in Iraq Leading up to the Spring of 1935', *Journal of Royal Central Asia Society* (1936), 23:27–44.

Mardin, Serif. 'Ideology and Religion in the Turkish Revolution', *International Journal for Middle East Studies* (1971), 2:197–211.

Marr, Phebe A. 'The Iraqi Revolution: A Case Study of Army Rule', *Orbis* (1970), 14:714–39.

——. 'Iraq's Leadership Dilemma: A Study in Leadership Trends 1948–1968', *Middle East Journal* (1970), 2:283–301.

——. 'The Political Elite in Iraq' in G. Lenczowski (ed.), *Political Elites in the Middle East*. Washington, DC 1975, pp. 109–49.

——. 'The Development of a Nationalist Ideology in Iraq 1920–1941', *Muslim World* (April 1985).

McDonald, A. D. 'The Political Development of Iraq Leading Up to the Rising in Spring 1935', *Royal Central Asian Society Journal* (1936).

Minorsky, V. 'Kurdistan', 'Kurds', *Encyclopedia of Islam*, Vol. II, 1927.

Owen, Roger. 'The Role of the Army in Middle Eastern Politics', *Review of Middle Eastern Studies* (3) (1978).

——. 'Class and Class Politics in Iraq before 1958. The Colonial and Post Colonial State' in Robert A. Fernea and William Roger Louis (eds), *The Iraqi Revolution of 1958: The Old Social Classes Revisited*, London, 1991.

Porath, Y. 'Al-Hajj Amin al-Husayni, Mufti of Jerusalem – His Rise to Power and the Consolidation of His Position', *Asian and African Studies* (1971), 7:121–56.

——. 'Palestinian and Pan-Arab Nationalism 1918–1939', *The Wiener Library Bulletin* (1978), 31 (N.S. 45/46):29–39.

——. 'Britain and Arab Unity', *Jerusalem Quarterly*, 15 (1980).

——. 'Nuri al-Sa'id's Arab Unity Programme', *Middle Eastern Studies*, 20 (1984).

——. 'Abdallah's Greater Syria Programme', *Middle Eastern Studies*, 20 (1984).

Porenti, M. 'Ethnic Politics and the Persistence of Ethnic Identification', *American Political Science Review*, LXI (Sept. 1967).

Al-Qazzaz, Ayad. 'Review of *Memoirs of Taha al Hashimi*, by Taha al-Hashimi', *Middle East Forum*, 45 (1969).

——. 'Power Elite in Iraq, 1920–1958: A Study of the Cabinet', *Muslim World* (1971), 61:267–82.

——. 'The Iraqi–British War of 1941: A Review Article', *International Journal of Middle Eastern Studies*, 7 (1976).

Schmidt, H. D. 'The Nazi Party in Palestine and the Levant 1932–1939', *International Affairs* (1952), 28:460–9.

Sheffer, Gabriel. 'The Involvement of Arab States in the Palestine Conflict and British–Arab Relationship before World War II', *Asian and African Studies*, 10 (1974).

Simon, R. 'The Teaching of History in Iraq before the Rashid 'Ali Coup of 1941', *Middle Eastern Studies* (Winter 1986).

Sluglett, Peter. 'Some Reflections on the Sunni Shi'a Question in Iraq', *British Society for Middle Eastern Studies Bulletin* (1978), 5:79–87.

Taggar, Y. 'The Iraqi Reaction to the Partition Plan for Palestine, 1937' in Gabriel Ben-Dor (ed.), *The Palestinians and the Middle East Conflict*. Ramat Gan, Israel, 1978.

Tomlinson, B. R. 'India and the British Empire, 1880–1935', *The Indian Economic and Social History Review*, 12 (1975).

Vinogradov, Amal. 'The 1920 Revolt in Iraq Reconsidered: The Role of the Tribes in National Politics', *International Journal of Middle Eastern Studies* (1972), 3:123–39.

Zubaida, Sami. 'Community, Class and Minorities in Iraqi Politics' in Robert A. Fernea and William Roger Louis (eds), *The Iraqi Revolution of 1958: The old Social Classes Revisited*, London, 1991.

Books in Arabic

'Ala' Jasim, Muhammad, *Al-Ja'far al 'Askari wa dawrahu al siyasi wal 'askari fi ta'rikh al 'Iraq hata 'amm 1936* (Ja'far al 'Askari and his Political and Military role in Iraq's History, until 1936). Baghdad, 1987.

Al-'Allaf, 'Abd al Karim. *Baghdad-al-qadima* (Old Baghdad). Baghdad, 1960.

Al-Ayyubi, 'Ali Jawdat. *Dhikrayat 'Ali Jawdat* (Ali Jawdat's Memoirs). Beirut, 1967.

Al-'Azzawi, 'Abbas. *Ta'rikh al 'Iraq baina ihtilalain* (The History of Iraq between Two Occupations), 7 vols. Baghdad, 1935–1956.

Al-Bazargan, 'Ali. *Al-waqa'i' al-haqiqiyya fi al-thawra-al-'Iraqiyya* (The Real Facts about the Iraqi Revolution). Baghdad, 1954.

——. *Min Awraq Kamel Jadirji* (From the Papers of Kamel Jadirji). Beirut, 1971.

Al Bazzaz, 'Abd al Rahman, *al-'Iraq min al-ihtilal hatta al-istiqlal* (Iraq from Occupation to Independence), Baghdad, 1967.

Al-Durra, Mahmud. *Al harb al 'Iraqiyya al-Britaniyya sanat 1941* (The Iraqi – British war of 1941). Beirut, 1969.

——. *Al-Qadiyya al Kurdiyya* (The Kurdish Question). Beirut, 1966 (2nd edn).

Al Far'un, Fariq al-Muzhir. *Al-Haqa'iq al-nasi'a fi-al-thawra-al-'Iraqiyya sanat 1920 wa nataijiha* (The Forgotten Facts about the Iraqi Revolution of 1920 and its Results). Vol. I. Baghdad, 1952.

Al-Hashimi, Taha. *Mudhakkirati* (Memoirs). 2 vols. Beirut, 1967 and 1969.

Al-Hassani, 'Abd al-Razzaq, *Ta'rikh al wizarat al 'Iraqiyya* (The History of Iraq's Cabinets). Sidon 1939 and 1940, Vols. III–IV.

——. *Ta'rikh al buldan al 'Iraqiyya* (History of the Iraqi Towns), Baghdad, 1930.

——. *Al Thawra al 'Iraqiyya al kubra sanat 1920* (The 1920 Great Iraqi Revolution), Beirut 1978 (3rd. edn).

——. *Al Asrar al khafiyya li harakat al-tahrir sanat 1941* (The Hidden Secrets of the 1941 Liberation Movement). Sidon, 1971.

——. *Ta'rikh al 'Iraq al siyasi al hadith* (Modern Political History of Iraq), 3 vols. Beirut, 1948.

——. *al-'Iraq: qadima wa haditha* (Iraq: Ancient and Modern). Beirut, 1973.

Al Hilali, 'Abd al Razzaq. *Dirasat wa tarajim 'Iraqiyya* (Iraqi Studies and Biographies). Baghdad 1992.

——. *Ta'rikh al ta'lim fi al 'ahd al 'Uthmani 1638–1917* (The History of Education in the Ottoman Period, 1638–1917). Baghdad, 1959.

——. *Ta'rikh al ta'lim fi al 'Iraq* (The History of Education in Iraq). 2 vols. Baghdad, 1959 and 1975.

Al-Hissan, 'Abd al-Razzaq. *Al-'Uruba fi al-mizan* (Arabism on the Scales). Baghdad, 1933.

Al Husri, Sati'. *Mudhakkirati fi-al-Iraq* (Memoirs from Iraq). 2 vols. Beirut, 1966 and 1967.

——. *Abhath mukhtara fi al qawmiyya al 'arabiyya* (Selected Studies in Arab Nationalism). Cairo, 1963.

——. *Thawrat 14 Tammuz wa haqiqat al shuyu'iyyin fi al 'Iraq* (The Revolution of July 14 and the Truth of the Communists in Iraq). Beirut, 1960.

Al Jamali, M. Fadel. *Mudhakkirat wa 'ibar* (Memoirs and Lessons). Beirut, 1964.

Al-Kailani, Rashid 'Ali. *Mudhakkirati* (Memoirs). In *Majalla Akhir Sa'a*, Cairo, 1957.

Al-Kassab, 'Abd al Aziz. *Min dhikrayati* (From my Memoirs). Beirut, 1962.

Al Kawakibi, 'Abd-al-Rahman. *Taba'i-al-istibdad* (The Attributes of Tyranny). Cairo, 1900(?).

Al Khattab, Raja'a Husayn. *Ta'sis al jaish al 'Iraqi wa tatawwur Dawrihi al-Siyasi 1921–1941* (The Establishment of the Iraqi Army and the Development of its Political Role 1921–1941). Baghdad, 1979.

Al-Mahbubah, Shaikh Bakir. *Madi al-Najaf wa hadiruha* (The Past of Najaf and its Present). 3 vols. Sidon and Najaf, 1934–1957.

Al Sabbagh, Salah al-Din, *Fursan al 'Uruba fi-al-Iraq* (The Knights of Arabism). Damascus, 1956.

Al-Suwaidi, Tawfiq. *Mudhakkirati* (Memoirs). Beirut, 1969.

Al Tahir, 'Abd al Jalil. *al-'Asha'ir al-'Iraqiyya* (The Tribes of Iraq). Baghdad, 1972.

Al-Wardi, 'Ali. *Dirasa fi tabi'at al-mujtama' al-'Iraqi* (A Study on the Nature of the Iraqi Society). Baghdad, 1965.

Al-Waqa'i'-al-'Iraqiyya (the Official Gazette of the Iraq Government). From 1920.

Al Ziyyadi, Muhammad Husein. *Mawlud Muhlis Pachachi wa dawrahu fi al thawra al 'arabiyya al kubra wa fi ta'rikh al 'Iraq al mu'asir* (Mawlud Muhlis Pachachi and his Role in the Arab Revolt and in Iraq's Modern History). Baghdad, 1979.

———. *Muhammad al Sheikh 'Ali* (Memoirs of Muhammad al Sheikh 'Ali, defence minister in Rashid Ali's cabinet of 1941). Baghdad, 1985.

Fawzi, Ahmed. *Faysal II, 'A'ilatuhu, hayatuhu, mu'allafatuhu* (Faysal II, his family, his life, and his books). Baghdad, 1988.

Haddad, 'Uthman Kemal. *Harakat Rashid 'Ali al-Kaylani 1941* (Rashid 'Ali al Gailani's Rebellion of 1941). Sidon, n.d.

Ibrahim, 'Abd-al-Faitah, *Mutala'a fi-al-Sha'biyya* (Studies in Populism). Baghdad, 1935.

Jadirji, Kamil. *Mudhakkirat Kamil Jadirji wa-ta'rikh al-hizb al-watani al-dimoqrati* (Kamil al Jadirji's Memoirs and the History of the Democratic National Party). Beirut, 1970.

Jamali, Muhammad Fadel. *Ittijahat al-tarbiyya wa-al-ta'lim fi Al-maniyya wa Ingiltira wa Faransa* (Cultural and Educational Trends in Germany, England and France). Baghdad, 1938.

Khalil, Kanna. *Al 'Iraq, amsuhu, wa ghaduhu* (Iraq, its Past and its future). Beirut, 1966.

Kubba, Muhammad Mahdi. *Mudhakkirati fi samim al ahdath* (Memoirs in the Course of the Events). Beirut, 1965.

Lutfi, Ja'far Faraj, 'Abd Allah. *'Abd al Muhsin al Sa'dun wa dawrahu fi ta'rikh al 'Iraq al siyasi al mu'asir* ('Abd al Muhsin al Sa'dun and

his role in the Modern Political History of Iraq). Baghdad, 1988.
Mushtaq, Talib. *Awraq ayyamy* (Records of My Days [1900–1958]). Beirut, 1968 and Baghdad, 1989.
Ni'ma, Kazim. *Al Malik Faysal al Awwal wal-Ingliz wal-Istiqlal* (King Faisal I, the British and the Independence). Baghdad, n.d.
Al Qaysi, Sami 'Abd al-Hafidh. *Yasin al-Hashimi*. 2 vols. Basra, 1975.
Sa'd Ru'uf, Sha'ir Muhammad. *Nuri al Sa'id wa dawrahu fi al Siyasa al 'Iraqiyya 1932–1945* (Nuri-al-Sa'id and his Role in Iraqi Politics), Baghdad, 1988.
Al Sabbagh, Salah al-Din. *Fursan al 'uruba fi-l-Iraq* (The Knights of Arabism in Iraq). Damascus, 1956.
Shawkat, Naji. *Awraq Naji Shawkat* (Naji Shawkat's Records). Baghdad, 1977.
Shawkat, Sami. *Hadhihi ahdafuna* (These Are Our Goals). Baghdad, 1939.
Suwaidi, Tawfiq. *Mudhakkirati* (Memoirs). Beirut, 1969.
Zaki, Muhammad Amin. *Ta'rikh-al-Sulaimaniyya wa anha'iha* (The History of Sulaimaniya and its Districts). Translated from Kurdish by Mulla Jamil Ahmad al-Ruzbayani. Baghdad, 1951.
Zu'aytir, Akram and al-Miqdadi, Darwish. *Ta'rikhuna bi-uslub qisasi* (Our History in Form of Tales). Baghdad, 1939.

Hebrew

Eliraz, David. 'Markiveha shel ha-Leumiut ha-Aravit etzel Sati al-Husri' (Components of Arab Nationalism in Sati al Husri's Thought). *HaMizrah HeHadash*, No. 22 (1972).

Doctoral Dissertations

Haider, S. 'Land problems in Iraq'. Unpublished Doctoral Dissertation, University of London, 1942.
Nadhmi, W.J.O. 'The Political, Social and Intellectual Roots of the Iraqi Independence Movement of 1920'. Unpublished Doctoral Dissertation, University of Durham, 1974.
Sassoon, Yosef. 'Economic Policy in Iraq 1932–1950'. University of Oxford, 1980.

German

Grobba, Fritz. *Männer und Mächte im Orient* (Men and Power in the East). Göttingen: Musterschmitt, 1967.

French

Baban, Isma'il Haqqi Bey. *De Stamboul à Bagdad. Notes d'un homme d'état Turc* (From Istanbul to Baghdad. Notes of a Turkish Statesman). 1910. Translated from Turkish, *Collection de la Revue du Monde Musulman*, Paris, 1911. Also in *Revue du Monde Musulman* (Paris) (1911), XIV: 5, 185–296.

Guerreau, Alain and Anita Guerreau-Jalabert. *L'Irak: Dévéloppement et contradictions*. Paris, 1978.

Al-Hadid, 'Ajjan. 'Le Dévéloppement de l'éducation nationale en Iraq', *Revue des Etudes Islamiques* (1932), 6:231–67.

Vernier, Bernard. *Armée et Politique au Moyen-Orient*. Paris, 1966.

Italian

Rossi, E. 'L'Istituzione scolastica militare al-Futuwwa' nell 'Iraq', *Oriente Moderno* (1940), 20:297–302.

Iraqi Newspapers

Al Ahali
Al 'Alam al 'Arabi
Al Daftar
Al Fajr al Jadid
Al Hurriyya
Al Istiqlal
Al Ittihad al Sha'b
Al Muwatan al Arab
Al Nahar
Al Ra'i al 'Amm
Al Thawra
Al Umma
Al Yaqza
Al Yawm
Liwa' al Istiqlal
Sawt al Ahali
Sawt al Ahrar

Index

'Abbas, Hajji, 123
'Abbas, Khawwam al, 70, 86, 133
Abdul Hamid, Sultan, 53
Abu Sukhair, 67
Abu Sultan confederation, 66
Afghanistan, 97
Aflaq, Michel, 142
aghas, Kurdish, 49, 57, 109, 122–5, 145, 150–2
Agricultural Credit Bank, 83
agriculture, 123–4, 144–5, 152; crop shares, 138
Ahali group, 85–6, 130
Ahmed, Sheikh, 46–7
Albu Mutaiwit tribe, 143
Aleppo, 44, 151
'Ali, Muhammad al Sheikh, 157
Ali, Baba, 145
Alliance Israelite Universelle, 113
Alwan, Musa al, 133
'Amadiya, 36, 128
'Amara tribe, 140
Anatolia, Eastern, 36
Anglo-Ottoman Convention (1913), 102
'Aqra, 36, 67
Arabic language, 48–9, 110, 114–17, 149
Arabism, 62, 74, 112, 120–1; see also Pan-Arabism
Arabs, 3–4, 22, 72, 143, 150–2; and Jews, 100; and Kurds, 34, 36–8, 42–7, 49, 125; Shi'is, 60, 62, 80, 149
Arbil, 27, 35–6, 42–3, 118, 126
Arbil tribe, 122
Aref, Colonel 'Abd al Salam, 141
Armenians, 23, 27, 29, 134
Ashraf, Naqib al, 73, 84
'Askari, Ja'far al, 13, 20, 46, 76, 83, 87–9, 157
Association of People's Reforms, 85
Assyrian National Pact (1932), 26
Assyrians, 5, 22–33, 37, 45, 127, 134, 143, 146–7, 158; Levies, 18, 24, 26, 92, 99, 123
Atatürk, Mustafa Kemal, 26, 33
'Atiyya, Hajj Rayeh al, 138
'Atiyya, Sheikh Sha'lan al, 61, 67–8, 70
awqaf, 83–4, 95, 138–9
Awqaf Department, 48–9, 64
Ayyubi, Jawdat al, 67

Aziz, Tariq, 156

Ba'th Party, 142, 145, 147, 152–3, 157
Baban, Jamal, 131
Baban emirs, 35
'badal' system, 91
Bader, Ja'far al, 132
Badinan, 126
Baghdad, 33, 37, 44, 49, 56, 151–2; British Embassy, 99–100; British troops, 18; German activity, 94–5; Iraqi Communist Party, 142; Jews, 100; Military Academy, 123; 1936 coup d'état, 81–3; Ottoman vilayet, 13; schools, 69, 112–13; Shi'i community, 112–13, 132, 145; social structure, 72
Baghdad Pact, 144
Bahrani, Ra'uf al, 68
Bang-al-Haqq, 40
Bani Hasan, 70
Bani Zuraij, 70, 86
Ba'quba camp, 23–4
Baradost project, 27
Barazani, Mulla Mustapha al, 127–8, 135, 152
Barazani, Sheikh Ahmed, 127
Barzinji, 34, 40–1, 46
Basha'yan, Burhaniddin, 132
Basra, 15, 102, 137, 140, 145, 151; British troops, 18, 60, 98, 100; Naqib of, 130; Ottoman vilayet, 13; schools, 112–13
Batatu, Hanna, 6, 144, 152–3
Bedouin, 59
Beg, 'Ali Muhsin, 23
Beg, Hamid, 145
Beg, Hasan, 145
Beg, Murad, 84
Beirut, 72, 158; American University, 115, 118
Bell, Gertrude, 14
Bitlis, 34
bombardment, aerial, 20, 35, 37, 76, 86
Britain, see Great Britain
British Oil Development Company, 84
British Petroleum Company, 140
Brussels Line, 24
Bühtan River, 34

206